PERTH & KINROSS

AN ILLUSTRATED ARCHITECTURAL GUIDE

Architecture acquires depth and meaning when seen under Sir Banister Fletcher's six major influences – geographical, geological, climatic, religious, social and historical. Place it into the timeframe of centuries, generations, and more recently five-year spans, and it emerges as a rich story that patently engages the minds of the curious, of critics and of patrons. Above all architecture has the power to engender a sense of pride and personal identity with one's surroundings.

Nick Haynes' attractive guide presents the architecture of Perth and Kinross in this way. I was amazed to see the diversity of buildings in an area I thought I knew well, and to reflect that this heartland of Scotland retains evidence of settlement and exploitation since prehistoric times. Great ideas and themes have been tried and imported over the centuries. Some have been given strong form based on primitive techniques and local materials, contrasting beautifully with the 18th-century Improvers' notions of model villages, or the industrial archaeology of the textile industry. Nick's criticisms of recent building should make us all reflect on whether we agree with him, and what we should all demand as the future evolves.

This is an exciting publication for all, and a fitting companion to the other guides in the series.

David R Penman
FRTPI ARIAS FSA Scot

© Author: Nick Haynes
Series editor: Charles McKean
Series consultant: David Walker
Editorial consultant: Kate Blackadder
Cover design: The Almond Consultancy
Index: Oula Jones

Cover illustrations
Front *Balvaird by David Henrie (Crown copyright: Historic Scotland)*.
Back *Kinross-shire from Dowhill Castle (Haynes)*.
    Inset *Commercial Street, Perth (SCRAN)*.

The Rutland Press
ISBN 1873190123
1st published 2000

Typesetting and picture scans by
The Almond Consultancy, Edinburgh
Printed by Pillans & Wilson Greenaway, Edinburgh

British Library Cataloguing in Publication Data.
A catalogue record for this book is available from the British Library.

'*Among all the provinces in Scotland, if an intelligent stranger were asked to describe the most varied and the most beautiful, it is probable he would name the county of Perth. A native also of any other district of Caledonia, though his partialities might lead him to prefer his native county in the first instance, would certainly class that of Perth in the second, and thus give its inhabitants a fair right to plead that, prejudice apart, Perthshire forms the fairest portion of the Northern kingdom.*' Sir Walter Scott, *The Fair Maid of Perth*, 1828

Vast, and infinite in beauty and variety of scenery, Perthshire lies at the heart of Scotland, bounded by Kinross, Fife, Dundee, Angus, Aberdeenshire, Highland, Argyll & Bute, Stirling and Clackmannan. Divided south-west to north-east by the Highland Boundary Fault, the county is half lowland, with the lazy meanders and fertile carses of the great River Tay and its tributaries, and half highland, encompassing the wild and spectacular southern Grampians. North of the fault, hard crystalline metamorphic rock; south, younger sedimentary formations. This natural diversity reflected in the county's extraordinary cultural wealth, and resulting buildings comprising its towns, villages, estates and farms.

Old county of Perth, some 1.5 million acres, which extended westward to include Dunblane, Callander, Crianlarich and Tyndrum, was much reduced by local government reorganisation, 1974. What remains is still enormous, taking in ancient districts of Strathearn, Methven, Breadalbane, Atholl, Strathardle, Glenshee, Stormont, Gowrie and Perth itself. As might be expected, pattern of building is densest in the fertile hinterland of Perth and along the communications routes through the river valleys. History too has coursed along Perthshire's glens, from coronations at Scone, via the first sparks of the Reformation fanned by John Knox in Perth, to Cromwell's occupation and the Jacobite Risings. Great families that have shaped that history and built its monuments include the houses of Murray, Drummond, Campbell and Hay.

Perthshire more than makes up for its lack of coast in its abundance of rivers, which craze the county from top to bottom and side to side. Mightiest of them all, the Tay, even yet carries sea trade to the harbour in Perth. Commercial net fishing by the Richardsons of Pitfour took Tay salmon to the dinner tables of Venice in the 18th and 19th centuries, but now the rod and line provide the main source of income from the river beats. Bridging the rivers began with the Romans at Bertha, where the Almond meets the Tay, but shifting paths and sheer force of water have

Victoria Ball

Carved grotesque from former Duncrub House, monogrammed R for Rollo, set in park wall, Dunning.

Opposite *Crieff Hydro, Knock Hill and the southern Grampians by G S R Photographic.* Below *Inchyra Lodge with Cottown Schoolhouse.* Bottom *Meikleour Cross.*

David Walker

Irene Hemmings

Bridges have long been essential to the infrastructure of the area, and there are many of interest including General Wade's bridge over Allt A' Chrombaidh in Clunes Wood, **Gow's** and **Gilbert's** bridges of 1759 over the River Tilt, the pretty suspension footbridge over the River Garry at the West Lodge to Blair Castle, and the concrete bridges along the old A9, built by Owen Williams & Partners in the late 1920s.

undone many fine structures, including Bertha, several attempts in Perth and the beautiful old Bridge of Earn. However, it is still impossible to travel far in Perthshire without encountering the art of the bridge-builder, from the baroque splendours of William Adam's Tay Bridge at Aberfeldy to the contrived picturesque of W H Playfair's Dry Bridge at Lynedoch and plain measured elegance of the Bridge of Isla at Meikleour. Harnessing immense water power has long been a Perthshire speciality, as testified by the mills at Stanley and Blairgowrie. After the Second World War new temples to the water gods peppered the highland tributaries in the form of power stations for the colossal Tummel and Breadalbane hydro-electric schemes.

Glens Artney, Lednock, Almond, Lyon, Garry, Tilt and Shee compete with Rannoch Moor for wild grandeur, whilst straths of Earn, Braan, Tummel, Tay and Ardle fight it out for gentler charms. Ben Vorlich, Ben Chonzie, Ben Lawers, Schiehallion, Farragon Hill and Ben Vrackie head the roll-call of famous peaks, more for distinctive shapes rather than height. Highland visitor trail began in the 18th century when timid tourists came to seek out the horror and beauty of savage nature. At Acharn and Dunkeld the landowners played up to their thrill-seeking guests by building artificial 'hermitages' to dramatise and magnify the experience of the nearby waterfalls. In the 19th century, visitors to Dunkeld, such as Dorothy Wordsworth (1803) and Felix Mendelssohn (1829), sought more contemplative and romantic pleasures from the scenery. Country house architects too began to respond to the romantic qualities of the landscape by designing new fairy-tale castles in place of rigidly formal classical boxes. Robert Adam led the way at Pitfour (1784), but it was Alexander Nasmyth at Taymouth and Kinfauns who invented the Picturesque castle in Perthshire, in most literal sense, by composing designs for new buildings and their settings as a picture. Queen Victoria's visit to completed Taymouth Castle, 1842, and accompanying medievalising revelry, set the seal of

Top *Haugh Cottages, Acharn.* Above *Stair Hall, Taymouth Castle.* Left *Pitfour Castle, drawn by David Walker when compiling the Statutory List of Listed Buildings, 1961–4.*

ST MADOES

approval on the county. Mass tourism followed
with arrival of the railway, establishing Aberfeldy,
Crieff, Birnam and Pitlochry as holiday towns.
Ancient peoples too set up their homes and
temples in the county. Several generations of
Neolithic man built the extraordinary ritual oval
barrow and 2km earthwork approach of the
Cleaven Dyke, near Meikleour, *c*.3300 BC. The
dramatic forts of Dunsinane Hill, Collace, and
Barry Hill, Alyth, and the artificial islands or
'crannogs' of Loch Tay indicate a significant area of
settlement in the Iron Age (*c*.700 BC to *c*.500 AD).

Roman soldiers hailed the Tay as a second Tiber,
and the 'Painted Ones', or Picts, established
Forteviot, Dunkeld and Scone as centres of power.
These retained and enhanced their importance in
the reign of Kenneth mac Alpin, who ruled from
the Pictish royal seat at Forteviot and is generally
credited with final uniting of the Picts and Scots.
Political power in early medieval Scotland
focused on Scone, place of coronation and original
home of the Stone of Destiny. Along with the
Augustinian abbey here, the foundation of the
Cistercian abbey at Coupar Angus and the
cathedral at Dunkeld had a profound effect on the
physical and social fabric of the area, as it
transformed from largely royal demesne to
monastic estate and secular lordships. The
establishment of parishes produced the
characteristic long, low, rectangular churches,
which survived throughout the county in
remarkable numbers until the end of the 18th
century, when the fashion for larger and even more
boxy Improvement kirks left most of them either in
ruins or remodelled beyond recognition.

Little remains of the once-dominant textile
industry, but whisky, insurance, buses, tourism,
and the traditional industries of agriculture,
forestry and fishing still drive the economy. Rich
loamy soils of lower valleys to less fertile uplands
enable extraordinary range of crops and stock,
famously Blairgowrie raspberries and Aberdeen-
Angus cattle. Perthshire was at the forefront of the
agricultural revolution of the earlier 19th century,
resulting in construction of large numbers of fine
farmhouses and Improvement steadings, such as
William Mackenzie's model farm at Elcho.
Any guide to this extraordinary county can only
paint a partial picture. Some building types, in
particular agricultural, vernacular and industrial,
are under-represented. It is hoped that this volume
will stimulate an awareness of the quality and
variety of Perthshire's architecture, past and
present, and encourage further exploration.

From top *Blair Atholl Railway Station; St
Madoes Parish Church and cross; Collace
Parish Church; Errol Park stables.*

Top *St Bean's Parish Church, Fowlis Wester.* Above *Greenhall, Madderty.*

List of tolls, Barnhill Tollhouse.

Organisation of the guide

The guide is divided into the two former counties of Perthshire and Kinross-shire, each with its own introduction. The city of **Perth**, with its medieval core, gracious residential streets overlooking the North and South Inches, and outer suburbs begins the guide. Perthshire is continued in a series of road routes from Perth and Dunkeld, starting along **Strathearn** to Auchterarder and back via Aberdalgie. Next the A85 from **Huntingtower** to Crieff and Comrie, returning Perthwards on the back roads of Glenalmond. Following on, the guide travels the A9 to the Highlands, including Dunkeld and **Aberfeldy**. A circular route from **Dunkeld** around the Loch of Clunie takes in Stanley, before continuing north to **Pitlochry**, Rannoch Station and Blair Atholl. Returning to Perth, the guide sets out to **Glen Shee** and Strathardle, via Scone Palace and Blairgowrie (A93), then from Perth again on the A94, from **New Scone** to Coupar Angus, Meigle and Alyth. Perth along the **Carse of Gowrie** (A90) towards Dundee and back is the last major route before heading south via **Abernethy** and Glenfarg to Kinross-shire, which begins in the old county town, **Kinross**, heading south to Keltybridge, west via Cleish to Blairingone, and east around Loch Leven, to Scotlandwell.

Text Arrangement

Entries for principal buildings follow the sequence of name (or number), address, date and architect (if known). Lesser buildings are contained within paragraphs. In general, the dates given are those of the design or of the beginning of construction. Marginal text offers anecdotal and less technical aspects of the story of the Heartland of Scotland.

Map References

Maps are included for the main towns and villages and are guideline only. Numbers do not refer to page numbers but those in the text itself. Where buildings are concentrated, space has allowed only a few numbers sufficient for visitors to take bearings.

Access to properties

Many of the buildings described in this guide are **private** and readers **are requested to respect the occupiers' privacy**. Several are open to the public or are visible from a public road or footpath.

Sponsors

Perth & Kinross Heritage Trust, Perth & Kinross District Council, Scottish Enterprise Tayside, The Russell Trust, Kinross-shire Civic Trust, Perth Civic Trust, Forteviot Charitable Trust, Thomson Charitable Trust, Perth Partnership, Guildry Incorporation of Perth, CGU Insurance, Atholl Estate, United Distillers and The Landmark Trust.

RIAS Collection

CITY OF PERTH

The origin of the name is disputed, but likely to derive from Aber-tha (mouth of the Tay). Certainly the town's location at the lowest bridging point and tidal extremity of the River Tay, and its proximity to the ancient coronation site at Scone, played a key role in its trading prosperity and rise to burghal status under David I.

The earliest developments appear to have been along the Watergate, with riggs stretching behind and wharves built out into the river. Construction of a bridge at the end of what is now the High Street shifted the main axis of the town from the Watergate. First mention of a parish church occurs in an 1126 grant to the Benedictines of Dunfermline. The flourishing hides, cloth and timber industries, and the export of wool to the Low Countries made Perth second only to Berwick in terms of wealth by 1200. Perth Castle, which stood to the north of the Skinnergate, was destroyed in 1209 by one of the many floods which still occasionally inundate the town. The resulting damp soil conditions in Perth have preserved exceptional archaeological remains of burgh life from the late 12th century onwards, including wattle, plank and clay-walled structures.

Royal revenues and patronage in Perth increased in tandem, leading to the foundation of a number of religious houses, most significantly the Dominican friary (1231) on the old castle lands, the Carmelite friary (1262) at Tullylumb, the Franciscan friary (late 15th century) between Tay and Princes Streets, and the only Carthusian

National Library of Scotland

Top *View of Perth by John Slezer, published 1693.* Above *City of Perth, late 16th century by Timothy Pont.*

Perth Bridge and North Inch, early 19th century.

RCAHMS

Right *City of Perth*. Below *Pullar Building, Mill Street.*

Millais' Viewpoint by Tim Shutter, 1997.

monastery (1429) in Scotland, sited near the present King James VI Hospital. The Treaty of Perth, between Alexander III and Magnus IV of Norway, was made in the church of the Dominican friary in 1266. Parliaments and general councils met frequently in various other Perth venues throughout the 14th and 15th centuries. Unusually for a Scottish burgh, Perth developed defensive stone walls and fortifications, probably as a result of its involvement in the Wars of Independence. A fosse or lade surrounded the walls. Perth is also unique as the only burgh known to have had suburbs (Curfew Row area to the north and New Row area to the west) before the 16th century.

Nestled at the foot of Kirkton and Moncreiffe Hills to the south, and Kinnoull Hill to the east, Perth lies on what was once a small promontory between the North and South Inches.

Like many old Scots burghs, Perth developed on a plan of two parallel streets (High and South) linked by a herringbone pattern of vennels. The old Watergate gained in status as nobles built sophisticated new town houses and laid out gardens down to the river. A tolbooth, market cross, guildhall and town mills were built, but all are now lost or replaced by more modern buildings.

In 1559 the appearance of the town was radically transformed by the Reformation mob, who destroyed all the monastic foundations. Nearly a century later, Cromwell's troops robbed stone from over 140 houses, the grammar school, the hospital, the market cross and even the Greyfriars' Churchyard to build a massive square-plan citadel on the South Inch (excavated 1999). In turn this hated symbol of occupation suffered demolition by attrition, finally being swept away in the early 19th century. Relative stability returned after the Restoration, interrupted only by the Jacobite risings of 1715 and 1745, which saw increased prosperity based on the linen trade, and the gradual replacement of the early structures with stone-built tenements.

John Smeaton's new bridge of 1766 provided the catalyst for an extraordinary burst of building activity, breaking the confines of the old town walls. The plans were exceptionally ambitious: not only the creation of two new grid-iron pattern developments grafted onto the north and south sides of the town, but also a rationalisation of the existing medieval plan to link the new developments through the centre of the old town. The north/south links were George Street from 1771, and St John Street, opened 1801. The northern new town started with Charlotte Street (1783), Atholl Crescent and Rose Terrace. From 1801 the monumental terraces of Marshall Place fronted the southern new town. Although the street layouts survive, the pattern of development continued in a more piecemeal fashion into the mid-19th century. Tay Street, the last great frontage to the town, was completed in the 1870s. Apart from its strength as an agricultural trading centre, Perth generated a broad industrial base during the 19th century encompassing the manufacture of glass, ink, carpets, umbrellas, ropes, linens and bricks, and whisky-blending, printing, dyeing, brewing, ship-building and iron-founding, to name but a few. The arrival of the railway in 1848 tended to concentrate the industries on the north and west sides of town. Consequently the smartest villa-dwellers moved east and created their own *rus in urbe* on Barnhill. An early 20th-century boom, particularly in insurance and banking, produced some very fine flourishes of Edwardian baroque.

The late 20th-century losses include the 16th-century Kinnoull Lodging in the Watergate, 17th-century buildings in High Street and South Street, the early 19th-century Star Inn in Canal Street, Ruskin's House at Bridgend, Wallace's linen works in Barrack Street, H E Clifford's 1912 Glasgow Road whisky bond for Dewars, and Smart, Stewart & Mitchell's 1934 United Free Church in Kinnoull Street. Like many towns, Perth faces pressures of increasing traffic, the retail-barn culture versus town centre shops, and the provision of new housing and offices. In these difficult areas the 'Fair City' continues to build on recent successes such as Gaia Architects' Fairfield scheme, Keppie Architects' redevelopment of the old Pullar building and the Nelson Street flats.

Below *Perth City crest.* Bottom *Council Offices (former Sharp's Educational Institute), 6-8 South Methven Street.*

9

St John's Parish Kirk, proposed alterations by Robert Lorimer.

On his return from France and Geneva in May 1559, **John Knox**, *c.*1513–72, delivered his famous sermon against idolatry in St John's Kirk. The resulting riot was the first crisis of the Reformation in Scotland: '*So was menis consciences befoir beattin with the worde, that thei had no respect to thare awin particulare proffeit, bot onlie to abolishe idolatrie, the places and monumentis thareof: in which thei wer so busye, and so laborious, that within two dayis, these three great places, monuments of idolatrie, to witt, the Gray and Black theves, and Charter-housse monkis (a buylding of a wonderouse coast and greatness) was so destroyed, that the walles onlie did remane of all these great edificationis.*'

Below Spire, St John's Parish Kirk. *Bottom* Partially built scheme by James Gillespie Graham, 1825.

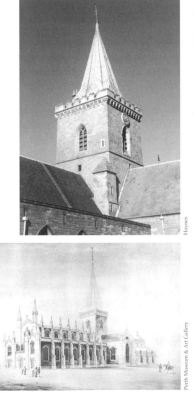

1 **St John's Parish Kirk**, St John's Place, from 1440
A church has stood on this site since at least early 12th century, giving rise to the city's alternative name, 'St John's toun', its most frequent title in the 16th century. Rebuilding of the Kirk of St John took place in stages, beginning with the choir *c.*1440, followed by the transepts and tower, and finally the nave and Halkerston Tower (or north porch) by the end of the 15th century. Subsequent repairs, subdivisions and restorations, including major campaigns by James Gillespie Graham in the 1820s, Andrew Heiton Jr in the 1890s and Robert Lorimer in the 1920s, have taken their toll on the 15th-century fabric, but the core of the building, including original choir roof, survives. Leadwork on ribbed broach spire dates predominantly from repairs of 1747 and 1767, and tower contains a remarkable collection of bells, some of pre-Reformation origin. The 1923–6 restoration of St John's in memory of the First World War dead was Lorimer's last major gothic work. Externally, the crisp stonework of the heightened aisles (previously the aisle roofs formed a near-continuous sweep from the nave roof) and tidying up of Halkerston Tower has a slightly clinical effect. Interior works were much more successful removing post-Reformation divisions and galleries to reveal something like the original spaces and unifying the fitting out with high quality materials and craftsmanship (Scott Morton). Iron lectern and font, 1970, Schomberg Scott. Fine early 20th-century stained glass by William Wilson, Douglas Strachan, Herbert Hendrie and Marjorie Kemp (colour p.52).
Guidebooks available

K D Farquharson

Below *City Hall*. Bottom *King Edward VII Memorial*.

Haynes

2 **City Hall**, King Edward Street, 1909–14,
H E Clifford & T Lunan
Big, bold and baroque. Giant paired Ionic
columns dominate the recessed portico, windows
are garlanded with rich decorative carving and
oversized putti perch above. All done with
considerable swagger and much energy. The
more understated interior has a continuous
gallery, swept down at the east end to
accommodate stage and organ.

King Edward VII Memorial, King Edward
Street, 1913, A K Beaton
Modelled on the 1885 Sydney Mitchell restoration
of Edinburgh's Mercat Cross. Original Perth
Mercat Cross stood in the middle of High Street
at the junction with Kirkgate, but was destroyed
by Cromwell's army in 1651. New cross,
designed 1669, by Robert Mylne, was removed as
an impediment to traffic in 1765, and the shaft
now stands at Fingask Castle. **St John's Centre**,
1987, behind, a deceptively large and bland retail
development, spruced up by Reiach & Hall, 1998.

Internaçionale, King Edward Street,
earlier 20th century
Appropriately Edwardian in design, with two-
storey colonnade above shopfronts, in the style of

Haynes

Selfridge's, but detailed in the contemporary 1930s fashion with bronze panels and stylised block capitals to the columns.

Salvation Army Hall.

The Watergate's long decline began in 1796, when fickle fashion shifted to the parallel, but newly built, St John Street. By the end of the 19th century, residential use had declined and business moved in, as can be seen in the brick temple front to the wine and whisky warehouse at **56 Watergate**, 1891, David Smart – perhaps a rather cheeky jibe at the Temperance Movement by the merchant Alexander Dingwall.

Clydesdale Bank.

3 **Salvation Army Hall**, 30-36 King Edward Street/75-81 South Street, 1904, John Hamilton
Perhaps best described as in Glasgow Free Style, the Sally Army Hall touches obliquely on every style from classical and gothic to Art Nouveau. Light and airy original shopfronts at ground floor with crisp red sandstone to hall above. Sculptural effect, particularly in strong sunlight, with bold shadows cast by oversailing eaves and other exaggerated details such as hoodmoulds, wallhead coping and roof ventilators. Good internal finishing, but not dramatic like the exterior.

St John Street, from 1796
Elegant terraces of largely plain early 19th-century tenements with shops below and broad brick stacks above, **Nos 26-30** on the east side distinguished by Venetian windows, and a pair of wallhead gables at **Nos 62-76**.

Clydesdale Bank, 3-5 St John Street, *c.*1845, James Smith
Appropriately genteel bankers' palazzo, built for the Bank of Scotland by master mason to the Crown, with Ionic-columned doorpieces in outer bays, a delicate lacy iron balcony stretching along the pedimented first-floor windows and a modestly projecting cornice.

4 **Bank of Scotland**, 48-50 St John Street, 1846–7, David Rhind
By comparison, there is nothing restrained about

this opulent Italian renaissance palazzo, originally headquarters for the Central Bank. Rhind was never a man to let his clients' budgets get in his way, and it shows in the high quality of materials and expensive detailing: sturdy balustrades at top and bottom, Corinthian pilasters to first-floor windows, paired stone brackets to balcony, chunky quoins and deep bracketed cornice. Extraordinary plasterwork of the banking hall is even more lavish. Unfortunately the grand staircase with a screen of columns to the palatial accommodation above is now lost.

Watergate was probably the earliest site of settlement in Perth, although it is not documented until the 13th century. Street's heyday was in late 16th and early 17th centuries, when lined with fashionable town houses or lodgings, those on the east side enjoying long narrow plots stretching down to the river. Last remaining timber-fronted house in the burgh, early 17th-century **Kinnoull Lodging** or **Dower House**, survived at the southeast end until demolition in 1966, although old refronted buildings still exist, for example at **13 Watergate**. The artisan classical doorpiece to **No 27** is dated 1725 and displays the monogram of the Wrights' Incorporation, whose panelled meeting hall there was dismantled, late 1960s.

Top *Bank of Scotland.* Above *Compartmental ceiling, Bank of Scotland.*

Left *Kinnoull Lodging, late 19th century.* Below *Kinnoull Lodging, reconstruction drawings.*

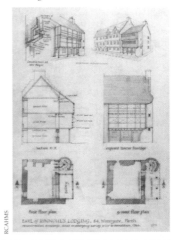

Tay Street
An embankment and street along the river from South Inch to new Perth Bridge had been planned as early as 1806, but it was not until the mid-1880s that the grand tree-lined boulevard was finally completed. Last remnants of the medieval backlands were tidied away, and for the first time the city presented a grand civic face

13

J D Fergusson Gallery.

Fergusson Gallery
The second great age of water engineering is aptly celebrated by Anderson's Roman Doric temple. Following the complete collapse of the water supply for two weeks in 1827, Anderson was called in by the burgh water commissioners to design a new system. Fresh clean water was drawn from filter beds at Moncreiffe Island in the Tay, and pumped by steam engine to an enormous domed cast-iron cistern. The waterworks served the town's pumps, commercial concerns, and eventually private houses. Motto *'Aquam igne et aqua haurio'* means *'I draw water by fire and water'* (steam). Anderson also promoted Perth's gas supply, standardised weights, improved navigation of the Tay, and Perth/Dundee railway.

Below *Pillars designed and cut for Broomhall House, Fife, used at Sheriff Court.* Right *Sheriff Court.*

towards the river. Flood prevention scheme replaced 19th-century embankment, 1999–2000.

5 **J D Fergusson Gallery**, Tay Street and Marshall Place, 1830–2, Adam Anderson
Highly original neoclassical former waterworks designed 1832 by the rector of Perth Academy, in form of a Roman temple. Restoration and later 19th-century additions removed to form Tourist Information Centre, 1973, Morris & Steedman. Converted 1992, Perth & Kinross District Council Architects, to bright and well-planned gallery for the display of works by Scottish Colourist, J D Fergusson (colour p.52).

The former Caledonian Railway line sweeps in behind the gallery on the curved 1180ft **viaduct** of 1864. **56-70 Tay Street**, 1887–96, John Young, Teutonic Romanesque former home of the Natural History Museum and Working Boys' and Girls' Hall. Yellow brick tenement, **70 Tay Street**, 1992, replaces Young's corner block and Baptist Church, which were destroyed by fire in 1984.

6 **Sheriff Court**, 1819–22, Robert Smirke
Although adjoining felons' and debtors' prisons were demolished, 1968, the full weight and majesty of the law are reflected in Smirke's Greek Revival design for courthouses and former county buildings. Columns re-used from unexecuted portico at Broomhall (see *The Kingdom of Fife* in this series). Complexities of later Victorian planning are latent in the segregation of judiciary, jurors, witnesses, accused and public. An underground passage led directly from dock to prison. King's Architect, Robert Reid, prepared plans for a neoclassical palace block, and also designs in Greek Revival style, similar to William Stark's Glasgow Justiciary Courthouse (see *Central*

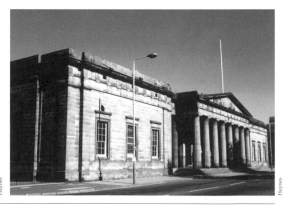

Glasgow), but the Commissioners of Supply were unimpressed and awarded the project to Smirke. Fine interior to Courtroom No 1, rebuilt in square format, 1866–7, David Smart, from original D-plan layout; Assembly Room now subdivided and missing its superb eagle chimneypiece (colour p.51).

7 **Queen's Bridge**, Tay Street, 1960, Consulting Engineers F A Macdonall & Ptnrs (Glasgow) Ponderous old Victoria Bridge of 1900 was jacked up to support new pre-stressed concrete structure as it was built. The result is a beautifully light and elegant triple span of shallow arches.

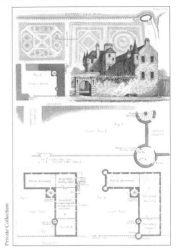

Private Collection

Old Gowrie House, *c*.1570 (*above, mid-19th-century engraving*), was demolished in 1805 to make way for the County Buildings. Town house of Lords Ruthven, the most magnificent of many nobles' lodgings which backed onto the Tay along Speygate and Watergate. L-plan with enclosing courtyard wall, it was the scene of the notorious Gowrie Conspiracy of 1600, from which James VI escaped assassination at the hands of John 3rd Earl of Gowrie and his younger brother Alexander Ruthven. Formal gardens incorporated parts of the old town wall and its defences at Monk's Tower and Spey Tower.

Gowrie House, 46-52 Tay Street, *c*.1865, possibly Andrew Heiton Jr
Near symmetrical three-storey French Gothic office block with spiky roofline of bargeboarded dormers and wallhead stacks. Well-detailed throughout, from its polished pink granite columns flanking the pend to cast-iron window guards.

Victoria Buildings, 36-44 Tay Street, 1872, Andrew Heiton Jr
Grandiose symmetrical palace block of offices, in the style of Alexander 'Greek' Thomson. Four pedimented bays with tripartite windows break forward from serried ranks of single windows. Ornament is reserved for the pedimented doorways. The perils of stone cleaning are well-illustrated by the offices of the *Perthshire Advertiser*, which barely read as part of the block.

Left *Queen's Bridge and Gowrie House*.
Below *Victoria Buildings*.

8 **St Matthew's Church** (formerly Free West Church), Tay Street, 1871, John Honeyman
The undoubted glory of Honeyman's Gothic Revival essay in the First Pointed style is the

elegant 212ft tower and slender stone spire. Base of tower incorporates porch; above a blind arcade at second stage and an open belfry at the third; pinnacles on angles of the tower and four lucarnes ease the transition from tower to spire. Internally, cast-iron columns with oversized floreate capitals support the gallery and barrel-vaulted roof. Church opened for public worship in November 1871. Cost of the building was estimated at £6,000. In 1965 congregations of Wilson Church, Scott Street, West and Middle Churches, Tay Street, and Bridgend Church merged in St Matthew's.

The Jazz Bank, 26 Tay Street, c.1873, Andrew Heiton Jr
The stylistic melting pot of Tay Street continues with a French renaissance roof (decorative ironwork sadly missing) and Venetian Gothic windows at No 26, the old Savings Bank of the County and City of Perth.

9 **Middle Church and Halls**, 4-6 Tay Street, 1887, Hippolyte Jean Blanc
Exuding confidence in design and quality in materials. Blanc practised from Edinburgh, but generally preferred to use red sandstones from the west. Here, the capable handling of Early Pointed Gothic, including flying buttresses, rose window, clerestory and plate tracery, is crowned by a high roof and modest Continental style flèche. Externally sensitive conversion to flats, 1995, McLaren, Murdoch & Hamilton.

Top *St Matthew's Church*. Above *The Jazz Bank*. Right *Middle Church, 1904*.

Perth Bridge, 1766–72, John Smeaton
Previous bridges had stood at the east end of High Street, but following the demise of Robert Mylne's 1617 bridge, swept away in a flood of 1621, no new crossing was attempted until Lord Provost William Stewart commissioned John

Smeaton to design the present bridge in 1766. The result was a structure of great strength and supreme elegance: seven main arches in red sandstone with oculi (now bricked up, but originally hollow to reduce weight and spread load) set in the spandrels, gently cambered to centre to throw off rainwater to the sides. Footpaths added, 1869, by engineer A D Stewart and lamps by Laidlaws of Glasgow.

10 **Council Offices**, 3 High Street and 8-18 Tay Street, 1877–9, Andrew Heiton Jr
Outwardly subdued Continental Gothic style for former Municipal Buildings. Short four-bay High Street elevation was extended by two bays as part of works by Andrew Grainger Heiton following a disastrous fire in 1895. Corner oriel is loosely based on tower of the ancient chapel of St Mary, which formed part of the former town house and police offices on site. Chief interest of interior is Council Chamber, a mock medieval hall with hammerbeam roof, timber panelled dado, hooded baronial fireplace and magnificent stained glass windows illustrating scenes from Sir Walter Scott's *The Fair Maid of Perth* and the capture of Perth by Robert the Bruce in 1313. Victoria and Albert guard window to grand stairhall (colour p.49). More oak panelling in former District Courtroom adjoining Council Chamber.

Severe earlier 19th-century bank building at **7-11 High Street**, with suitably centurion pairs of Doric columns flanking entrance. Splendid late renaissance doorway to pend of plain classical

Top Perth Bridge. *Middle* Council Offices. *Above* Pediment, 13-19 High Street.

11 tenement at **13-19 High Street**; pediment initialled 'RG EC' (Robert Graham and Elspeth Cunningham), dated 1699. Impressive unbroken run of four-storey tenements and shops from **21-43 High Street**, dated 1774 on gable to George Street. **55-57 High Street** is taller and later, with classical trimmings and smart balustrade. **Woolworths**, 1960, Festival of Britain in inspiration – symmetrical grid design above shop floor, with alternate strips of glazing and coloured tiles, and rooftop flagpoles to cheer up shoppers. Good 19th-century shopfront, adapted, 1950s, to **Watson's**.

12 **Perth Theatre**, 177-187 High Street, 1898, William Alexander
Theatre reconstructed following fire, 1924, G P K Young. Cleverly designed as mixed development of shops and tenements to street, linked to the theatre behind, the architect saved his fireworks

High Street developed from the early 12th century, starting at the east end where it met the Tay at right angles, probably linking to a bridge. Evidence of wattle houses and workshops, the earliest High Street structures, was found during archaeological work prior to the construction of Marks and Spencer in 1977. By the early 14th century, the Turretbrig Port (demolished 1766) closed the western end of the High Street, at the junction of North and South Methven Streets. Development began to spill outside burgh boundary during the 15th and 16th centuries. Much of the High Street was re-developed for shops and tenements in the late 18th and early 19th centuries. A number of these plain classical tenements survive above the much-altered shopfronts. The major junctions were beefed up with good solid corner buildings c.1900.

Laura Ashley.

Glasites were the followers of John Glas, the Minister of Tealing Parish, who split from the established church in 1728. After the marriage of Glas's daughter to Robert Sandeman of the Luncarty bleaching family, the sect also became known as Sandemanians. Meetings were followed by a common meal, often of kail, or cabbage, which led to further nicknames of *'kailites'* for followers and *'Kail Kirk'* for their church (see *Dundee* in this series).

Below *249 High Street.* Bottom *Detail, Council Chambers.* Right *Council Chambers.*

for the interior. Relief of Marjorie Dence by Scott Sutherland, 1969, adorns glass-roofed foyer. Auditorium has horseshoe plan, with two balconies on cast-iron columns (colour p.49). Frilly cast-iron glazed canopy, which once stretched the full length of street frontage, is now replaced by a simple canopy over theatre entrance.

Dutch classical in red sandstone at **Laura Ashley**, 189-191 High Street. The west corner of High Street and Kinnoull Street is secured by the substantial presence of the **Woolwich**, 197 High Street, 1900, David Smart, with its mixture of Italian and French renaissance details. Next door, **199 High Street**, a rare late 18th-century survival of a tenement with wallhead gable to street – did it once have a lum too? **Cafe Paco**, on the corner of High Street and South Methven Street, 1894, Peter Roy Jackson, was a speculative development for Thomas Roy, arcaded at ground floor in readiness for a bank, now missing lantern to its dome.

13 **249 High Street**, late 18th century
Former Glasite Meeting House. Odd piece of vernacular classicism, with symmetrical arrangement of doors and windows at ground floor and three Venetian windows to hall at first floor. Blank gable walls suggest it was intended to be part of a terrace or close-knit group.

14 **Council Chambers**, 2 High Street and Tay Street, 1899, George P K Young
Built as sumptuous power house of the General Accident Fire and Life Assurance Corporation, on site of old post office. Strongly influenced by J J Burnet in Beaux Arts detailing and colonnaded second floor tucked under the heavy bracketed

cornice (Young's son, Cedric, was a favourite assistant and friend of Burnet). Yellow freestone from Woodburn Quarry in Cumberland, sets the building apart as a bold interloper. Converted for council use in 1984 by Technical Services Department; large ground-floor counting room subdivided and council chamber created at top of building, but magnificent marble staircase, mahogany panelled board room and general manager's office survive. Arcaded extension, 1957–8, well managed, continuing along High Street with variation on Thomsonesque colonnade.

15 Opposite, **28-30 High Street/1-5 Watergate**, late 18th-century tenement with Gibbsian doorpiece to No 3 Watergate, refronted in smart mid-19th-century classical garb, incorporating arms of the Mercers of Aldie at first floor. Late 19th-century commercial Venetian at **32-34 High Street**. A distinctive feature of Perth tenements, particularly in High Street and South Street, from mid-18th century to early 19th century was the open stair to street. Although rather mutilated at first floor, **44-46 High Street/1 St John Street** is a good example, *c*.1835. **Dolland & Aitchison**, 1900, squeezed inwards and upwards in ashlar sandstone Dutch renaissance.

16 **Halifax** (former Guildhall), 104-106 High Street, 1907–8, A G Heiton
Two broad arches to ground-floor shops, first floor a direct quotation from centrepiece of Wren's Privy Garden elevation at Hampton Court. Sculpture in niche below central pediment by H H Morton. Former Guildhall of 1722 previously occupied site. Elegant panelling of hall now sadly removed.

Top *28-30 High Street/1-5 Watergate.*
Above *Halifax.*

Hydro-Electric, 108-112 High Street, 1904, Menart & Jarvie
Powerful Edwardian baroque shops and tenements appropriately announcing the entrance to King Edward Street. Corner tower with its bulbous attic columns, pediments, scrolls and dome is particularly effective.

17 **Former St Paul's Church**, High Street and South Methven Street, 1806–7, John Paterson
Possibly the earliest example in Scotland of a hybrid gothic-classical church. Result is strange, but striking. Awkward juxtaposition of spiky tower with octagonal body of the church is largely obscured in the principal view of the building from the eastern part of High Street.

The Guildry Incorporation of Perth originally comprised merchants, maltmen, surgeons and dyers, who exercised their judicial and membership functions through the Guild Court. A separate body, the Incorporated Trades, represented hammermen, bakers, glovers, wrights, tailors, fleshers, and shoemakers, through the Convenor Court.

St Paul's Church
It had often been remarked, that another steeple would much improve the appearance of Perth; but to have a steeple, it was necessary to have a church, and therefore the foundation was laid of St Paul's Church!
Anonymous Guide to Perth, 1822

Right *29-37 South Street.* Below *SEPA Offices.*

18 **SEPA Offices**, 1-3 South Street, 1863–6, David Smart, built for Sheriff Clerk and Procurator Fiscal in Italian renaissance dress, forming a distinguished introduction to South Street. **29-37 South Street**, *c.*1825, paired pilasters to shopfronts, pends to outer bays and Venetian window in central pediment to tenement above. More confidence than strict classical correctness, but still a fine termination to Princes Street opposite. Panel below pediment records history of the site. **91-95 South Street**, late 18th century, remains of once-impressive tenement with wallhead gable, now mutilated by unsympathetic glazing. **Royal Bar**, 139-141 South Street, has interesting stained glass windows. Polygonal corner tower anchors **The Illicit Still**, 89 South Street, 1900–1, McLaren & Mackay, sturdy Edwardian renaissance pub and tenement. Liberal use of raised blocks breaking window architraves, carved volutes to tower and strapwork parapet.

8-12 South Street/3 Speygate, mid-18th century Large vernacular classical tenement with steep gables and broad chimneystack, marking start of South Street proper. Rare bow-fronted late 18th-century shopfront survives at ground floor. Rear wing on Speygate has crowstepped gable. More vernacular classical at **26-32 South Street**, this time sporting a wallhead gable.

Watergate continues as Speygate, once a dense urban landscape with old prison defining the east boundary of street, now shot through with car park and gap sites. Particularly good tenement front with wallhead gable and stack at Nos 17-21, dated 1802. No 15 is the Old Customs Bond.

8-12 South Street/3 Speygate.

19 **Salutation Hotel**, 36 South Street, *c.*1800 Claimed to be the oldest established hotel in Scotland, dating from 1699. Externally, it is expressed in two parts. The left, containing the enormous Venetian window of the Adam Restaurant, *c.*1800, terminates the view along St John Street giving the illusion that it is the centre of an impressive palace block. The illusion is

shattered on arriving in South Street, where it is clear that the palace block was never built. The right is a 19th-century remodelling of an earlier building, visually linked to the main block by balustraded parapet. Much modified inside, but retains the splendid vaulted Adam Restaurant and stone fireplace of 1699 in the Stewart Room. Stone bearing arms of the Earl of Moray, dated 1619, in courtyard behind.

20 **38 South Street**, 1858, David Rhind
Ten years on from the Central Bank in St John Street, Rhind adopted a Florentine palazzo mode – round-headed windows and arcade between chimneystacks – for this branch office of his principal clients, the Commercial Bank. Quality is still there in beautifully detailed stonework and trademark keystone masques. The last two bays on Princes Street are later additions in same style.

170-178 South Street, c.1810
Former Wesleyan Church in plain Gothicky style, four pointed windows at first floor. Converted to new use.

21 **Bank of Scotland**, 220 South Street/17 Canal Crescent, 1903–4, Dunn & Findlay
Renaissance Freestyle with exotic ogee dome to corbelled corner tower. Unsympathetic replacement shopfronts.

South Street continues westwards as County Place and York Place. **2-8 County Place**, early 19th century, plain classical tenements with shops below, on gushet site with Hospital Street. Bowed corner bay, stacks rebuilt in brick.

22 **A K Bell Library & Theatre**, York Place, 1836–8, William Mackenzie
Mackenzie's *'elegant and spacious'* infirmary building survives at the heart of new library

Top *38 South Street*. Above *2-8 County Place*. Left *A K Bell Library & Theatre*.

William Macdonald Mackenzie, 1797–1856, Perth's City Architect, hailed from a remarkable architectural dynasty that lasted for a century and a half. W M Mackenzie held the post of City Architect for some thirty years, and his influence extended well beyond the burgh boundaries into the provision of many churches and farms throughout the county. One of his designs for a model farm (see Elcho, p.46) was published as an exemplar by John Claudius Loudon in his *Encyclopaedia of Cottage, Farm & Villa Architecture* (1833), and he won a medal from the Highland Society for other farm designs. Mackenzie also designed the triumphal arch erected for Queen Victoria's visit to Perth in 1842. The dynasty:

Father	Alexander (Scone) d.1827
Son 1	William Macdonald (City Architect, Perth) 1797–1856
Son 2	David I (Dundee) d.1842
Son 3	Thomas (Elgin & Aberdeen) 1814–54
Grandson	Alexander Marshall Mackenzie (Aberdeen & London) 1848–1933
Grandson	David II (Dundee) 1832–75
Gt Grandson	Alexander G R Mackenzie (Aberdeen) 1879–1963

complex on commanding site at head of South Street and County Place. Symmetrical design with central block linked to advanced wings, including quirky features such as a *porte-cochère*, tapering window surrounds *à-la-Grec* to first-floor windows of wings and strange scrolls in the form of pediments. Post-modern additions, 1994, Perth & Kinross District Council Architects, toy playfully with circular motifs from the old building, leading to fully fledged portholes in places, which lend a nautical feel. Mackenzie's shallow-domed entrance hall remains an impressive space. Enormous window in new east wing makes good use of spectacular views across town to Kinnoull Hill. **Lodge** was part of 1836 scheme, again with Greek tendencies, but moved and rebuilt, *c.*1867, David Smart; refurbished as offices for Perth & Kinross Heritage Trust, 2000.

Above right *Lodge, A K Bell Library & Theatre.* Right and below *1-9 York Place.*

1-9 York Place, 1907, G P K Young, has splendid copper dome to corner tower. Upper floors boldly modelled with crisp baroque carving and detailing. Beautifully delicate cast-iron shopfronts below. Scale of buildings on York Place drops away to two-storey villas west of Library. **Nos 18-20**, later 19th century, have columned doorpieces and bay windows. **32 York Place**, also later 19th century, pair of pattern book villas made exceptional by lavish use of Thomsonesque Greek ornament on front elevation. **Trinity Church**, 1860, built for the United Presbyterians, appears defiantly Germanic with its twin towers capped by tall pyramidal roofs and gabled bell louvres, influenced by Bryce's Dundee Congregational church.

23 **6-8 South Methven Street**, 1860, David Smart Handsome symmetrical design with central Italianate tower, set back from the street. Established as Educational Institute before advent of board schools, by bequest of John Sharp, Perth baker. As well as junior and senior departments, it provided an industrial school for girls and technical school for boys. Special provision was made *for branches of education peculiar to girls* (*Groome's Gazetteer*, 1884). Now council offices.

24 **King James VI Hospital**, Hospital Street, 1750 Perhaps designed by James Cree, who laid the foundation stone. Classical H-plan paupers' palace of some magnificence, built by voluntary subscription under day labour supervised by Baillie Robertson and Deacon Gardiner. Buildings of original hospital, founded by James VI, 1589, were largely destroyed by Cromwell during his occupancy of the city in 1651. Anachronistic turnpike stair suggests some parts of earlier building may have been incorporated. Third Duke of Atholl presented the cupola in 1764, salvaged from the demolition of the House of Nairne (see p.108). Trustees' Room survives inside, fitted with panels recording hospital benefactors. Remainder was converted to 21 flats, 1973–5, by James Morrison.

25 **Free Presbyterian Church of Scotland**, Pomarium Street, 1938, Erskine Thomson & Glass Picturesque grouping of neatly crowstepped Arts

From top *Trinity Church; King James VI Hospital, Cupola, and Trustees Room.* Left *Free Presbyterian Church of Scotland.*

The **culmination** of the seasonal railway traffic through Perth was the rush north for the Glorious Twelfth, the first day of the grouse shooting season. On 7th August 1888, the 7.50 left Perth Station with 36 carriages belonging to nine different companies, including 13 horse boxes and a meat van.

& Crafts church and houses, originally built as hall and caretaker's house for Forteviot Charitable Trust. Largely overshadowed by first of Perth's small and precocious developments of highish-rise (eight- and 11-storey) flats, **Nos 7-51** and **52-95**, 1958, by Burgh Council Housing Department.

Perth Museum & Art Gallery

Right Perth Railway Station, pre 1885. *Below* Station Clock. *Middle* Station Hotel. *Bottom* 40-42 Leonard Street.

Haynes

26 **Perth Railway Station**, Leonard Street, 1848, Sir William Tite (London)
Aptly known as the Gateway to the Highlands, Perth Station's key strategic position made it the busy marshalling point for the Highland, Caledonian, and North British railways from 1866. Earliest part of building is long range of Tudor-Gothic offices and waiting rooms with octagonal tower between platforms 4 and 7, which closely resemble Tite's station at Carlisle, 1847. Next came the Tudor-Gothic ramp and exotic Moorish arches at platforms 1 and 2, set on a curve to the Dundee line. Blyth & Westland expanded the station, 1885, with formation of platforms 3 and 4, enclosing Tite's buildings on east side. Frilly canopies over platforms 5 to 7, 1893, for Caledonian Railway. Latest part of jigsaw is Scotrail booking office, late 20th century.

Haynes

Station Hotel, Leonard Street, 1888, Andrew Heiton Jr
Built jointly by the railway companies. Flemish Gothic style perhaps an allusion to lowland start of journey north. Much frequented on journeys to and from Balmoral by Queen Victoria, who was said to dislike dining on trains. More hotels opposite in Leonard Street: the **Queen's** has vestigial remains of early 19th-century scheme; old **Royal British** has politely vernacular seven-bay frontage of late 18th-century origin.

Haynes

40-42 Leonard Street, 1904
Deceptively simple pair of shops and tenements in red brick and harl. Nicely detailed throughout – roof gently swept at eaves, glazed oculus in

gablehead, sinuous shopfronts (doorways glazed to form one shop) and central moulded doorway with another oculus above.

27 **Caledonian Road School**, 1892, Andrew Heiton Jr Handsome Dutch-gabled Board School, built from deep red sandstone from Corncockle Quarry, Dumfries. Light and ventilation were primary concerns, as demonstrated by the enormous mullion windows and rooftop ventilators. Impressive double stair lit by a large cupola.

Princes Street

28 **St John the Baptist Episcopal Church**, 1851, J, W H & J M Hay, solid Mid-Pointed Gothic by church specialists, the Hay brothers of Liverpool. Arcaded tower with broached spire. Impressive open timber roof. **No 55**, 1923–4, James Miller, built as lodging house for the homeless by Lord Forteviot. Perth's finest surviving warehouse at **Nos 38-48**, c.1890, long nine-bay front, pedimented at centre and arcaded at ground floor; converted to shops below and flats above. **No 52**, 1866, by contrast has short triple arcade at first floor. **No 62**, 1883, rippling renaissance details at first floor, gutted inside, was the studio of photographer Magnus Jackson.

Top and above *Caledonian Road School.* Left *Warehouse, 38-48 Princes Street*

Magnus Jackson, Perth's major late 19th-century photographer, travelled extensively throughout the county and specialised in architectural subjects. An extensive collection of Jackson's glass plate negatives is held in Perth Archives.

62 Princes Street by Magnus Jackson.

Canal Street
Laid out, 1790s, on site of city wall, South Stank and Spy Ridge. From the beginning it had a back-quarter character, home to granaries, warehouses, livery stables, gasworks, a brewery, coachworks and two commercial inns (including fine early 19th-century Star Inn, demolished late 20th century). Gap sites, car parks and pastiche housing

25

have taken their place to enhance backland feel. Only **Love's Auction Rooms**, 52-54 Canal Street, exotic half-timbered former coachworks, enlivens the dreary scene. **Charterhouse Lane**, continuation of Canal Street, has fared better, retaining its long, low terraces of early 19th-century houses and axial view of St Leonard's Church.

29 **Telephone Exchange**, Canal Crescent, 1962, GPO Technology and modernity are reflected in the glass wall with its jolly zigzag entrance canopy and coloured panels below the windows, but not at the expense of the gentle curve of the old street pattern. A sensitive design for its time.

James Street
Mixed residential development in southern new town. On east side, imposing corniced doorpieces to **Nos 28-40**, a terrace of earlier 19th-century town houses. To west, a series of mid-19th-century single-storey villas, **Nos 25-27** with pair of console doorpieces, **No 31** with pilastered doorpiece, all weighted down with substantial dormers.

King Street
Largely populated with polite classical villas of earlier 19th century. Loss of original details, in particular window astragals, is a shame, as it has clearly been a development of high quality. Pair of double villas at **1-4 Graham's Place** are finest, with Doric-columned doorpieces, rusticated ground floors and pedimented dormers.

Top *Telephone Exchange*. Middle *King Street*. Above *Former St Leonard's Parish Church by Magnus Jackson*. Below *Nelson Street Flats*.

30 **Former St Leonard's Parish Church**, King Street, 1834, W M Mackenzie
Closing vista along Canal Street, striking neoclassical design of three huge round-arched doorways, capped with bellcote in the style of choragic monument (erected in Athens by ancient Greek Lysicrates to commemorate his success in a choral competition). Interior recast in more florid style and extended by addition of an apse, 1891. Now an auction room.

22 South William Street, early 19th century
Pretty piend-roofed villa with pilastered doorpiece and rear stairtower.

31 **Nelson Street Flats**, 1998,
James F Stephen Architects
Energy-efficient flats for Perthshire Housing Association, designed around 'sun spaces'; internal south-facing conservatories absorb heat during the day and channel warm air into the building.

32 1-14 and 15-28 Marshall Place, 1801, Robert Reid
Two monumental palace block terraces of houses
and tenements, still under construction early 1820s.
In their day they would have rivalled the great
development schemes of Edinburgh's Second New
Town, Glasgow's Blythswood and Aberdeen's
King Street and Union Street. Reid's distinctive
attic lunettes mark centres of main blocks and
pavilions. Sadly, original unity of scheme is now
barely discernible (following removal of astragals,
truncation of chimneystacks, addition of dormers
and painting of individual properties). **King James
Place**, begun *c.*1820, was intended to continue
palace block theme, but was completed to
shortened design *c.*1885, following construction of
St Leonard's-in-the-Fields on the site of intended
eastern section. Scheme peters out completely to
west in later 19th-century villas of **King's Place**.

33 St Leonard's-in-the-Fields, Marshall Place, 1885,
J J Stevenson
First, and arguably best, scholarly revival of late
Scots Gothic forms of late 15th/early 16th
century, most conspicuously in crown spire,
clerestory, polygonal apse and sturdy buttressing.
Internally restrained, much more in preaching
box tradition of the Free Church than revivalist
spirit of the exterior. Stevenson was London-

Marshall Place by Magnus Jackson c.1870.

Provost Thomas Hay Marshall,
1770–1808, son of Thomas Marshall, a
previous Provost from 1784–86, was a
businessman, property developer, and
amateur soldier. Marshall's impact on
the appearance of the city was
enormous, initiating great public
improvement schemes such as doubling
the size of the North Inch, widening
streets, lighting and paving the main
thoroughfares, re-housing the Academy,
and developing new fronts to the North
and South Inches.

*Presentation drawing, St Leonard's-in-the-
Fields by J J Stevenson*

based, but in his last years designed small series of expensive Free Churches for his native country. **Halls** behind part of scheme.

St Leonard's Bank contrasts with the monumental front grafted on to the city in Marshall Place and eases the transition from the open space of South Inch to the buildings of the suburbs by a series of large and imposing villas set in expansive grounds. More informal, but still a show front to the city: all villas face east towards Edinburgh Road, not west towards street. Most are earlier 19th-century two-storey, three-bay villas. **No 5** has Ionic-columned doorcase, **No 7** similarly, but with elegant balustrade to roof. Fine Greek Doric doorcase at **No 9**, let down by modern windows. **No 10**, *c.*1835, grandest of all, four-bay garden front with pedimented windows at ground floor, attic storey over two central bays (dislocated by loss of original six-pane glazing pattern) and balustrade all round. Roman Doric porch, unfortunately glazed, flanked by niches on south front.

Kinnoull Street
High Street end is very grand in scale, particularly on west side, effectively five storeys high. **Nos 6-12**, 1895, the earliest part of David Smart's scheme for the corner with High Street.

34 **14-16 Kinnoull Street** (former Sandeman Public Library), 1898, Campbell, Douglas & Morrison Crisply detailed renaissance Freestyle by Glasgow firm in red sandstone with black granite Ionic columns to portico and curious pepperpot clocktower on corner with Mill Street. Now council offices.

31-33 Kinnoull Street, 1907, McLaren & McKay Arcaded shops with tenements above. Good Edwardian Baroque doorway on corner with Mill Street. Glasgow influence is felt here in the use of red sandstone, bay windows, wallhead chimneys and attenuated mouldings, keystones and corbels.

35 **Congregational Church**, Kinnoull Street, 1897, H B W Steele & Balfour
Another Glasgow firm at work in a compact design for a corner site, resulting in not-unpleasant proportions of a medieval casket.

From top *7 St Leonard's Bank; 10 St Leonard's Bank; 14-16 Kinnoull Street; 31-33 Kinnoull Street; Congregational Church.*

Towards Atholl Street, the scale of Kinnoull Street diminishes, finishing in elegant mid-19th-century corner block at **No 52**.

36 Pullar Building, Kinnoull Street and Mill Street, from 1865

Former Pullar's dyeworks complex occupies an enormous triangular site next to the Town Lade, bounded by Mill Street, Kinnoull Street and Blackfriars Wynd. Most dramatic external aspect is view of two main blocks along Mill Street, both immensely long and relentlessly regular. Two-storey block in attenuated classical style is the earliest (1865). Later three-storey block on Mill Street and four-storey block on Kinnoull Street have exaggerated crowstepped gables in manner of Flemish cloth halls. Behind these fronts, accomplished high-tech council offices, 2000, Keppie Architects (colour p.51).

Rear, Pullar Building.

Perth had long been famous for its linen industry, producing damasks, napkins, and fine sheetings. By the time Robert Pullar set up a factory in 1819, cotton was king – particularly umbrella gingham. His son, John, established a dye works, which flourished on the arrival of the railways, and the award of a Royal Warrant in 1852. The family firm branched out into dry cleaning from 1857. Prince Albert's death in 1861 sent the dye business into overdrive, as the demand for mourning attire soared. By 1900 Pullar's North British Dye Works in Mill Street was Perth's biggest enterprise, employing over 2,600 people. The First World War saw a collapse in trade and shortages of materials to a point where short time and low wages triggered 'The Battle of the Gates', a violent industrial dispute, in 1917. Following this, the company was taken over by Eastman & Sons, but continued to trade under the Pullar name.

Left *North Church by Magnus Jackson c.1880.* Below *Interior, North Church.*

37 North Church, Mill Street, 1880, T L Watson

Designed in flamboyant Italian Romanesque style for United Presbyterian Church by Glasgow architect. Tall round-headed lancet windows with slender colonnettes dominate design. Above arches on main elevation and porch, stone is cut like a honeycomb to imitate Romanesque decorative techniques. Slender cast-iron columns support galleries and barrel roof inside. Much remains of original fittings including pulpit and arcaded timber screen beneath organ. Richly painted decorative scheme may survive under present pink paintwork of chancel arch.

38 Playhouse Cinema, Murray Street, 1933, Alex Cattanach

Enormous Art Deco cinema and tearoom constructed in a record nine weeks for Caledonian Associated Cinemas, as a flagship to seat 1,700 patrons. Relatively restrained by Deco standards, but still flashy enough to stand out. Marble facings to two shops, originally confectioner and tobacconist, flanking entrance tower, with layers of red facing brick and horizontal wrap-around windows above (colour p.50). Although now divided into three cinemas, cantilevered balcony, proscenium arch and some of the Deco fittings and finishings remain. Thomas Bowhill Gibson was consultant.

61-71 South Methven Street, c.1840

Impressive late classical 11-window block, formerly premises of Alexanders Seedsmen. Centre slightly advanced, quoined and pedimented with centre windows tripartite. Later ground-floor shops, good detail at centre shop with scrolled pediment.

34-44 South Methven Street, mid-19th century

Long, low block of shops and tenements with a central pediment; pilasters of vermiculated rustication at ground-floor shops. Boldly detailed windows at first floor, right hand 10 have lugged architraves, left-hand six are architraved with triple keyblocks, modillioned cornice and blocking course.

39 City Mills, Mill Street and West Mill Street, later 18th century

Of the substantial industry which had been built up on the City Mills site by the beginning of the 19th century, two particularly fascinating buildings remain. The **Jarvis City Mills Hotel**, formerly Upper City Mills, comprises two wheat mills linked by large three-storey, five-bay granary, completed, 1792. Uncompromisingly converted to hotel in 1970–1 by T M Miller & Partners, but two undershot wheels remain visible beneath foyer and splendid king-post roof survives above the ballroom. The two **Lower City Mills**, complete to their current plan by 1805, straddle the lade, for oatmeal and pot barley/malt. Distinctive pagoda roof to old kiln. Restored by Perth & Kinross District Council, 1982–8, with working machinery, including massive undershot waterwheel.
Open to the public; leaflet

From top *Playhouse Cinema by Alex Cattanach; 61-71 South Methven Street; 34-44 South Methven Street; Lower City Mills.*

Milling has an extraordinary history in Perth, dating back to at least the 12th century, when David I granted 10 shillings from the income of his Perth mills to the canons of Scone Abbey. Robert II gave these King's Mills to the town in 1374. The route of the **Town Lade** appears to be of similar antiquity, drawing water from the River Almond some four miles away, both to power the mills and also to feed the ditch surrounding the medieval town walls.

Fair Maid's House.

Walter Scott's 1828 romance, set in Perth at the close of the 14th century, is a fictionalised version of the intrigue and feuding surrounding the court of mild-mannered Robert III. A tripartite struggle to win the hand of the Fair Maid, Catherine Glover, ends in the carnage of the Battle of the Clans Quhele and Chattan, fought on the North Inch. Georges Bizet's opera of 1867, *La Jolie Fille de Perth,* is based on the novel.

Mid-18th-century **Bakers' Granary**, 61 West Mill Street, north of hotel, converted to office and residential use by National Trust for Scotland.

40 **Fair Maid's House**, 21-23 North Port, 1893–4, J & G Young
Bought by the Glover Incorporation in 1629, and used as meeting hall for 150 years, it became immortalised by Sir Walter Scott as the Curfew Row home of Catherine Glover, *The Fair Maid of Perth*. Its picturesque qualities, including rickety forestair, were largely lost during reconstruction for William Japp of Alyth in 1893. Pointed-arched niche, home of the curfew bell in Scott's novel, remains high up on the left-hand side. **Hal o' the Wynd's House**, Mill Wynd, late 18th century, much restored, is Scott's model for the house of Catherine's suitor.

17-19 North Port, early 18th century
Again much reconstructed, the only remnant in Perth of an arcaded shop with tenement above, prevalent in all major burghs (see Elgin, *The District of Moray* in this series) from the 17th century. Known as the town house of Lord John Murray from 1755–87, when MP for Perthshire.

41 **Blackfriars House**, North Port, later 18th century
Elegant white harled classical town house of the Richardsons of Tullybelton, the lands of which were sold to develop the New Town streets of Atholl Place, Atholl Crescent and Rose Terrace. Five-bay piend-roofed *corps-de-logis* with refined pilastered doorpiece. Two-storey wings not quite symmetrical. Extended to Atholl Place, 1950, and now converted to council offices.

George Street
Broad and handsome planned street, opened in 1771 to form an appropriately elegant link between the new bridge over the Tay and High

Below 17-19 North Port. Middle *Blackfriars House.* Bottom *George Street.*

Street. Earlier tenements on east side are wide and low, usually no more than three storeys. Later west side largely four storey. Good sprinkling of traditional wallhead gables at **Nos 23-27**, **35-39**, **59-65** and **54-58**. **Glovers' Hall** is at 36-38.

15-21 George Street, mid-19th century
Three Venetian windows form an arcade at first floor with balustrade above. Remodelled from upholsterer's shop, 1887, by Andrew Heiton Jr for newly formed Perth Conservative Club.

Royal George Hotel, 47-51 George Street, 1790
Originally a coaching inn, it acquired its 'Royal' prefix and weighty classical make-over after a number of visits by Queen Victoria on her way to and from Balmoral. The artist D Y Cameron died here in 1945.

Strangeways, 22-24 George Street, 1857–8, Andrew Heiton Sr & Son
Unusual paired doorways to robust palazzo headquarters of Perth Bank. Ground floor details similar to Dunkeld and Blairgowrie branches.

42 **Camerons**, 26-34 George Street, 1836, William Mackenzie
Fine neoclassical former Exchange Coffee Room, with incised decoration in Sir John Soane manner, floats above improbably delicate Edwardian shopfronts at ground floor. Giant incised pilasters define end blocks and five impressive corniced windows light old coffee room on first floor; square windows above. Roof is discreetly hidden behind parapet. Little original interior work survives, and the coffee room is divided by an additional floor.

43 **Perth Museum and Art Gallery**, George Street, 1824, David Morison
Reduced version of Roman Pantheon, complete with dome (modified 1954) and giant Ionic portico, built in memory of Lord Provost Thomas Marshall to house city's library and museum of Literary and Antiquarian Society. Equally monumental, with dash of Imperial classicism in cut-away corner and hint of Art Deco in doorpiece, is Smart, Stewart and Mitchell's large new addition of 1931. Inside, mosaic floor of impressive entrance hall is lit by shallow glazed dome (colour p.49).

Laid out on broad scale in 1783, **Charlotte Street** was once a model of genteel city dwelling. During brief lulls in traffic, it is possible to evoke

Charlotte Street.

Below *1 Charlotte Street.* Middle *1 Atholl Crescent.* Bottom *2-8 Atholl Crescent.*

the haven of order and elegance which made it a much-prized address. North side came first.

44 **No 1**, terminating George Street, a beautiful later 18th-century classical house with Corinthian pilasters to corniced doorpiece, pilaster quoins and delicate frieze. Remaining buildings maintain a constant eaves line, but gradually increase in height to take account of falling ground towards **Nos 9-13**, five-bay tenement with Venetian window set in wallhead gable. South side is all early 19th-century tenements, **Nos 10-18** with channelled quoins and stonework at first floor. Outstanding quality at **20 Charlotte**

45 **Street/2-4 Charlotte Place**, *c.*1830, which completes the block and turns the corner with three bowed bays and Greek Doric colonnade at ground floor.

1-7 Atholl Place, from 1795
Short terrace of town houses, probably developed by Thomas Hay Marshall. **No 7**, on corner with Blackfriars Street, a storey taller and complete by 1805.

2-8 Atholl Crescent, from 1795
Early property development by Thomas Hay Marshall. Centre of terrace of two-storey-and-basement houses, each with three over-widely spaced bays, is marked by a pediment. Now a bit toothless where window astragals have been removed. Some good interiors, particularly staircases with Adamesque plasterwork. **1-3 Atholl Street**, early 19th century, turns the corner in similar style.

Atholl Street was planned as the main street through Thomas Hay Marshall's New Town, which it remains to this day, but any unity the building scheme may have had has long since been lost. **Nos 5-7** were built as the Theatre Royal,

Theatre Royal
Despite the appearance here of Edmund Kean as Richard III in 1822, the *New Statistical Account* commented: *This place of amusement has fallen very much into disrepute. Few inhabitants of any respectability frequent it. Prices of admission have lately been lowered, not to the improvement of the morals of the place, for that has brought to it the lowest and most questionable characters of society.* A correspondent of the *Perth Constitutional Newspaper*, Dec. 21 1836, identifies the multitude of its frequenters: *with the baser sort who squander their means in tippling-houses.* Closed 1845 on completion of Old City Hall by W M Mackenzie.

Top Atholl Street. Above *St Andrew's Parish Church.*

1820. **1-3 Atholl Court**, 1985–8, for Northern Housing Association, a replica elevation of early 19th-century terrace which stood on the site. **Nos 11-17**, early 19th century, were re-fronted in more ornate classical dress in the mid-19th century. **Nos 14-36** were complete by 1823, as was **No 56** on the corner with Melville Street. Apart from concrete roof tiles, **Nos 58-66** are an extremely smart earlier 19th-century development of house and two shops with tenements above. Exceptionally fine Roman Doric doorpiece to No 58.

St Andrew's Parish Church, Atholl Street, 1884–5, Andrew Heiton Jr
Cost £3,785. Began as Chapel of Ease to the East Church. Became *quoad sacra* parish in 1889.

46 **St Ninian's Episcopal Cathedral**, Atholl Street and North Methven Street, begun 1849, William Butterfield
Chancel, transepts, flèche, one bay of nave and three bays of aisle walls were completed 1849–50. Remainder of nave, north porch and lower part of intended west tower built to Butterfield's Early Middle Pointed Gothic design from 1888–90. J L Pearson redesigned the west end, recast the east end and added Lady Chapel, cloister, vestries, chapter house and library for Bishop Wilkinson, 1896–7. F L Pearson executed the work, 1901–11, incorporating projected tower into nave and adding octagonal pinnacles. Building was finally completed following addition of a new cloister, recreation hall and entrance hall by Tarbolton & Ochterlony, 1939. Rich interior of similarly complicated descent – particularly noteworthy are magnificent carved bishop's throne, stone pulpit, Butterfield's reredos (now divided

St Ninian's Episcopal Cathedral by Magnus Jackson c.1890.

between vestries), F L Pearson's font cover, 1919, and Sir J Ninian Comper's replacement rood screen, 1924.

8-10 Blackfrairs Street, early 19th century
Pair of two-storey, three-bay houses with pilastered and corniced doorpieces.

Prince Albert Statue, North Inch, 1864, William Brodie, originally unveiled at foot of High Street by Queen Victoria. At 8ft tall, the Consort's figure is heroic in scale, but not unbelievably larger than life. His amateur architectural interest is recorded in the clasped plans of Crystal Palace. **Obelisk**, 1895, in memory of the 90th Perthshire Light Infantry and Thomas Graham of Balgowan, later Lord Lynedoch (see p.81). **51st Highland Division Memorial**, 1995, bronze figure of soldier receiving flowers of peace from girl.

Above *Prince Albert Statue.* Left *2 Atholl Street/Rose Terrace.*

2 Atholl Street/Rose Terrace, late 18th century
Four-bay corner block with delicate wrought-iron balcony to lengthened windows of *piano nobile* and fluted giant Doric pilasters, curiously lacking an obvious entrance now that doorway in the far left bay of Atholl Street elevation has been converted to window. Probably built as mansion for developer of Rose Terrace, Lord Provost Thomas Hay Marshall, though never occupied by him. Intended corresponding pavilion block at other end of terrace not built.

1-5 and **8-17 Rose Terrace**, 1795–1808, probably Robert Reid
Two extremely fashionable terraces of three-storey houses with arcaded ground floors, flanking Old Academy. Terraces first conceived by Thomas Anderson, as part of ambitious scheme to build a New Town on former lands of the Blackfriars to north of High Street. Likely that

The elite **51st Highland Division**, whose kilted soldiers were termed 'the ladies from hell' by German opponents during World War I, famously saw action under Montgomery at Alamein, Mareth and Wadi Akarit in World War II. The well-known *Reel of the 51st Division* was created by the Division's prisoners of war at Laufen in 1940, after two of its three brigades were forced to surrender at St Valéry-en-Caux.

Anderson's wife, Sarah Rose, lent her name to the development, later bought out and completed by their son-in-law, Thomas Hay Marshall. Unfortunately, stonework has deteriorated beyond redemption in many places, much being replaced with cement render, lined out in imitation of original. **No 10** was childhood home of the great art critic, John Ruskin.

Right *Old Academy, 1968.* Below *School Room, Old Academy by Robert Reid.* Middle *7 Barossa Place.* Bottom *1-9 Barossa Place.*

47 **Old Academy**, 6-7 Rose Terrace, 1803–4, Robert Reid

Thomas Hay Marshall called on his friend, later King's Architect, to design centrepiece of his development scheme on North Inch, the Seminaries – a gathering together under one roof of the Academy, Grammar School and other educational establishments. Reid produced a beautifully balanced classical arrangement with large lunettes to pavilions and paired pilasters to central block. Internally, showy effects of pair of elegant oval staircases, and refined Adamesque plasterwork of remarkable domed octagonal classroom to rear, were achieved at the expense of more practical considerations such as adequate acoustics and heating. Balustraded parapet, clock and statue of Britannia by John Rhind, added in 1886. Academy moved to Viewlands in 1932, building now used as offices.

Barossa Place

A later development of the New Town, begun by Thomas Hay Marshall. Street begins as reduced version of Rose Terrace, with short block of two-storey houses, **Nos 1-5**, early 19th century, arcaded at ground floor. **No 7**, taller, with paired pilasters at ground floor, huge windows and extraordinary spider's web fanlight. Terrace finishes with **No 9**, early 19th century. Character of the street then changes to an exclusive regiment of mainly two-storey, three-bay villas, set in their own grounds. **No 31**, one of the finest, with giant pilasters and Greek Doric porch. More of a mixture on south side, but some good mid-19th-century paired villas at **Nos 14-18** and **Nos 22-24**. **26-52 Barossa Street**, late 18th century, long, low terrace of artisan housing, backing the Rose Terrace scheme. Prominent wallhead chimneys to **Nos 42-52**.

Melville Street
Initially planned as part of Thomas Anderson's 1790s new town grid, the street was skewed to current alignment by 1805, but not developed until earlier to mid-19th century. **Nos 7-11**, *c*.1860, an unusual two-storey tenement with large triple doorpiece (colour p.50). **No 23** is earlier, grand classical town house with rusticated ground floor, pedimented tripartite window at first floor and high roof. Rounded corner of **No 25**, mid-19th century, eases the way into Barossa Place.

St John's Roman Catholic Church,
Melville Street, 1832
Andrew Heiton Jr did his best to pull together the disparate parts of this much-altered building in 1892, but not with enormous success. Open belfry still caps first stage of intended tower. **Presbytery**, 1932, Reginald Fairlie, Scots 17th-century style.

48 **Balhousie Castle**, Black Watch Regimental Museum, Hay Street, 1631
Owes its bristling skyline of crowstepped gables, towers and bartizans to David Smart, who virtually rebuilt old L-plan courtier's palace in 1864 for the Earl of Kinnoull.

49 **Gannochy Trust Sports Centre**, Hay Street, 1968, J B Davidson (Burgh Architects' Department)
The space age arrived in Perth with the great saucer dome of the sports hall, gifted to the city by the Gannochy Trust in memory of the Trust's founder, A K Bell. Linked by tented canopy, 1991, to interlocking brick cubes and cylinders of **Gannochy Pavilion**, clubhouse to Perthshire Cricket & Rugby Club.

Top 7-11 Melville Street. Above Balhousie Castle.

Balhousie
A castle is said to have stood on the site since the time of Alexander I, passing through various notable families, including the Eviots, Mercers, and Hays. The old house was dated 1631 on one of the skewputts, and enclosed by a high wall with an arched gateway. The arms of the Earls of Kinnoull, perhaps those of the 1st Earl (see p.45), adorned a panel set in a wall.

Gannochy Trust Sports Centre under construction.

The depot's internal finishings were minimal, with hammocks slung between iron columns, perforated for ventilation. Within two years of completion, French prisoners were sent home, to the regret of the townspeople: '*Vast multitudes went daily to view the market and buy from the prisoners their toys, of which they had a great variety …*'. New general prison halls, housing prisoners from all over Scotland sentenced to more than nine months, based on American '*separate system*' of individual cells.

Right *Old Prison, 1810*. Below from top *Outer Entrance, Perth Prison; Prisoners exercising in yard, c.1900; Craigie Primary School; St Stephen's Parish Church; Inglelowe and Hollybrook.*

50 **Perth Prison**, Edinburgh Road, 1810–12, Robert Reid
Built at a staggering cost of £130,000 as depot for 7,000 French prisoners-of-war. Five three-storey halls set on polygonal-ended plan around central offices and chimney tower. Replaced by Thomas Brown's bleak four-storey whinstone halls on more fashionable radial plan around same tower, as part of conversion to Scotland's first general prison, 1839–42. More chilling is Robert Matheson's completion of main halls in formidable castle style, 1852–7. Tower now gone, but arcaded guard houses fronting Edinburgh Road, much of North Square, and perimeter wall and canal are all part of Reid's original scheme.

Old Tollhouse, 79 Edinburgh Road, early 19th century
Shallow piended roof with deep eaves and entrance breaking forward in a canted bay.

51 **Craigie Primary School**, Abbot Street, late 19th century, C S Robertson
Symmetrical arrangement of three projecting gabled bays, convenient for the usual separate boys' and girls' entrances. Appropriately intimate scale for primary school.

St Stephen's Parish Church, Abbot Street, 1894–5, J & G Young
Magnificent boat-builder's gothic, well-crafted in crisp red Dumfriesshire sandstone, with splendid rooftop flèche. Projected tower and transepts unfortunately never built.

52 **Inglelowe** and **Hollybrook**, 27-29 Wilson Street, 1923, Soutar & McQueen, joiner-builders
Apparently a pair of inter-war bungalows with continuous glazing and open porches suggestive of verandas; in fact much more substantial

38

custom-made houses, disguising two storeys to rear. Left-hand house, built for poet William Soutar by his father's firm, retains fine panelled interior and room modified for view of back garden during his bedridden years.

53 **113-119 Glover Street**, 1903, James Marshall Factory designed in semi-Art Nouveau style and jolly red brick for bobbin manufacturer John McArthur. Slender Dutch gables hint playfully at the shape of bobbins within (colour p.51).

54 **Perth Leisure Centre**, Glover Street, 1985–8, Faulkner Browns
Competition-winning design with indoor and outdoor leisure pools, training and competition pools, waterfalls, geysers and computer-controlled wave machine. Excellent fun. RIBA Architecture Award 1989 (colour p.51)

William Soutar, 1898–1943, was born and brought up in Perth. During wartime service in the Navy, Soutar contracted a form of spondylitis which was to confine him to bed from 1930. Soutar wrote in both Scots and English, publishing some 10 volumes of poetry, including *Poems in Scots* and *Seeds in the Wind* (a book of 'bairnrhymes'), and kept a diary from 1917 which formed the basis of a selection published posthumously in 1954 as *The Diary of a Dying Man*.

Top *113-119 Glover Street.* Above *Perth Leisure Centre.*

Pitheavlis: left *Mid-19th-century drawing by W F Lyon;* below *Third floor plan;* bottom *Front elevation.*

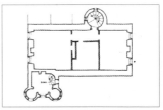

55 **Pitheavlis**, 50 Needless Road, late 16th century Possibly built by 'James Ross of Petthevels', and largely occupied by Oliphant and Murray families until 1920. L-plan laird's house of considerable sophistication, with 17th-century two-storey wing to rear. Unusual in a number of respects: square-plan stairtower with pair of pepperpot turrets to the front is lower than the main body of the house; further circular-plan stairtower is set towards centre of rear elevation; apart from normal gablehead stacks, the house is served by a massive wallhead chimney. Now subdivided into flats.

Already a sizeable village by 1845, **Cherrybank** developed with Glasgow Road as a suburb. Little remains of pre-suburban vintage, apart from early 19th-century farmhouse at **Oakbank Road**. **Cherrybank Cottages**, 1-4 Pickembere, *c.*1920, probably by James Miller for Lord Forteviot.

Top *United Distillers Reception Centre.*
Above *Bell's Cherrybank Gardens Visitor
Centre.* Right *Norwich Union Offices.*

Below *Pitheavlis Cottages.* Bottom *Youth
Hostel.*

56 **United Distillers Offices**, Necessity Brae, 1980
Built for the Perth whisky firm Bell's. Like flares, big collars and wide lapels, this is a building of its time – a utilitarian concrete frame with buff facing brick, clip-on parapet and modular office fronts. **Reception Centre** opposite is much better. Here the light timber structure, deep overhanging eaves and light airy interior have a definite oriental feel, no doubt with an eye to giving a particular welcome to Far Eastern buyers. **Bell's Cherrybank Gardens Visitor Centre**, late 20th century, built on a curve to enjoy panoramic views.

57 **Norwich Union Offices**, Necessity Brae, 1986–8, James Parr & Partners
Built as the world headquarters of General Accident. Low-rise ziggurat sensitively following contour of spectacular site on Craigie Hill. Staggered horizontal terraces of offices with roof gardens. Deep plan around nine courtyards. Reinforced concrete structure and exposed concrete finish. Modular 10m grid of columns supporting elm-clad coffered slab ceilings. Terrace planting enhances organic approach. Largely open plan. Bottocino marble entrance foyer; Hills of Perth tapestry by Samantha Ainsley and Edinburgh Tapestry Co. Rosewood panelling to board room. Executive floor batik panels by Norma Starszakowna. Ceramic wall by Mike de Haan incorporates names of employees.

Pitheavlis Cottages, Low Road, earlier 20th century, James Miller
Built for Lord Forteviot. Half-timbered porches, tall brick chimneys, casement windows and tiled roofs lend the air of English almshouses. All done with great charm, and beautifully maintained.

Glasgow Road
Built up and laid out on a broad scale from mid-19th century. Large and bleak neo-Jacobean **Rosslyn House**, 1858, Andrew Heiton Jr, former poorhouse, now missing its symmetrical lodges. Heiton again, SYHA's **Youth Hostel**, No 107, *c.*1865, in more exuberant Italianate mode, with

fine **lodge** to match. **Nos 109-135**, an impressive series of blowsy later 19th-century villas with quirky details. Fine columned porch and small paned windows at **12 Tullylumb Terrace**, 1902, James Miller, for Misses Ann and Cathi McLaren.

From top Perth Academy; Royal Infirmary; Letham St Mark's Church; Fairfield Housing; Perth Northern District Primary School.

58 **Perth Academy**, Viewlands Road, 1932, T Aikman Swan
Its visual impact in the drab inter-war years was shocking. White, bright, spacious and airy, the new building embraced the southerly aspect in its plan, and blew away the cobwebs, smells and diseases supposedly harboured by its predecessor.

59 **Royal Infirmary**, Taymount Terrace, *c.*1905, James Miller
Formal arrangement of four pavilions with cupolas to corner towers, linked to central quadrangular block, in semi-'Wrenaissance' style. Red brick and rendered infill.

60 **Letham St Mark's Church**, Rannoch Road, 1950s
Basic harled church transformed to more active community evangelism by addition of blockish bell tower and striking monopitch church hall with enormous geometric west window, later 20th century. Built to serve burgeoning post-war local authority housing, surprisingly modish, opposite, two storey with flat roofs, tapered chimneys, fins and portholes in jolly Festival of Britain spirit.

61 **Fairfield Estate**, off Crieff and Tulloch Roads, 1930s, Burgh Architect
Interesting scheme of tenements, with piended roofs, big broad chimneys and early 18th-century classical features, in south-facing blocks. Revivified from 1991 by refurbishment, new landscaping and Gaia Architects' addition of an ecologically designed block, arranged in 'sun-scoop' form for maximum light, passive heat-gain and shelter.

62 **Perth Northern District Primary School**, Dunkeld Road, 1908, G P K Young
Late 17th-century Dutch classical revival in red sandstone, including carved swags over entrances, oculi, channelled quoins and louvred cupolas. Matching **janitor's lodge**.

Muirton Estate, off Dunkeld Road, 1930s, Burgh Architect
Perth's biggest inter-war scheme of generously planned two- and three-storey tenements, like Fairfield, harled and slated, and ornamented with occasional early 18th-century motifs.

Bridgend
A settlement existed on the east bank of the Tay from at least the 16th century, and survived without a bridge through much of the 17th and 18th centuries by serving as a small ferry terminal. Its renaissance dates from the construction of Smeaton's new bridge in 1771.

Top *Main Street*. Above *Villas, Main Street/Isla Road.*

Much concerned by the plight of Perth's unemployed railway workers at the height of the Depression, whisky magnate A K Bell set his **Gannochy Trust** about the task of providing cheap rented accommodation for them. As the scheme progressed, Bell would take his morning walk from his home, Kincarrathie House, through the estate to make sure that everything was properly maintained, and also that the occupants kept the windows open. A great fresh air fanatic, Bell was known to lecture tenants on the spot about closed windows, and distributed posters explaining that cold could be combated by an extra blanket on the bed!

Gannochy House.

Bridgend
Although now traffic-mired and jaded in places, **Main Street** is recognisably a fine New Town development of early 19th-century tenements regimented along a broad planned street parallel with the Tay. Unfortunately most lack their original small-pane timber windows and some have been re-roofed in concrete tiles. **Bridgend Court**, 1973, Keystone Development, creditable attempt to introduce well-scaled modernity, particularly successful at the rear, where the court steps down to the river. Solitary street-facing villa, **Inchbank**, *c.*1800, most refined with elaborate doorpiece, giant pilasters and Venetian window in wallhead gable. Behind and in **Isla Road**, beautiful necklace of mainly classical early 19th-century villas stretching along river front, each with its own substantial garden (colour p.49). **Newlands** and **Inveraven**, Main Street, *c.*1810, have imposing giant Ionic order pilasters facing the town across the river. Pretty Gothick boathouse/gazebo, *c.*1800, at **Springland**, Isla Road. **Croft House**, Keir Street, early 19th century, sophisticated villa with umbrella fanlight, giant order pilasters and central pediment. In Bryce baronial manner is **Ardchoille House**, Strathmore Street, 1851, probably Andrew Heiton Sr & Son.

63 **Kincarrathie House**, Pitcullen Crescent, later 18th century, retains five-window west front, but much extended and altered. In the grounds, little Gothick summerhouse, reputedly former chapel, and lean-to doocot dated 1694. **Doocot Park Cricket Pavilion**, 1925, Smart, Stewart & Mitchell, extraordinary pantiled concoction with rustic balcony akin to an African hunting lodge, built for A K Bell's Gannochy Estate.

64 **Gannochy Housing Estate**, Bridgend, 1925–32, R M Mitchell
Perth's garden suburb, laid out to semi-formal plan of parallel streets. Gannochy Trust built 150 high quality cottages with a garden, each costing £1,200 and slightly different from its neighbour. Uniformity was achieved in common use of red Locharbriggs sandstone, white sash-and-case windows, overhanging eaves, slate roofs and hedge boundaries. Much-praised scheme includes an ornamental pond at junction of Dupplin and Annat Roads. Beautifully maintained.

65 **Murray Royal Hospital**, Muirhall Road, 1827, William Burn
Stern whinstone neoclassical palace built into Kinnoull Hill on H-plan. Long south front

dominated by central entrance pavilion and
rooftop octagon. Burn later built asylums in
Dumfries and Edinburgh. Quirky late Scots
gothic **chapel**, 1901, designed by Physician
Superintendent, Dr A R Urquhart, partly built by
patients. Neighbouring **Birnam Day Centre** and
Elcho Ward built as half-timbered **villas**, 1904.
Nurses' Home, 1939, long rectangular box with
cylinder on front is Perth's only large
International Style building. **Child & Family
Psychiatric Unit**, former Pitcullen House, fine
early 19th-century classical villa.

Annat Lodge, Muirhall Road, later 18th century
Famous as the home and studio taken by artist
John Everett Millais following his marriage to
Effie Gray (former Mrs Ruskin). House itself, a
large classical villa with large west-facing bow
and Venetian-windowed wings, thought to have
been remodelled, 1813, James Gillespie (Graham).

66 **St Mary's Monastery**, Hatton Road, 1868–70,
Andrew Heiton Jr
Loosely gothic in style, four-storey buildings
arranged in U-plan with chapel forming the north
side, a slated spire caps the tower on main west
entrance front of accommodation blocks.
Cruciform in plan, chapel incorporates short four-
bay nave with aisles and clerestory, and conical-
roofed bell-turret. Internally the chapel is
particularly lavish and in keeping with
ecclesiological thinking. Tiered chancel arch
corbelled on carved angels soaring up into ribbed
vaulted roof. Beautiful brightly painted iron gates
open through marble rail in front of exuberantly
carved altar and reredos.

Bowerswell, Bowerswell Road, 1848,
probably Andrew Heiton Sr & Son
Attributed to David Bryce by Urquhart, this
straightforward Italianate villa more likely to be

Murray Royal Hospital: left *Chapel;* top
Entrance front; above *Nurses' Home.*

Murray Royal Hospital was founded as
a lunatic asylum by James Murray, a
day labourer, who inherited his half
brother's Indian fortune in 1809, when
the ship carrying him home sank in a
storm. The endowment was such that:
*the meanest patient could be well fed and
clothed, and those among the higher classes
who could pay for it were as well lodged and
cared for as they could be in a palace.* The
regime was notably relaxed by the
standards of the day, allowing patients
plenty of room to exercise in the
parkland or enjoy the views from the
balconies: *While all is sufficiently secure to
prevent injury or escape, all is free from the
gloomy aspect of confinement, and there is
an air of quiet and of comfort which never
fails to strike the visitor …*
New Statistical Account, 1842

St Mary's Monastery was established
by the Congregation of the Most Holy
Redeemer, a Roman Catholic Order
founded by St Alphonsus Ligouri in
1732 to encourage priests to imitate the
virtues and example of Christ, and to
preach to the poor.

Bowerswell.

Bowerswell is famously the childhood home of Euphemia or Effie Gray, who married John Ruskin in the drawing room here.

Commercial Street and Potterhill Flats.

Sir Patrick Geddes, 1854–1932, biologist and town planner, spent his formative years, from 1857 to 1874, at the earlier 19th-century **Mount Tabor Cottage**, Mount Tabor Road. Geddes' idyllic childhood, exploring the natural delights of Kinnoull Hill, devouring the contents of the Mechanics Library, excelling at the Academy and experimenting in the makeshift laboratory/workshop constructed by his father, laid the foundations for his unorthodox and extraordinarily wide-ranging career. Aged 25, Geddes discovered chlorophyll, the basic substance of plants. In 1886 he founded an ambitious urban renewal programme in the Old Town of Edinburgh, and the following year established the first summer school held in Europe. Geddes set up the world's first 'sociological laboratory' in the Outlook Tower (see *Edinburgh* in this series), 1895, and in 1915 wrote his influential *Cities in Evolution*. Much of the rest of his life was spent abroad. He was knighted in 1931.

Kinnoull Parish Church.

the work of Bryce's local pupil, Andrew Heiton Jr, for George Gray. Modest tower with shallow roof marks entrance to house, otherwise characterised by broad eaves, tall chimneys and bay windows. Interior restrained apart from compartmental ceilings of principal rooms. Converted to retirement home as Perth's War Memorial, 1950, when 20 cottages were built in the grounds.

67 **Commercial Street**, 1978, James Parr & Partners
Modern interpretation in miniature of traditional Scots burgh High Street, perhaps in reaction to the monolithic assertiveness of **Potterhill Flats**, 1961, Wimpey, which dominate the skyline behind. By contrast, Commercial Street presents an irregular grouping of gabled flats with individual houses stepped along the bank of the Tay. Sandblasted pink concrete block walls, gabled roofs with re-used slate and stained timber windows. Picturesque effect achieved through careful massing and orientation of gables. Roofline broken by use of differing heights, dormers and staggered positioning. Simple unfussy detailing with splashes of colour. Balconies positioned to enjoy westerly views of River Tay and Perth. Civic Trust and Saltire Society awards, 1980 (colour p.52).

68 **Kinnoull Parish Church**, Dundee Road, 1826, William Burn
Buttressed and pinnacled neo-perpendicular gothic, in Greek cross plan. Praised for *chasteness* by the minister in the 1842 *Statistical Account*, crisp detailing, fine ashlar stonework, ample accommodation and symmetrical plan a stark contrast to the old kirk. Refurbishment, 1930, saw removal of galleries, new seating and furnishings, and re-siting of 1894 organ. Glory of interior is stained glass, particularly 'Parables of Our Lord' west window, 1870, to designs by Sir John Millais (colour p.50), and two memorial windows, 1942 and 1946, by Douglas Strachan.

Kinnoull Primary School, Dundee Road, *c.*1876,
Andrew Heiton Jr
Plain at first glance, but nicely detailed in 'Greek'
Thomson manner, including end bays with
pediments and acroteria, and mannered tapering
pilasters of the tripartite windows.

In the same way that the smartest of the early
19th-century smart set 'The Beautiful Order'
moved out of the city to the villas of Bridgend and
Isla Road, the newer, and brasher, industrial
money of the later century jostled for prime sites
and views on Dundee Road and Kinnoull Terrace
(colour p.49). Best are **Knowehead**, 1852,
crowstepped Jacobethan, **Rio**, *c.*1860, David
Smart, Italianate, both Dundee Road, and in
Kinnoull Terrace **Witchhill House**, *c.*1860, also
Smart, French renaissance, and Andrew Heiton's
Cragievar and **Darnick** (for himself), *c.*1870, semi-
detached villas in robust French gothic. **St
Leonard's Manse**, Dundee Road, 1905, C J
Menart, beautifully detailed Edwardian
renaissance, harling and red sandstone dressings.

69 **Kinnoull Aisle and Monument**, off Dundee
Road, 1635
Unprepossessing in its solitary state, Aisle once
formed part of 16th-century parish kirk, rebuilt in
1779 and demolished in 1836. Existing aisle
probably adapted to accommodate outstanding
early Baroque monument to George Hay, 1st Earl
of Kinnoull, in 1635. Elaborately carved sandstone
from pedestal to crowning heraldic panel, and
originally brightly painted, two bays of the
monument depict angels revealing the Privy
Purse to life-size figure of Hay in Chancellor's
robes. Rich decorative work and Latin inscriptions
contain erudite allusions to Hay's life and
achievements. Design may have emanated from
workshops of London sculptor, Nicholas Stone,
and been executed by Royal Master Mason, John
Mylne II. Re-roofed and repaired by Benjamin
Tindall Architects for Perth & Kinross Heritage
Trust, 1995; ongoing consolidation of monument.
Further along Dundee Road, **No 101**, mid-19th
century, polygonal-ended with traceried
windows and big brick chimney, is Gothick lodge
70 to Barnhill House. **Barnhill Tollhouse**, early 19th
century, effectively marking the entrance to the
city from the south-east, is a tiny Greek Doric
masterpiece, complete with its table of toll dues.
Probably built at the behest of Lord Gray of
Kinfauns who championed Robert Smirke's
Greek scheme for the Sheriff Court (see p.14).

Top *Kinnoull Primary School.*
Above *Kinnoull Aisle.*

George Hay, educated at the Scots
College at Pont-à-Mousson, returned to
the court of James VI in 1596 on the
death of his father. As a reward for his
part in foiling the Gowrie conspiracy of
1600, Hay was granted the Perth estates
of the disgraced Earl of Gowrie.
Industrial initiatives, such as the
production of iron ore and glass, and
political astuteness increased his wealth
and standing. In 1622 Hay was
appointed Chancellor of Scotland.
Further honours followed, culminating
in 1633 with the title of Earl of Kinnoull.

Barnhill Tollhouse.

Rhynd.

The first standard telephone kiosk, the K1 of 1921, was much disliked by public authorities, largely on aesthetic grounds. As a result, the architects Robert Lorimer, John James Burnet, and Giles Gilbert Scott were invited to enter a limited competition for the design of a new box in 1924. Scott won with his classical cast-iron construction, painted pillar-box red, which became the K2. The K3 was a concrete version, this time painted a stone colour with red glazing bars. The easily damaged concrete was not a widespread success, and led eventually to the ubiquitous 'Jubilee' kiosk or K6 of 1936, still much loved and used throughout the country.

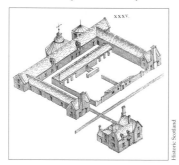

Above *Elcho Farm, much admired and illustrated in John Claudius Loudon's* Encyclopaedia of Cottage, Farm and Villa Architecture, *1833. Right Rhynd Parish Church.*

Surprisingly little is known about the genesis of Elcho, the magnificent Wemyss family seat, other than that it was largely complete to its current plan by about 1600. Theories abound about whether it was built in one campaign, or whether the south-west tower existed and was radically altered and extended in the late 16th century – stylistic evidence suggests the latter.

RHYND

Enclosed by the River Tay to north, the Earn to west and Moncreiffe Hill to south, modern Rhynd feels off the beaten track, but is an area of considerable variety and beauty. Once the garden of central Scotland, home of key families and location of significant building, 1500–1700. The Tay provided the principal source of trade and access to the parish and its principal seat, Elcho, but the landing has long been derelict and the road is now king.

Barely more than a small, but picturesque, hamlet of late 19th-century cottages, once known as Newhiggle. Notable as the site of Scotland's only K3 **telephone kiosk**, produced from 1929 to designs by Sir Giles Gilbert Scott.

Rhynd Parish Church, 1842, William Mackenzie Solid Tudor-gothic T-plan with crenellations and dumpy pinnacles to square tower. Built at centre of parish to replace 17th-century **Old Parish Church**, remains of which can be found near confluence of the Earn and the Tay.

The serpentine land approach to Elcho is through **Elcho Farm**, *c.*1830, a model farmhouse and steading designed by William Mackenzie – the grand courtyard was covered over, 1966, but a fine range of cartsheds, a horse-mill and unusual circular feeding house survive. Beehive **doocot** is a reproduction.

71 **Elcho**, complete *c.*1600
Extraordinarily luxurious mansion arranged in palace form around a courtyard, of which only principal north range remains substantially intact. Viewed from north-west river approach from Perth, it presents an impressive array of round and square towers, crowstepped gables and chimneys. From entrance door and yett, a broad ceremonial

RCAHMS

stair rises to hall and laird's chambers on first floor. Two storeys above contain remarkable sequence of lodgings and bedchambers, serviced by three turnpike stairs and an astonishing number of latrines. Clearly this was a house for entertaining on a grand scale (colour p.50). The mansion ceased to be used regularly after 1781, when the 7th Earl acquired the Gosford estate in East Lothian. Orchard to west recently replanted. *Historic Scotland; open to the public; leaflet*

Custodian's House, *c.*1830, sports a fine rustic porch, built perhaps as the factor's house.

Kinmonth House, 1875–6, Peddie & Kinnear
Enjoying a commanding site at eastern end of Moncreiffe Hill, Kinmonth is a wonderful baronial fantasy. Romantic effect particularly successful when summer evening light glows off the sandstone and top-heavy skyline of crowstepped gables, bartizans and towers casts its shadow. Contemporary **stables** and **lodges** are stylistic offspring. Double-chambered **doocot**, early 18th century, has unusual back wall, swept up into curved gablet.

Wallacetown Farmhouse, *c.*1830
Attractive two-storey, three-bay farmhouse with a polygonal porch and broad spreading eaves to the piended roof.

Elcho Castle engraved by R W Billings, 1845–52.

The lands of Elcho were confirmed to Sir John Wemyss of Wemyss by James III, 1468. Another Sir John Wemyss, confirmed in the lands, 1552, may have initiated the building we see. Initials IEW, on gable of ruined courtyard range, and fragments of Unionist plasterwork in laird's chamber, depicting the thistle, rose and fleur-de-lys, probably date from ownership of John, 1st Earl of Wemyss, ennobled by Charles I in 1633.

Below *Kinmonth House.*
Bottom *Wallacetown Farmhouse.*

Perth Museum & Art Gallery

RCAHMS

Old Moncreiffe House, late 19th century.

Moncreiffe House: *a neat little seat ... built of Freestone after the Manner of the Country-Seats in the Villages about London, with a Glass Cupola or Lanthorn at Top, and very neatly wainscoted and furnish'd within.*
John Macky, *A Journey through Scotland,* 1723

Perth Museum & Art Gallery

Sir William Bruce, *c.*1630–1710, was the younger son of Robert Bruce of Blairhall, Fife. Bruce's wealth and success derived largely from his part in the restoration of Charles II, which secured him a series of official posts including Clerk of Supply to the Lords in council, Collector of Taxes to the Royal Force, Commissioner of Excise for Fife, and *'surveyor, contriver, and overseer of all the works at the Palace of Holyroodhouse, and of such other castles and palaces in Scotland as the king shall appoint to be repaired.'* He acquired the Balcaskie Estate, Fife, in 1665, and was created a baronet in 1668. Bruce bought New House, Kinross (see p.218) in 1675, and planned his own magnificent seat on an adjacent site from 1685, the year of his appointment as a Scottish Privy Councillor. The following year saw the beginning of his downfall, when he was dismissed from the Privy Council, probably on account of his Episcopalian activities, which were regarded with deep suspicion by both the Catholic faction of James II and the increasingly influential Presbyterian groupings. As gentleman-architect, Bruce was involved in the design or re-design of a number of other significant houses including Thirlestane and Mertoun (see *Borders & Berwick* in this series), Brunstane and Craigiehall (see *Edinburgh*), Hopetoun (see *West Lothian*), Dunkeld (see p.115) and Nairne (see p.108).

Old Moncreiffe House, 1679, attributed to Sir William Bruce (demolished, 1962)
Built adjacent to the old house on the lower slopes of Moncreiffe Hill for Thomas Moncreiffe of that Ilk. At first glance a severely classical box, relieved only by magnificent pedimented doorpiece and decorative quoins, it was particularly sophisticated in its planning. Along with a glazed rooftop cupola, the closer grouping of central windows of the front elevation increased the light to the large rooms running through the middle of the house. Broader bays lit the stair and rooms also served by windows in side elevations. Attic windows, tucked neatly under the eaves cornice, predated similar arrangement at Bruce's own Kinross House. Following a disastrous fire, 1957, William Kininmonth incorporated old doorpiece into new **Moncreiffe House,** 1962, an intriguing example of Gothick revival – classical symmetry and proportions with gothic crenellations. Fine range of 18th-century **stables,** crowned with an ogee-roofed clocktower and doocot – the top stage of Bruce's cupola removed from the old house during 19th-century re-roofing, or, perhaps, an echo of the original Tudor-gothic **South-East Lodge,** *c.*1825, probably by William Burn, who produced a Tudor design for main house at this time. Large roofless lean-to **doocot,** 1729.

Moncreiffe Chapel, pre-Reformation
First mention of a chapel here is 1208. Existing ruins much altered. Core a plain rectangular-plan structure with bellcote perched on remaining east gable. Buttressed transepts and apse added, 1887, employing masonry from partially demolished Bridge of Earn and coat of arms from the old tower house which once stood between the chapel and site of Bruce's house.

Top *Main Street/Isla Road houses.* Middle *Auditorium, Perth Theatre.* Above left *Victoria and Albert, Council Offices.* Left *Perth Museum & Art Gallery.* Above *Villas, Kinnoull Hill.*

49

Top *7-11 Melville Street.* Right *Elcho Castle.* Above *Millais window, Kinnoull Parish Church.* Below *Playhouse Cinema.*

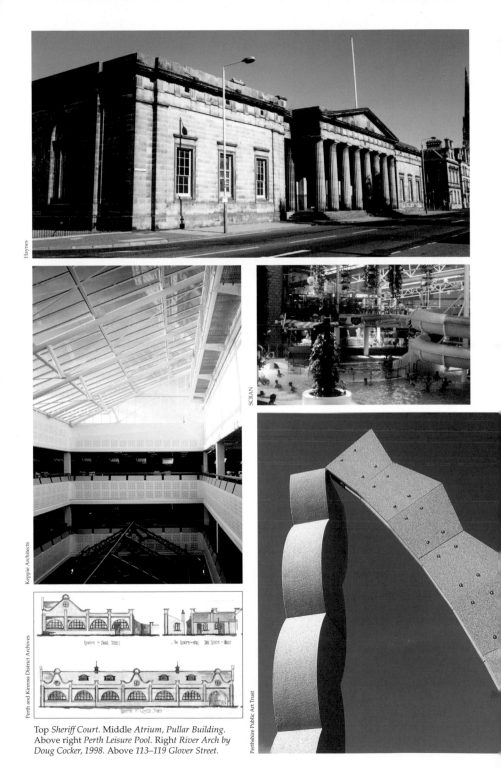

Top *Sheriff Court.* Middle *Atrium, Pullar Building.*
Above right *Perth Leisure Pool.* Right *River Arch by
Doug Cocker, 1998.* Above *113–119 Glover Street.*

Haynes

Keppie Architects

SCRAN

Perth and Kinross District Archives

Perthshire Public Art Trust

51

Top left and middle *J D Fergusson Gallery*. Top *Spire, St John's Parish Kirk*. Above *St John's Parish Kirk*. Left *Commercial Street, Bridgend*.

Hilton House, 1732
Exceptionally interesting example of a small laird's house which draws from two distinct traditions: the relatively new classicising tendency of fashionable professionals' and merchants' houses, and the asymmetry of old gentry houses. Plain horizontal format – a two-storey gabled rectangular block with serried rows of windows aligned in bays – derives from merchant tradition. So too does high wallhead above first-floor windows, accommodating attic service rooms lit by small windows in gables. In other respects the house looks back to the Scottish tradition of asymmetry, in which the elevation is generated from requirements of the plan. Off-centre doorway, roll-moulded in 17th-century manner, irregular spacing of bays. Above the door, corniced date stone a cross between merchant's marriage lintel and heraldic panel of a tower house, perhaps reflecting the builder's status and aspirations.

Hilton House, 1960s.

BRIDGE OF EARN
The roads south from Perth wind through the complicated web of bridges and underpasses at Craigend Interchange between Kirkton and Moncreiffe Hills, and the landscape opens into the broad strath of the lower Earn. Bridge of Earn lies ahead, long a key river crossing point on the north/south route, and a junction for the roads east to Fife and west along Strathearn. Dramatic wooded slopes and cliffs of Moncreiffe Hill form the backdrop to the village.

The oldest part, **Back Street**, dates from 1769 and was developed by wright and undertaker John Gilloch, on a dog-leg plan from the south side of the old bridge. Scale remains, but 18th-century details largely lost. Least altered are **Cyprus Inn**, 1790, and **Burnbrae**, 1800, retaining their distinctive *nepus* gables. **Earnbank House**, 1788, once a classy small mansion in its own grounds, may have provided more polite model for these wallhead gables. Characterful shaped gables and oculi added *c*.1900, countered by a less than sensitive conversion as part of retirement housing complex *c*.1990.

Dunbarney Parish Church, 1787
Large boxy design, originally similar to that at Abernethy, remodelled *c*.1880 when galleries were removed, windows standardised and flèche added. Adjacent former **manse** dates from 1775.

First reference to a stone bridge over the Earn is 1326, when Robert I requested stone for construction from local quarries of Scone Abbey. Tidal position caused frequent collapses, probably resulting in four-arch **Auld Brig**, early 16th century, contemporary with that at Stirling. This required numerous repairs, and a further arch and re-alignment of north end, undertaken 1766 on the advice of John Adam and John Smeaton. Old bridge partially dismantled to prevent toll-dodgers on completion of John Rennie's elegant **New Bridge**, 1822, further upstream, but two southern arches remained until demolition, 1976.

Below *Old Bridge of Earn, 1976*. Middle *Burnbrae*. Bottom *Dunbarney Parish Church*.

From top *New Bridge, Bridge of Earn; Main Street, Bridge of Earn, late 19th century; Bridge of Earn Institute; Kintillo, late 19th century.*

Kilgraston School: below *First-floor hall;* right *Entrance front.*

The opening of the **new bridge** and rising popularity of the spa at Pitkeathly Wells (see p.56) were accompanied by a second flourish of building activity. The tenant of the wells built sprawling **Moncreiffe Arms**, *c.*1825, *one of the most commodious coaching inns in Scotland* (*New Statistical Account*, 1845), now a nursing home. No aspiring spa town was complete without its douce terraces of boarding houses, so William Burn's 1823 design for **Main Street** palace blocks was partially carried out 1832–4. Main block now barely recognisable as an integrated classical design.

Bridge of Earn Institute, 1909, G P K Young
Public hall and institute incorporating typical features of Glasgow Free Style such as contrasting white harl and red sandstone, tapering chimneystack, swept eaves and buttresses. Attractively grouped with Celtic cross of village **War Memorial**.

KINTILLO

Claimed to be the oldest village in Scotland, probably largely rebuilt as neat thatched cottages from late 18th century. Narrow unenclosed strips of arable land or *pendicles*, each with low byre and shed, lay to the south, all now swamped with modern housing and subsumed into Bridge of Earn.

Kilgraston School, 1793, Francis Grant
Designed by the laird in rather schizophrenic mixture of Adamesque classical and crenellated Gothick styles, executed in red sandstone. Following a devastating fire, 1872, interiors were revamped in believable neoclassical style. Details a little heavy but spaces are exciting, from the pilastered entrance hall and double stair to the magnificent central hall at the top, lit by a domed cupola. On conversion to school, 1930s, the

immediate setting was compromised by barrack-like accommodation blocks. Unusual D-plan office court to rear rebuilt by Gillespie, Kidd & Coia. Interesting estate buildings survive, including a particularly accomplished quadrant arrangement of entrance gateways after the manner of James Gillespie Graham and pedimented stable block, both *c.*1820, domed ice house and remains of a small gothic chapel. At Old Kilgraston, a Spanish oak, reputed to have been planted when Cromwell took Perth in 1651.

72 **Dron Parish Church**, 1824, William Stirling
Pretty English perpendicular box with pinnacled tower by progenitor of the distinguished Dunblane firm of architect-builders (colour p.120). Equally attractive **manse**, 1810, extended by Perth's principal architect William Mackenzie, 1838, and his adjacent **school**, much altered in conversion to house.

Balmanno, *c.*1580
Gleaming white ultra-romantic interpretation of late 16th-century laird's house, lovingly restored, 1916–21, for Glasgow shipowner William Miller by Sir Robert Lorimer. Four-storey L-plan with square tower and corbelled circular stairtower in re-entrant angle, George Auchinleck's original house was a sophisticated and early example of a type which culminated in William Aytoun's 1640 Innes House (see *The District of Moray* in this series). Complete with broad wheel-stair to first and second floors, viewing platform at top of tower, steeply crowstepped gables, massy gablehead chimneys and mock-defensive moat (now infilled), Balmanno must have been at the forefront of domestic fashion. Under Lorimer's direction the accretions of later centuries were stripped away, and his favourite craftsmen were let loose to create a sensuous evocation of the late 17th century, from the plasterwork, ironwork, joinery and furnishings of the interior to the stonework of the new service wing, gatehouse, gazebo and interlocking courtyard gardens. External alterations to house itself relatively restrained, such as heightened turret capped with ogee roof, new gabled dormers and roof-ridge carvings of monkeys by Louis Deuchars, but all beautifully detailed and quirky in typical Lorimer manner. Small 1960s' addition, Ian G Lindsay.

Glenearn House, *c.*1830
Small symmetrical country house, harled and trimmed with Picturesque features: broad eaves,

Dron Parish Church by William Stirling.

Of all the houses Sir Robert Lorimer built or restored, Balmanno was said to be the one he would most like to live in, perhaps from the similarities with his childhood home, Kellie, Fife. The commission to transform it from dilapidated farmhouse to fantasy holiday retreat arrived with the First World War. Top-to-bottom project included house, landscaping and furnishings from the Edinburgh firm Whytock & Reid. Work delayed by wartime restrictions, and locally sourced elm, ash, oak and larch used, probably to the benefit of overall quality. Mrs Miller non-plussed by the effort, preferred to stay in more refined comfort of her Pollockshields home.

Balmanno.

Top *Glenearn House.*
Above *Ecclesiamagirdle House.*

The plan of Drummonie House is in the tradition of the Court Style established by Sir James Murray at Baberton in 1623 (see *Edinburgh* in this series) and continued throughout the 17th century in such houses as Methven, remodelled in 1664 (see p.80).

Pitkeathly Wells
Pronounced *'Pitcaithly'*, the medicinal qualities of the mineral waters found here were recognised from at least the 17th century. By 1711 the church session were concerned about the number of people visiting the well every Sabbath morning, and had constables posted to stop the practice. Both imbibing and bathing were encouraged to cure an enormous range of ailments from hiccups to chronic liver disease. The Regency vogue for spa towns began a frenzy of building activity to cater for visitors, most ambitiously in Bridge of Earn. By 1829 the Perth Courier regarded Pitkeathly as *'undoubtedly the most delightful watering-place in Scotland, crowded with beauty and fashion'.*

Right *Drummonie House, early 19th-century engraving* . Below *Pitkeathly Wellhouse.*

bowed window bays and trellised verandas. **Glenearn Farmhouse**, plainer red rubble sandstone offspring, maintaining shallow piended roof profile and distinction in size between windows of the principal floor and bedrooms above.

Ecclesiamagirdle
Pronounced 'Exmagriddle', the remarkable name derived from the chapel of St Grill or Gillan, one of St Columba's harpers. **Chapel**, a small roofless rectangular-plan ruin, possibly just pre-Reformation. Adjacent kirkyard wall is dated *DSC 1651 STIL REA DEI*. Idyllically sited next to the loch, **Ecclesiamagirdle House**, 1648, T-plan laird's house of great charm, similar to Pilmuir House (1624), East Lothian. Characterised by steeply pitched crowstepped gables and gabled dormerheads, house originally entered by doorway to projecting stairtower. Columned recess over door marks the location of missing coat of arms, probably that of the Carmichael family, whose initials still adorn gateway to old courtyard (colour p.118). Contemporary **doocot** of unusual circular lean-to form with crowsteps.

Drummonie House, 1697
Handsome laird's house, U-plan with lower infill between crowstepped gables of projecting wings. By 1818 the commercial activity at Pitkeathly Wells reached fever pitch and Drummonie was converted to hotel, gaining a grand Doric entrance and obligatory ballroom to rear. Now returned to private use.

73 **Pitkeathly Wellhouse**, early 19th century
Circular tower pierced with openings in the form of Crusader crosses. Girth of lean-to cubicles around base, a late 19th-century addition. Broad-eaved well-keeper's cottage, *c.*1830, adjoins to north. **Pitkeathly Wells Farmhouse**, late 18th century, was fitted out as a hotel at the height of spa mania.

Ballendrick House, 1825
Plain classical lairdly residence built for
Alexander Stoddart. Roman Doric doorpiece and
umbrella fanlight are particularly well executed.

Ballendrick House.

Dunbarney House, 1697
Three-storey house for John Craigie, probably
originally three ground-floor bays and four bays
above, later extended to six bays and doubled in
depth. Extension of front elevation nicely done.
Addition of columned porch at new centre
creates a very pleasing proportion and credible
classical arrangement. Late 18th-century parallel
rear wing comprises series of huge round-arched
windows to light the public rooms. Strange
arcaded service wing dated 1772. **Belfry Cottage**
probably incorporates belfry from old Dunbarney
Church, removed from its site near surviving
churchyard to Bridge of Earn in 1684.
Contemporary lean-to **doocot**.

An auld man stands abune the hill;
Crick-crack, crick-crack,
He's unco comfie gin he's still:
Crick-crack, creeshie.
But when his airms flee round and round.
Crick-crack, crick-crack:
He deaves the clachan wi his sound.
Crick-crack, creeshie.

William Soutar, from *Seeds in the Wind*,
1933

Dunbarney Windmill, early 18th century
Rare substantial stump of a windmill – rotating
timber cap and sails are long-since gone. Grain
was delivered to, and meal dispatched from, the
vaulted basement; milling took place on ground
floor.

Left *Dunbarney House*. Below *Dunbarney Windmill*.

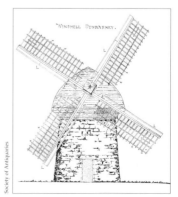

Dunbarney Cottage, mid-19th century
From the front a rather unassuming single-storey
cottage, but in fact a surprisingly large dower
house, serviced by half-timbered offices around a
courtyard.

Carmichael Cottages, early 19th century
Small group of former estate cottages on the
Forgandenny road distinguished by artisan
classical timber porches.

FORGANDENNY
Attractive estate village on the old main
approach to Freeland House. Mainly picturesque
single-storey cottages with overhanging eaves,
c.1820 to 1900, replacing their mid-18th-century
predecessors. **The Croft**, *c*.1820, two-storey,
befitting status as former factor's house, as are
Forgandenny Schoolhouse and **Earlston**, the old
manse, both *c*.1840. **Forgandenny Hall**, former
Free Church, 1885, perhaps the least expensive of
several contemporary Free churches by London-
based architect J J Stevenson. Competently
executed in red rubble and contrasting dressings,
with stocky belfry and cusped heads to windows.

Forgandenny Parish Church, from 12th century
One of a handful of pre-Reformation Perthshire
churches to escape total demolition or
abandonment in the 19th century. This said, it has
been much knocked about, leaving only the
Norman dog-tooth ornament of the old door-arch
as evidence of early origins. Scale and
arrangement similar to ruinous church at
Kinfauns (see p.193), a plain rectangular block,
without distinction between nave and chancel.
Transepts added later: north transept is long
gone, but the south was reconstructed as Ruthven
burial vault and laird's loft, probably late 16th
century, and remodelled with a Venetian
doorway in the 18th. Dr Thomas Ross, of
MacGibbon & Ross fame, prepared a restoration
scheme in 1899, but was beaten to the job in 1903
by the more local T S Robertson of Dundee, who
ironed out the irregularities and patina of age by
installing new windows, re-building the roof,
adding the west porch, and removing the
galleries and Oliphant aisle. Even so, the result is
not without charm and its own century of patina.

Top *Forgandenny*. Middle *Forgandenny
Hall*. Above *Forgandenny Parish Church*.

An impressive Iron Age fort on Castle
Law, just to the east of the summit of
Culteuchar Hill (1028ft), occupies a key
defensive position over the strath,
commanding views of much of
Perthshire, Angus and parts of Fife. A
smaller, but strongly fortified, mound
stands to the east of Netherholm Farm.
Romans set up a small camp near
Ardargie Mains.

74 **Strathallan School**, 1825, Edward Blore and
William Burn
Mid-18th-century Freeland House largely
reconstructed for Lord Ruthven. Unusually,
authorship is shared between two major country
house architects, Blore and Burn, although
division of labour is not clear. Horizontal
emphasis and details such as clusters of tall
chimneys, mullioned bay windows and
hoodmoulds, all derived from early 16th-century
English vernacular houses. Picturesque
asymmetry of vast rambling layout also allowed
for highly sophisticated interior planning of
which Burn was the master. R R Anderson
alterations/additions, 1891–1905. Converted for

Strathallan School.

Strathallan School

Harry Riley's relocated Bridge of Allan school, 1919. **Riley House**, old stable block and offices, also by Burn. Vaulted well-house, probably associated with the 17th-century mansion (destroyed by fire, 1750), covers **Lady's Well**.

Forgandenny Station, 1848
Set apart from the village, built as a cottagey homage to Freeland House. Closed 1956.

Rossie House, from 1657
Built for William Oliphant and Isabella Duncan, originally known as Forgan House. The 17th-century building is largely subsumed by 18th- and 19th-century additions, creating a grand seven-bay classical front; recessed arch created mid-20th century to replace more natural 18th-century pedimented centrepiece. Octagonal gothic **doocot**, c.1800.

Kildinny Steading, early 19th century
The west range houses a splendid arcade of cartsheds with two-storey end pavilions.

FORTEVIOT

A fascinating experiment in rural regeneration, planned before the First World War by the whisky magnate, John Alexander Dewar, 1st Baron Forteviot of Dupplin. The centre of the scheme, by Glasgow architect James Miller, is 75 **The Square**, 1925, actually U-plan, with an English Garden City feel with broad gabled bays, casement windows, tiled roofs and brick detailing. Miller's **Village Hall** flirts coyly with a more Scandinavian approach in its flat-roofed vestibule blocks and clocktower. Essential to the regeneration programme were the single-storey **Smithy** and **Carpenter's Workshop**, again by

Haynes

Stephen Stuart

Top *Garden front, Strathallan School.* Middle *Forgandenny Station.* Above *Rossie House.*

The field sloping from Rossie to the River Earn witnessed early experiments in powered flight by the Dundee engineer, Preston Watson. In 1906 he attached a Santos Dumont engine to a glider of his own design. Ten wooden propellers were destroyed before a successful lift-off. Two years later Watson built a stronger model with a 30 horse power and three-cylinder engine.

The Square, Forteviot.

Haynes

Miller. Boxy **Parish Church**, 1778, an earlier remnant repaired by William Stirling and Andrew Heiton Sr & Son in 1830, recast by David Smart, 1867. Stirling too was responsible for elegant classical **manse**, 1825–6, unusually three bays in depth as well as width. William Mackenzie reconstructed the **Old School** in 1839, David Smart remodelled it with a semi-baronial tower in 1863, and further additions were made, 1887.

Former **Forteviot Hotel**, an early 19th-century coaching inn, north-west of the village, over the railway on the Dupplin road. **Forteviot Bridge**, 1766, a distinguished five-arch span over the Earn, rubble-built with triangular buttresses and cutwaters, lies beyond.

Invermay House, 1750–70

Described as *'neat and commodious'* by *'a friend to Statistical Inquiries'* in 1798, and so it remains today, a brightly harled classical box with five-window frontage, central tripartite window and pediment and piended roof, on a wonderful site with stupendous views. Internal idiosyncrasies suggest it is almost certainly a reworking of a major earlier house, perhaps incorporating late 17th-century alterations by Sir William Bruce. Robert Burn, father of William, proposed an ambitious extension and rebuilding of the front in 1806, but thankfully a more modest scheme of bowed windows and porch was built to the design of Alexander Laing for Colonel Belshes. Laing had been responsible for the quirky, originally thatched **dairy/doocot**, 1803, the paired cubes of the **West Lodges** in the same year and now ruinous Gothick **gazebo** of 1804. Although incomplete, the two ranges of a projected classical U-plan **stable block**, *c.*1810, are very grand indeed. Universally high quality of all estate buildings and bridges is notable.

Top *Parish Church*. Above *Forteviot Bridge*.

Crop marks to the south of Forteviot have revealed a significant prehistoric ritual complex, including evidence of late Neolithic henges. Forteviot (*Forthiurtabaicht*) continued as an important centre under the kings of Picts and Scots, housing a royal *palacium* and probably a chapel, well into the 12th century; the ruins survived to the 17th century. The exact site is now lost, but an elaborately decorated arch (now in the National Museum of Scotland) from the presumed late 9th-century chapel was found in the Water of May, to the west of the village. *Cináed mac Ailpín* (Kenneth I), traditionally the first King of Scots, died here in 858. Edward Balliol's army encamped at Miller's Acre, before the Battle of Dupplin, 1332.

Situated above the beautiful wooded glen of the Water of May, **Invermay** was admired as *'one of the most romantic and pleasant spots in this part of Perthshire'* (First Statistical Account, 1798), and celebrated in the ballad *'The Birks* [birches] *of Invermay'*. The Humble Bumble, where the river rumbles through a long and deep gully in the rock, provided a natural focus for the 18th-century landscape gardens. In 1802 the celebrated gardener and prolific author, Walter Nicol, laid out a new western approach to the house, designed new peach- and grape-houses, and proposed an eccentric domed Gothick temple to mark the Humble Bumble. Neither the temple, nor an equally extraordinary two-storey classical tea-house/conservatory, were built.

Invermay House.

Old House of Invermay, late 16th century
Fragment, perhaps gallery wing, of very
substantial seat of the Lords Innermeath. True
height of two storeys and attic obscured on north
front by later outshoot and old entrance tower.
South elevation, facing the new house, has central
circular stairtower with steep batter from base to
top. Larger window openings indicate that
principal rooms were located on first floor.
Dormerhead of 1633 inserted over ground-floor
opening of stairtower is decoy, probably relating
to later remodelling.

Muckersie Chapel, reconstructed c.1840
Old parish church of Muckersie, united with
Forteviot in 1618. First mention of a church on the
site is 1181. Reconstructed as burial chapel for the
Belshes of Invermay, plain crowstepped rectangle
with round-arched doorway, now roofless.

Rossie Ochill House, 1691
Long back range is original part of house, but
greatly altered. South-east wing with tripartite
windows followed, probably earlier 19th century.
Finally, north-east wing built to match, and new
entrance created in-between, making
symmetrical front.

Pathgreen Farm, Path of Condie, 1742
House appears to be little altered apart from pair
of later dormers, and is probably typical of the
vast majority of pre-Improvement farmhouses
throughout Scotland, many of which were swept
away in late 18th and early 19th centuries.
Adjacent steading and **horse-mill** are very much
products of this agricultural improvement drive.

From top *Old House of Invermay; Rossie
Ochill House; Pathgreen Farm; horse-mill.*

Newton of Condie, from 16th century
Owned, and perhaps built, by William Oliphant,
one of the ablest lawyers of James VI's reign.
Burnt in 1866, ruins comprise L-plan tower house
and early 17th-century wing with late 18th-
century classical mansion block tacked on to
north. Roofless lean-to **doocot** appears
contemporary with this wing.

DUNNING
Picturesquely sited at the foot of the Ochil Hills,
Dunning forms the hub of six roads leading
respectively to Forteviot, Invermay, Path of
Condie, Yetts o' Muckhart, Auchterarder and
Dalreoch. Its strategic location on main Stirling/
Perth route, weaving and agriculture ensured
revival during late 18th into 19th century.

St Serf (see p.234) is reputed to have built a small chapel in Dunning, and slain the local dragon with only a staff.

Dupplin Cross depicts a king, possibly Constantín mac Fergusa (c.789–820), seated on a horse, with ranks of foot-soldiers on panels below. Military representations mark a departure from earlier crosses depicting hunting scenes, interpreted as a symbol of strengthening royal authority. Similar **Dronachy Cross**, fragments of which survive in Forteviot Church, stood at Invermay.

Top and right *Former St Serf's Parish Kirk.* Above *Dupplin Cross.*

An ancient ecclesiastical centre, testified by the parish kirk, which stands at the heart of the nucleated village plan. Like many of the neighbouring villages, Dunning was burnt to the ground by the Jacobites in 1715 to slow the advance of government troops after the Battle of Sherrifmuir.

Tron Square.

76 **Former St Serf's Parish Kirk**, early 13th century The most distinctive feature in the village-scape is the 75ft Romanesque tower, tapering in three unequal stages, topped with crowstepped saddleback roof, built sometime between 1200 and 1219. Round-arched belfry openings bisected by a column to each face of tower. Remains of 13th-century stonework at lower levels of north and east walls, most notably at round-arched north doorway. Laird's loft added 1687 at east end. Utilitarian north aisle and south front rebuilt and interior galleried on three sides, 1808–10, Alexander Bowie, rather brutally at the expense of early fabric. Still surviving inside, but interrupted by the west gallery, remarkable 13th-century decorative tower archway. Base of tower is the new home, from November 2001, of **Dupplin Cross**, early 9th century, Perthshire's most spectacular Pictish monument removed from site east of Bankhead Farm, Dupplin. Remainder of interior plainly refurnished, 1868, and further alterations of 1890s including stained glass by A Ballantine & Son.
Historic Scotland; open to the public

The heart of Dunning is at **Tron Square**, where the tight winding medieval street pattern broadens into the former bleaching green and market place around stocky gothic **Alexander Martin Memorial**, 1874, in front of St Serf's. Here and in **Kirk Wynd** and **Yetts o' Muckhart Road** the scale is low, predominantly two storey, mainly houses dating from the 19th century. Grander three-storey block
77 including **Dunning Hotel**, early 19th century, on corner of **Auchterarder** and **Station Roads**, and incongruously gothic corner shop and tenement with frilly iron balcony, 1874, at Tron Square and
78 Yetts o' Muckhart Road. **Dunning Primary School**, Station Road, 1867, prettily gabled in cottage style, with unusual gothic window heads over sashes and decorative pyramid ventilator.

79 **Auchterarder Road** contains **Town Hall and Council Offices**, 1858 in origin, with mildly
80 moderne gothic addition of 1909. **Kirkstyle Inn**, Kirkstyle Square, early 19th century, has replacement double stair up to its smartly corniced doorpiece. Intimate **Thorntree Square** commemorates the Jacobite burning of the village in 1717, although tree itself has been replaced several times since.

Dunning Burn Bridge, 1777, subsequently widened, marks the divide between the extent of the old village and its expansion east of the burn to a plan feued by the 6th Lord Rollo of Duncrub. Two fine doorpieces and eaves cornices to houses at **Bridgend**. To north and east the scale is low, but houses are more regimented in terraces, particularly where **Perth Road** and **Chalmers Street** surround the green and Celtic cross **War**
81 **Memorial**, 1919. **Granco Street**, more late 18th/early 19th-century artisan housing, is divided into Upper and Lower parts. In garden at Willowbank, Upper Granco Street, is the **Straw Bale Shed**, 2000, Gaia Architects, the ultimate eco-friendly office, constructed using a larchpole frame and lime-rendered straw-bale walls – the modern equivalent of the 18th-century picturesque 'primitive hut' retreat (colour p.120).
82 Plain gothic **Parish Church**, Perth Road, 1910, with witch's hat ventilator, was built for a United Free congregation, but became Church of Scotland after 1929 union, eventually replacing St Serf's on closure. Open timber roof and simple, but well-crafted, furnishings. **St John's Masonic Lodge**, Yetts o' Muckhart Road, 1806, plain rectangle with large round-arched Gothick windows, is the former Relief Church.

Garvock House, from 17th century
Hybrid F-plan house replacing the old Ha' Tower of Garvock. Low harled rear wing probably 17th century. Late 18th/early 19th-century main front has classical elements, such as pediment and columned porch, but does not conform to classical rules of symmetry, perhaps as the result of major remodelling in 1826 for Robert Graeme. Square tower and Jacobean north-west wing added at this time.

NEWTON OF PITCAIRNS
Newton of Pitcairns School, 1839, an attractive 'cottage' with octagonal chimneys and latticed windows; southern block added, 1847, as hall and school of the Free Church.

From top *Kirkstyle Inn c.1875; War Memorial; Parish Church; Garvock House; Newton of Pitcairns School.*

DUNNING

Established immediately to the south-east of Dunning as a new and distinct planned village by the Grahams of Orchill, late 18th century, **Newton of Pitcairns** is known as 'The Dragon', on account of the legend of St Serf's slaying of the Dun Knock dragon. The village forms a single street, now much altered, but never very uniform in its execution.

Pitcairns House, 1827–8, William Burn
Built for John Pitcairns in Burn's famed 'cottage style' – low and sprawling with lots of gables, tall octagonal chimneys and mullioned windows. Similar to now-demolished Snaigow (see p.139), and immediate predecessor to Burn's first Scots-Tudor house at Milton Lockhart, Lanarkshire.

Kippen House, Marcassie Bridge, 1874, Andrew Heiton Jr
Unlike surrounding country pads, Kippen was built for new money Angus Turner, Town Clerk of Glasgow, and the swagger shows in the blowsy baronial pile perched conspicuously above the Yetts o' Muckhart road at Marcassie Bridge. Tall and muscular entrance tower with corner turrets and lower gabled ranges gathered round. Ballroom added 1910 to mark coming-of-age of Jane Wilson, daughter of Sir John Wilson, coal magnate of Airdrie.

Below *Kippen House*. Right *Keltie Castle*.

Maggie Wall Monument (*above*), Auchterarder Road, of uncertain date, has a boulder base with tall slab and cross on top, erected in memory of Maggie Wall, allegedly burned as a witch in 1657. Dunning figured strongly in 17th-century witch-hunts, with some six people executed for witchcraft in 1663 alone. Nothing is known of Maggie Walls, or Wall, nor why she is commemorated by this monument.

Keltie Castle, *c*.1600
Small and sturdy unvaulted L-plan laird's house built for the Bonar family, perhaps incorporating earlier fabric in the 9ft thick walls, distinguished by unusual corbelled turret at north-east corner. Main wing widened, 1712, enclosing previous doorway (dated 1686) in re-entrant. Perhaps unfashionable crowsteps and attic dormerheads were removed at this time. Interior remodelled *c*.1920, when pointed arch was added to south doorway and large windows installed with concrete surrounds. Neighbouring **bridge** over Keltie Burn.

Duncrub House, 1861–3, Habershon & Pite (demolished 1950)
Colossal Continental Gothic mansion built by London firm for John Rogerson Rollo, 10th Lord

Rollo, on site of old Duncrub House, itself greatly extended by William Burn. Externally impressive through sheer scale rather than design, which was surprisingly dull – acres of rough-faced masonry and mullioned windows – enlivened only by Dutch crowsteps, pepperpot turrets and French pavilion roof on entrance tower.

Duncrub House Chapel, 1858, Habershon & Pite Appears as a somewhat incongruous, if charming, English parish church in the landscape, now that the dominant hulk of the house it served has been demolished. Converted to a sports hall with holiday accommodation above, the Early Pointed chapel is dominated by buttressed tower and wobbly looking needle spire. Splendid ogee-roofed **doocot**, 1725, another relic of the once great Duncrub estate in grounds of St Andrew's Cottage.

Inverdunning House and **Leadketty Farm**, early 19th century, appear to be by the same hand, both symmetrical with bowed bays flanking the entrance. Inverdunning has tripartite gothic window over the door, Leadketty has Venetian windows at ground floor and roof has been altered to form broad eaves linking the bows.

ABERUTHVEN
Although it must have been a kirkton at an early date, the village itself is now a linear settlement along the old Crieff to Perth road, mainly dating from the early 19th century in its present form, but its traditional character much damaged by double glazing and concrete roof tiles.

83 **St Kattan's Chapel**, Aberuthven, late medieval Ruinous rectangular-plan chapel with 17th-century bellcote on west gable, formerly parish kirk of Aberuthven before unification with Auchterarder, and traditional burial place of the Graham earls of Montrose. *John Adam fecet 1736* was apparently the inscription (no longer legible) on adjacent **Montrose Mausoleum** when MacGibbon & Ross recorded the building in 1896. This seems to be a misreading of the first name, as John Adam was only 15 in 1736 and documents in the National Archives of Scotland reveal his father, William Adam, as fully responsible for the construction, 1736–8. Built to contain remains of the 1st Duke of Montrose, it is a chaste square, beautifully detailed with raised margins, bold deep cornice, pyramid roof topped by urn and Ionic Venetian entrance (colour p.119).

Top *Duncrub House, late 19th century.* Middle *Duncrub House Chapel.* Above *Inverdunning House.*

St Kattan's Chapel and Montrose Mausoleum.

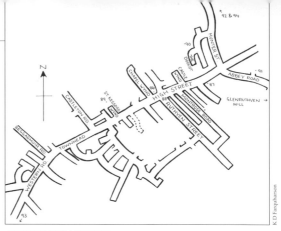

Tower from kirk built 1660.

Below *St Margaret's Hospital.*
Bottom *Aytoun Hall.*

AUCHTERARDER

Earliest records relate to a charter by Alexander II in 1227 conveying the teinds of the king's revenue from his Auchterarder lands to the Abbey of Inchaffray. The town was burnt by the Jacobites in 1715. A Report on the Annexed Estates (those forfeited to the Crown after the 1745 Rebellion) of 1778 concluded *Auchterarder was anciently one of the boroughs of Scotland, but it is now dwindled into a pitiful village.* The town flourished on agriculture and cotton weaving through the 19th century, developing in a long linear plan with wynds leading off. By 1894 it had recovered to the status of a police burgh, and in March 1951 was reinstated on the roll of the Royal Burghs of Scotland.

Remains of pre-Reformation kirk stand in the parish (see p.68), but the **tower** of the kirk built in 1660 from the stones of old Kincardine Castle

84 survives adjacent to the **War Memorial**, 1919, a shaft of white stone surmounted by a cross.

85 **St Margaret's Hospital**, Townhead, 1928–9, Stewart & Paterson
Very beautifully finished Scots 17th-century symmetrical design in red sandstone for the cottage hospital. Crowstepped gables, richly sculpted dormerheads and fine Ionic doorpiece.

High Street forms the backbone of the town, largely lined with two-storey traditional houses dating from late 18th century, also containing

86 most of the public buildings. **Aytoun Hall**, 1872, C S Robertson, looks like a church with clocktower, pinnacle and Romanesque windows, but flagpole and balcony reveal its secular purpose; columned fountain added to tower, 1905. Similarly domestic scale and fine doorpiece with niche above of the neighbouring **Girnal House**, *c.*1835, do not look municipal,

but in fact disguise library and institute additions to rear, 1896, G T Ewing. **Masonic Hall**, 85-89 High Street, late 18th century, has columned doorpiece c.1830 and three infilled archways at ground floor; hall itself at first floor with leaded windows, including central Venetian window. **65-67 High Street**, earlier 19th century, suave domestic and original shopfront. **Railway Hotel**, 1 High Street, c.1848, much altered, but has splendid bas-relief of locomotive incorporated in doorpiece.

87 **Barony Parish Church**, High Street, 1904, Honeyman Keppie and Mackintosh
Squat red sandstone tower with slated pyramidal roof of the kind favoured by J J Burnet in his 'low' churches, but here the bulky body of the church is nearly as high as the tower.

Top *Masonic Hall*. Above *Barony Parish Church.*

88 **Gleneagles Furniture Centre**, High Street, 1843, Cousin & Gale
Former Free Church started life as severe crowstepped box, but was extended forward by two bays in 1845 when distinctive 80ft pinnacled tower with open porch was added. Interior of note for galleries supported on wooden columns and arcaded upper level. Italianate **Mansefield**, 1847, Andrew Heiton Sr, former Free Church manse.

89 **St Kessog's Episcopal Church**, off High Street, 1897, Ross & Macbeth
Small plain gothic with gabled porch and pyramid ventilator. Rich interior including traceried chancel arch and east and west windows by Kempe of London.

Below *St Kessog's Episcopal Church.*
Bottom *Coll-Earn Castle Hotel.*

Behind High Street, the town expanded by the addition of some very large and sumptuous villas.

90 **Coll-Earn Castle Hotel**, off High Street, 1869–70, William Leiper
Early baronial work in Leiper's oeuvre for advocate Alexander Mackintosh. Earthy red sandstone with creamy coloured dressings (colour p.118). Circular tower anchors the design at north-east corner with the motto 'A Fast Tower is our God' and carved figure as finial. Menacing carved animals and birds perch on gables and dormers. Baronial theme is continued inside with stone fireplace in entrance hall and compartmental ceilings in principal rooms, but tempered by beautiful pine panelling and Aesthetic Movement stained glass stair windows. **Coll-Earn Lodge**, Hunter Road, is contemporary and finely detailed

Ruthven Tower Nursing Home.

From *Timothy Pont's late 16th-century*
map it would appear that the old
Kincardine Castle, was a very significant
structure – it stood south of the Mains, and
as the principal seat of James Graham, 5th
Earl and 1st Marquess of Montrose, was
destroyed by General Middleton's
Covenanter Army in 1646.

Let them bestow on every Airth a Limb;
Open all my Veins, that I may swim
To thee my Saviour, in that Crimson Lake;
Then place my par-boil'd Head upon a stake;
Scatter my Ashes, throw them in the Air:
Lord (since thow know'st where all these
Atoms are)
I'm hopeful, once Thou'lt recollect my Dust,
And confident Thou'lt raise me with the Just.
James Graham, His Metrical Prayer, 1650

Strathearn Home Institution.

with carved panels, as is conical-roofed
ornamental **doocot**, dated 1874, now rather
absurdly stranded in the driveway of 10 The
Doocot, part of a modern bungalow development.

91 **Ruthven Tower Nursing Home**, Abbey Hill,
1882, William Leiper
Second of Leiper's Auchterarder mansions, 12
years later than Coll-Earn, still in baronial style,
but tinged with renaissance detailing: mullioned
windows, richly carved dormerheads and
Flemish crowstepped gables. Again a conical-
roofed circular tower forms the hinge of design.
Anglo-Japanese glass by Cottier. Built for J Halley
of Halley & Co., power-loom weavers of nearby
Ruthvenvale Works.

Drumcharry, Montrose Road, *c*.1880,
A Macgregor
Medley of styles, lovingly detailed throughout.
Round-headed windows, corbelled oriel,
decorative bargeboards, curious catslide and
pagoda-roofed dormers.

92 **St Kessog's Kirk**, pre-Reformation
Ruinous rectangular remains of the original
parish kirk containing original piscina and plain
aumbry. East end converted to burial vault for
Hunter of Auchterarder, 1832, probably by
William Burn.

93 **Strathearn Home Institution**, 1863,
James Campbell Walker
Built as Upper Strathearn Combination
Poorhouse, a smaller version of Atholl &
Breadalbane poorhouse, built the following year
at Logierait (see p.149) by the same architect.
Plain symmetrical gabled frontage.

94 **Auchterarder House Hotel**, 1832, William Burn
Sumptuous red sandstone mansion house,
originally in Scots Jacobean style for Captain
James Hunter. Burn's work is best seen from the
back, where crowstepped gables, splendid curvy
dormerheads and strapwork balustrading are
clearly visible. Front and interior were given
treatment in Jacobean renaissance style by Burnet
Son & Campbell, 1887, to house the art collection
of locomotive magnate James Reid. Beautifully
sculpted Dumfries sandstone (brighter than
original local stone) adorns *porte-cochère*, winter
garden and elaborate billiard room additions.
Interior was equally lavish, particularly
magnificent timberwork of the principal rooms

crafted by William Sherriff, staircase ironwork,
banded tiles and marble-lining of the winter
garden, and ingleneuk of billiard room.
Handsome **stable court**, 1833, William Burn,
symmetrical front with crowstepped doocot tower
over entrance pend and little crowstepped
dormers. At main entrance, pretty Old English
style **West Lodge**, 1887, Burnet Son & Campbell,
central chimney, half-timbered gable and broad
enveloping roof forming veranda.

Kincardine Castle, 1805, James Gillespie (Graham)
Perched on spectacular hillside platform
overlooking Kincardine Glen and beyond to the
Ochil Hills, a small and pretty symmetrical Gothick
castle with battlements, octagonal turrets, pointed-
arched windows, hoodmoulds and huge south-
facing bow. Significant early work by Gillespie for
James Johnston. Restored and extended, 1995, Hurd
Rolland. Contemporary buttressed **lodge**, also by
Gillespie. Tall arched **Kincardine Glen Viaduct**,
1846–8, Locke & Errington, carries Stirling to Perth
railway over the deep gully cut by Ruthven Water.

Cloan.

Distinguished visitors to Viscount Haldane, owner of Cloan in the early years of the 20th century, included Henry Asquith, Sydney and Beatrice Webb, Field Marshal Haig, and the Maharajah of Sikhim.

Cloan, 1800
Originally modest two-storey, three-bay house. In 1855 Andrew Heiton Sr & Son prepared two extension schemes, one French, one Italian, and 10 years later the French one proceeded. East tower with angle turrets was added over existing wing, 1904–5, Harry Ramsay Taylor.

Foswell, late 18th century
Long two-storey laird's house with projecting crowstepped gables at outer ends, and bowed centre porch, distinguished by 1929 doorpiece partly constructed from moulded stones (probably James Smith vintage) salvaged from demolition of Hamilton Palace.

Gleneagles Station, 1919, James Miller
Light and airy canopied station built to welcome holidaymakers to the railway company's hotel.

95 **Gleneagles Hotel**, 1913–25, Miller & Matheson and Matthew Adam
Vast prestigious entertainment palace in blowsy classical style – an Edwardian country house run riot. Mostly harled brick of three floors with two rows of dormers in the mansard roof, entrance marked by Blaxter stone porch and balustraded tower. Although not quite symmetrical, an axis runs through the semicircular sunroom and ballroom. Amazingly sumptuous interior to public rooms by Charles W Swanson, dripping with plasterwork swags and all manner of rococo decoration, executed by Scott Morton & Co. Ballroom the *pièce-de-resistance* at the heart, top lit by cupolas and fitted with Morton's patent Valtor dancing floor. Conceived by Donald Matheson, senior executive of Caledonian Railways in 1909, and begun 1913, the war delayed construction until 1924–5. King's and Queen's golf courses laid out, 1910–19, by James Braid, five times Open Champion.

Above *Gleneagles Station.*
Right *Gleneagles Hotel.*

Gleneagles House, 1750

Idyllic site at northern entrance to wild Gleneagles, approached by a lime avenue planted to commemorate the Battle of Camperdown (1797). Bright white harled house takes linear form as consequence of incomplete scheme for a Palladian mansion, *c.*1750. Following normal practice, wings were constructed before the *corps-de-logis*, but centre block never built. Instead, wings were linked by wooden veranda, and west wing integrated with adjoining 17th-century house. All remodelled and raised to accommodate dormers in late 19th century.

Gleneagles Chapel, early 16th century

Sensitive restoration, 1925–6, by Reginald Fairlie perfectly retained the atmosphere of antiquity in this tiny crowstepped private chapel. Plain and largely original, just two windows in south wall, one window and door in north, slightly later arched doorway in west gable, and two-light east window installed by Fairlie, who also repaired the roof. Two colossal gatepiers, 1749, re-sited from old approach to main house, form the entrance to small courtyard in front.

Top *Gleneagles House.* Above *Gleneagles Chapel.*

Gleneagles Castle, early 16th century

Very fragmentary remains of ground and part of first floor of the old tower of the Haldanes.

GLENDEVON

See *Clackmannan and The Ochils* in this series.

BLACKFORD

96 **Old Parish Kirk**, 1738–9

Roofless ruin of unusually large long rubble rectangle with birdcage bellcote perched on west gable; abandoned on its hill east of the village in 1859. Symmetrical south front; three arched doorways with pairs of tall windows between. Minister's door at centre. Originally had east and west galleries, and narrow north gallery inserted by William Stirling, 1820–1, on advice of James Gillespie (Graham).

Below *Moray Street, Blackford.*
Bottom *Free Church, Blackford.*

Village laid out as two parallel streets, **Moray Street** the main thoroughfare. At east end, plain gothic **Parish Kirk** of Greek cross plan with slim tower and pyramid spire, 1858, David MacGibbon. On south side, eccentric half-timbered semi-detached villas with corner buttresses and wonderful Art Nouveau doors and leaded glass. Spired red sandstone tower of former **Free Church**, 1855–6, a landmark, but the

building forlornly derelict, the delicate Art Nouveau glazing installed after fire in 1914 now broken and falling apart. Black-and-white frontage of **Coaching Inn** appears to be an exuberant French baronial remodelling of existing modest hostelry; particularly lively skyline of castellated chimneypots, polygonal turrets and intricate iron cresting.

Top *Coaching Inn, Moray Street.*
Above *Former Gleneagles Maltings.*

Former Gleneagles Maltings, Moray Street, 1896–8

Large rubble-built range of maltings, only remnants of once-thriving brewing industry, and last independent commercial floor maltings in Scotland when closed in April 1989. Now re-used as mineral water factory, minus distinctive double kiln.

Greenloaning Church, 1787
Attractive small harled rectangle with square-headed windows in south wall and round-headed windows, *c.*1850, in north wall, interior of same date. Built as Antiburgher Church for faction of the Secession Church opposed to the Burgher Oath in 1747.

Below *Ardoch Parish Kirk.* Bottom *Ardoch Roman Fort.*

Ardoch Parish Kirk, Feddal Road, Braco, 1780
Simple harled rectangle with five arched and keystoned windows high up on south wall. Birdcage bellcote of 1836 recast in 1861. West porch and chancel additions, the latter 1890 by William Simpson. Established as Chapel of Ease, becoming the kirk on formation of the parish from parts of Muthill, Dunblane and Blackford in 1855. Forlorn tower of **Free Church**, 1844–5, is simple Romanesque, but the church itself is long demolished.

Ardoch House, late 18th century
Fine country house in post-Adam classical style. Five bays wide and three storeys high over basement, particularly handsome pedimented centre: Venetian doorway set in panelled arch; corniced tripartite window at principal floor above; and Diocletian window to attic storey. Semicircular bows to rear. Now ruinous.

97 **Ardoch Roman Fort**, later 1st century and mid-2nd century
Footpath signposted just north of Braco village. Exceptional remains of earthwork fort, perhaps the best preserved in the Roman Empire. Most impressive are works of the late 150s, a square rampart enclosing 1.95ha and surrounding series

of five ditches on north and east sides. Tombstone from the site, belonging to one of the earliest of many garrisons, the *cohors I Hispanorum*, now preserved in the Hunterian Museum, Glasgow. Evidence of temporary camps nearby.

Braco Castle, from 17th century
Magnificent setting. Stylistically, Braco has just about the lot: crowsteps, classical symmetry and oculi, Gothick crenellations, baronial turrets, Georgian bows and Victorian bays. Rich mélange the result of numerous chefs, and it is difficult to identify how it all took shape. Main house U-plan with two crowstepped gables facing entrance court, middle of the U filled with two-storey bowed entrance bay. Recently repaired re-instating some missing features.

Above Braco Castle. Left Hall, Old House of Orchill.

Old House of Orchill, mid-18th century
A curious marriage of traditional harled laird's house with 'space rocket' gothic tower and great hall. Origins of these latter parts are obscure, but both almost certainly by the then laird, James Gillespie Graham; the hall *c*.1840. Grand oriel lights north crowstepped gable of hall and two pointed-arched windows light the east; three Jacobean gablets sit on wallhead above. Interior of this room equally extraordinary – a miniature version of Pugin's Banner Hall ceiling at Taymouth Castle (see p.123), complete with ribbed gilded coffering. Fire 1991, restored 1991–4, Duncan Stirling. Excellent Tudor **North Lodge**, *c*.1840, also probably by Gillespie Graham. **Kaimes Cottage**, opposite, a pair of harled cottages with Gothick hoodmoulds, looks earlier, but could be by the same hand.

James Gillespie Graham, 1776–1855, was born at Dunblane, and, as James Gillespie, began his career as superintendent of 2nd Lord Macdonald's works on the Isle of Skye. From this promising beginning, Gillespie went on to become one of the most successful and fashionable architects in early 19th-century Scotland, with an unsurpassed feel for the picturesque. He designed Crawford Priory and Cupar County Buildings in Fife, Dr Gray's Hospital in Moray, Inveraray Court House and Jail in Argyll, the Moray Estate and Tolbooth St John's Church in Edinburgh, among many other major projects (see relevant guides in this series). In 1815 Gillespie married Margaret Graham of Orchill, a member of the cadet branch of the family of the Dukes of Montrose, and began to adopt her family name from 1823, two years before inheriting the Orchill estate. Gillespie Graham's Perthshire connections brought him significant commissions at Taymouth and Murthly Castles, where he collaborated with A W N Pugin, and numerous smaller schemes throughout the county.

Old House of Orchill.

Orchill New House.

William Murray, Marquis of Tullibardine, 1689–1746, was the second son of the 1st Duke of Atholl. He was one of the first to join the standard of 11th Earl of Mar in the 1715 Jacobite rising, and fled to France after the Battle of Sheriffmuir. In 1717 he was created Duke of Rannoch by the exiled Prince James Francis Edward Stewart (the Old Pretender). Murray returned with the Hispano-Scottish invasion of 1719, defeated at Glenshiel, and finally landed at Borrodale with Prince Charles Edward Stewart (the Young Pretender) in 1745, before capture at Loch Lomond, and death the following year in the Tower of London. In 1747 the old Castle of Tullibardine was partly dismantled by his younger brother, James, now 2nd Duke of Atholl, but William Adam's replacement was never built. The remains were swept away *c.1830*.

Right Tullibardine House from Vitruvius Scoticus. *Unexecuted scheme by William Adam for the Duke of Atholl's new house at Tullibardine. The old Castle of Tullibardine was dismantled in 1747 and completely demolished, c.1830.*

Robert Lindsay of Pitscottie's 1570 *Historie and Chronicles of Scotland* tells of a master shipwright involved in the construction of the *Great Michael* for James IV in 1508, who lived near Tullibardine Castle. So pestered by the locals for details of one of the wonders of the age, the shipwright dug deep ditches the width of the ship's sides, exactly shaped in length and breadth, to demonstrate its true scale. Planted round with hawthorns, the excavations remained visible into the 1880s.

Tullibardine Chapel.

Orchill New House, 1868, Andrew Heiton Jr
One of Heiton's most ambitious and successful country houses. Well composed in muscular baronial style around a tower with cap-house. Skyline bristles with turrets, chimneys and crowsteps, and use of bull-faced masonry heightens the dramatic rugged effect, set on its commanding bluff. Interior destroyed by fire during First World War, reinstated 1919, possibly by Heiton's nephew, Andrew Grainger Heiton; much of this work subsequently removed.

98 **Tullibardine Chapel**, 1446
Remarkable large family chapel in traditional Catholic arrangement of cruciform plan with tower – probably rather grander than most contemporary rural parish churches. Main body of chapel almost certainly intended as collegiate foundation by Sir David Murray (ancestor of the Murray Dukes of Atholl), whose arms adorn walls. Plain looped tracery in transepts and heavy moulding of south doorway suggest later date, *c.1500*, perhaps under patronage of Sir Andrew Murray (see Balvaird Castle, p.212), whose heraldry can be found on south transept gable. Tower probably of this vintage. Although worship ceased, use as a burial aisle ensured chapel's survival through the Reformation. Stark interior retaining much of original open timber roof, but providing little clue to probably a very rich decorative scheme.
Historic Scotland; open to the public

Trevor Wain

Strathallan Castle.

Strathallan Castle, 1817–18, Robert Smirke
Pervasiveness of Robert Adam's 'castle style' still
evident in Gothick remodelling of earlier house
for Perthshire Tory MP James Drummond, later
Viscount Strathallan, some 25 years after Adam's
death. Symmetrical front block with battlements
and turrets, *porte-cochère* and prominent
centrepiece lit by Venetian windows; gently
canted sides. Variety of towers to north front,
which is more complex and asymmetrical, partly
screening the service court. South front tends
towards ecclesiastical Gothick, including
buttresses and traceried Tudor windows.
Relatively plain treatment of interior, which looks
out over *'a veritable arborous sea'* (T Hunter).
Pavilions and central arch to classical **stable
court**, *c*.1800. Two curious gothic houses forming
Home Farm may also be by Smirke.

Trinity Gask Parish Kirk, 1770
Severe harled rectangle picturesquely sited on
ancient elevated site. Square-headed windows
and fine bellcote, 1816, James Scobie, on west
gable. Interior recast and porch added, 1865,
James Stevenson. **Trinity Gask House**, 1779, the
old manse in traditional two-storey, three-bay
format, extended to rear by William Stirling, 1820.

Gask House, 1801–5, Richard Crichton
Large neoclassical mansion built for Laurence
Oliphant. Restrained design of *corps-de-logis* with
columned links to single-storey pavilions, owing
much to late classical style of Crichton's former
employers, the Adam brothers. Originally three
storeys, the low attic storey was removed as part
of major remodelling in 1964–6 by prolific neo-
Georgian country house architect, Claude
Phillimore. Great Venetian window and

The Gask estate was long in the
ownership of the Oliphants until the
death of Kingston Oliphant in 1907. The
family paid the price for their staunch
Jacobitism following the '45, when the
estate was forfeited. Following George
III's award of a £111 pension to Mrs
Oliphant in 1763, the family returned to
the house. Celebrated lyricist, Carolina
Oliphant, later Lady Nairne, was born
at Gask in 1766. Apart from 'The Auld
Hoose' celebrating her beloved Gask,
other famous songs include 'The Laird
o' Cockpen', 'Charlie is my darling', and
'Will ye no come back again'. It was not
until her death in 1845 that the
pseudonym 'Mrs Bogan of Bogan' was
revealed as Lady Nairne.

Below *Trinity Gask Parish Kirk.*
Bottom *Gask House.*

RCAHMS

Trevor Wain

75

Top *Old House of Gask*. Above *Gask Episcopal Chapel*.

Gask Ridge formed part of the Roman frontier system probably constructed by Agricola in the early 80s AD, comprising forts and watchtowers straddling the Roman road, or *'The Street'*, from Bertha (north of Perth) to Camelon (north-west of Falkirk). Timber watchtowers were placed at regular half-mile intervals, possibly to control passage in and out of the Roman province, and to collect customs duties. Distance between sites seems too close for signalling, and towers too small for serious military purposes.

The unusual name, derived from St Findoc, distinguishes Findo Gask from Trinity Gask. The land rises from the Earn in the south to 400ft Gask Ridge bisecting the parish from east to west and down to the Cowgask Burn on northern boundary. Remains of Roman temporary camp and three watchtower sites have been found, one at Witches Knowe, the traditional site for burning witches in the 17th century.

Dupplin.

pediment of centrepiece remain at intended height. While appreciating the motivation of the day and the careful remodelling, loss of original proportions is regrettable.

Old House of Gask, 17th century
Substantial courtyard house, much reconstructed in 1932 for owner G A Buchanan. Entrance to courtyard through north gateway, crowned with splendid bellcote, dated 1632. Although repaired to wallhead in 1932, south range remains ruinous apart from a corner tower, which has extraordinary thatched conical roof. West range rebuilt above first-floor level, and roofed in pantiles to create cavernous Jacobite Hall running the length of the building. Result interesting as a 1930s' romantic view of the 17th century, rather than an archaeological exercise.

Gask Episcopal Chapel, 1845–6,
James Gillespie Graham
A letter of 1821 suggests that James Gillespie (Gillespie Graham from 1825) had *been at work with his own hands* on the new house of Gask, but in what capacity is unclear. Certainly by the 1810s the architect moved in county circles closely associated with the Oliphants of Gask. The chapel was probably erected as a memorial to Lady Nairne, née Oliphant, with whom the Gillespie Grahams were particular friends. Romanesque design is a more modest prototype for the spectacular private chapel at Murthly (see p.147).

Findo Gask Parish Church, 1800
Standard for its date, built on new site at centre of parish. Porch and bowed stair are later. Much altered internally. Plain three-bay **manse**, 1800, substantially extended by arcaded porch and red rubble addition, 1855, Andrew Heiton Sr & Son.

Dupplin, *c.*1970, W Schomberg Scott
Although commanding wonderful views, the site posed considerable difficulties. In the end, substructure of previous house retained to form basis of the new plan for Lord and Lady Forteviot. Loosely classical design, spread long and low across an enormous harled frontage. Central pavilion with splayed and columned porch. Internally, house is planned around large bow-ended drawing room, and serviced from western office court. Sinuous naturalistic ironwork winds its way up the staircase like delicate ivy. Fine A-plan **stable block**, *c.*1820, and Burn's **Estate Office**, 1831, survive. James Miller, who rebuilt

estate village of Forteviot, demonstrated his versatility in late Tudor-cum-Arts & Crafts style of **East Lodge**, *c*.1930, accompanying classical gatepiers and wrought-ironwork. **Burnside Lodge (South)** probably also by Miller.

Aberdalgie & Dupplin Parish Church, 1773 Originally T-plan with two large round-arched windows in the long elevation, Venetian windows with oculi above in gables. At Lord Forteviot's expense, remodelling, 1929, Lorimer & Matthew, constructing a new porch and replacing delicate columned bellcote with clumpy new design. Interior recast in typically restrained but beautifully crafted Austrian oak, including Ionic pilastered Forteviot Loft. Gothic arched recess contains extremely rare, and much damaged, Franco-Flemish carved relief slab of Tournai stone to Sir William Oliphant (d.1329). Large utilitarian **manse**, 1833, William Burn, architect to the sole heritor, the Earl of Kinnoull.

MILLTOWN OF ABERDALGIE
Early 19th-century estate hamlet, notable for its engaging Gothick cottages with pointed openings, overhanging eaves and brick chimneys.

The meandering River Earn forms the southern boundary of Aberdalgie parish, separated from Perth by the M90 to the east. The terrain rises sharply from the riverbanks, but is not as craggy as the neighbouring hills of Kirkton and Moncreiffe. Much of the parish is wooded, forming part of the extensive Dupplin Estate.

Top *Aberdalgie & Dupplin Parish Church.* Left *Milltown of Aberdalgie.*

Aberdalgie House, *c*.1800
Elegant classical house of modest pretension, nicely detailed with panelled pilasters, central pediment, corniced doorpiece and umbrella fanlight. **Offices**, *c*.1820, have gothic doors and windows, and broad-eaved pyramidal roof.

Kirkton of Mailer Burial Ground
Small square graveyard, the only reminder of the long-defunct Mailer Parish. Contains a number of interesting 18th-century stones, one depicting a salmon net – the principal industry associated with the Earn.

Dupplin has a long and distinguished history. Laurence, 1st Lord Oliphant, rebuilt a tower here in 1461. Charles I's Lord Chancellor, George Hay, 1st Earl of Kinnoull, acquired the estate in 1623. In 1688 a new classical house, possibly by James Smith of Whitehill (now Newhailes, East Lothian), incorporated part of the existing tower house for Thomas Hay, later 6th Earl of Kinnoull. The Earl of Mar executed agricultural improvements in 1707, and the following year his protégé James Gibbs produced a remarkable X-plan design for a new house. Instead of building afresh, the 7th Earl re-employed James Smith to construct a great Palladian arrangement of office wings, 1720–5. James Playfair altered these, built a *'Temple of Virtue and Honour'*, and designed a *'menagerie'* in 1789. The house was largely destroyed by fire in 1827. William Burn designed the spectacular and colossal Jacobean replacement, *'Burn's best'* according to Lord Cockburn, which was also badly fire-damaged in 1934 and finally demolished in 1967. Whisky tycoon and philanthropist Sir John Alexander Dewar purchased the estate in 1911, before his ennoblement as 1st Baron Forteviot of Dupplin in 1916.

Right Huntingtower. Above Huntingtower (Ruthve) by Timothy Pont, late 16th century.

The power and influence of the Ruthvens increased to the point of notoriety through the 16th century. The 2nd Lord Ruthven was Keeper of the Privy Seal. His son, Patrick, a leading Protestant reformer, entertained the Queen and Lord Darnley on their honeymoon in 1565, and conspired to murder Mary's Italian favourite, David Riccio, in 1566. William, 4th Lord Ruthven, became Treasurer under James VI in 1571, and was created Earl of Gowrie in 1581. The following year he instigated the 'Ruthven Raid', imprisoning the king at Ruthven to remove him from Roman Catholic influence at court, for which Gowrie was beheaded in 1584. The ultimate downfall of the Ruthvens came in 1600 following the 3rd Earl's execution for the 'Gowrie Conspiracy' (see p.15). An Act of Parliament annexed the estate to the Crown and *ordained the baronie and place of Ruthven to be changeit and callit in all tyme coming the place and baronie of Huntingtour* (although Nimmo still calls it the House of Ruthven in 1776). The house was granted to the 4th Earl of Tullibardine in 1663, and thence passed to the 2nd Earl of Atholl, in whose family it remained, until it was sold in a dilapidated state as a dormitory for the nearby calico printers in 1805.

Timber ceiling, Huntingtower.

99 Huntingtower, from early 15th century
One of Perthshire's most remarkable power houses, known as Place (palace) of Ruthven until 1600. Lower parts of the east tower, including remains of pend arches, appear to date from early 15th century. William, 1st Lord Ruthven, later James V's guardian, probably responsible for major remodelling in the late 15th century. L-plan west tower built shortly afterwards, on a detached site 9ft away. The reason for this proximity is unclear, but may relate to the royal guardianship, or to the division of Ruthven lands between two legitimised sons in 1480. Gap between the buildings became known as the *Maiden's Leap*, after a tradition that a daughter of the 1st Earl of Gowrie jumped the distance to avoid the Countess catching her with her lover. The later 17th century saw a scheme to avoid such inconvenience by linking the two towers. At this time, the fenestration was partially regularised, and the interior panelled and plastered in contemporary style. In 1913, the internal work was removed revealing miraculous survivals of late 15th/early 16th-century painted decoration on plaster walls and **timber ceilings**. Unfortunately nothing remains of the courtyard buildings or later 16th-century range of great hall or gallery and lodgings which adjoined the west tower to north (colour p.117).

Historic Scotland; open to the public; guidebook

Around 1800, the Duke of Atholl began to sell parts of Huntingtower estate, and a number of smart new classical lairds' houses and farmhouses sprang up as a result. **Ruthven House** and its curved **lodges**, *c.*1800, and **North Blackruthven**, *c.*1820 (and Tudor-gothic **lodge**, *c.*1833, John Bell), belong to the former category. **Newhouse Farmhouse** and **steading**, *c.*1835, just above the Perth bypass, is a fine example of the latter. **West Mains of Huntingtower**, *c.*1840, is more informal, with broad eaves, gothic tracery and an asymmetrical arrangement.

Huntingtowerfield Bleachworks, 1866
Slim Italianate bell tower fronting much-reduced remains of two-storey bleachworks, now converted for housing. Initially water-powered for the bleaching of linen, the firm of Lumsden & Mackenzie adapted the buildings for dyeing and mercerising before closure in 1982. Associated developments of workers' housing, the least spoilt of which are symmetrical single- and two-storey blocks at **Waterside Cottages**, Huntingtowerfield, *c.*1845. **Grey Row**, Ruthven, late 18th century, utilitarian terrace with forestairs. Bargeboarded gables and porches at **Low's Work Cottages**, mid-19th century, are more bucolic.

Low's Work Weir, rebuilt 1622–4
Medieval in origin, this 80ft weir was rebuilt in unmortared boulder rubble with ashlar groins to divert water from the River Almond to the King's Lade through Perth.

TIBBERMORE

The eastern part of the old parish is now subsumed into Perth, leaving the bypass as the effective boundary. The land slopes gently from the northern ridge of Strathearn to the flat plain surrounding the Pow Water and River Almond. Likely that the Roman road along Gask Ridge ran through the parish to the fort at Bertha, although only archaeological evidence of a fortlet remains.

Tibbermore Parish Church, medieval core
Remains of transept arches were discovered in 1920, suggesting pre-Reformation origin. Immediately striking elaborate bellcote of 1632 – perhaps the date when transepts were removed (colour p.118). Elsewhere, church remodelled, 1789, by 4th Duke of Atholl's factor, James Stobie, to form unexceptional preaching box, arranged around pulpit in long south wall. Ruthven Printfield Company added aisle in opposite wall, 1808 for their workers creating a T-plan. Whole refurnished in pitch pine, 1874, to designs by William Maclaren of Sir George Condie Conning & Co., all now very atmospheric in its decayed state. Interesting collection of 18th-century headstones in graveyard, and eccentric **monument** to James Ritchie (west side of the company aisle) depicting his prize bull and full array of curling accoutrements. Adjacent fine classical **manse**, 1823–4, by William Stirling.

Huntingtowerfield Bleachworks.

The Battle of Tibbermore provided Montrose with his first victory over the Covenanters in 1644. For centuries the parish was dominated by the Dupplin and Huntingtower (Ruthven) estates. In the late 18th century substantial textile bleaching and printing industries grew up around Huntingtowerfield and Ruthvenfield. Now the ubiquitous profiled steel sheds of the Inveralmond industrial units prevail in the north-east of the parish.

Tibbermore Parish Church:
below *bellcote*; middle *exterior*;
bottom *James Ritchie Monument.*

METHVEN

The narrow winding street pattern around the church reveals the kirkton origins of the village. The abundance of Logiealmond slate impacted at an early date on the local thatching tradition, which finally died out in 1902. Much of the village was reconstructed in the late 18th/early 19th century, at the height of the weaving trade here. **Main Street** and **The Square** were laid out at this time in plain and regular manner.

METHVEN

At the heart of Strathmore, Methven enjoys a beautiful location of rolling farmland and woodland largely south of the sinuous River Almond and north of the smaller canalised Pow Water. One of the battles of the Wars of Independence was fought at Methven in 1306, when the Earl of Pembroke routed Robert I. The parish was one of the most strident seats of the 18th-century Secession.

Right Front elevation, Methven Castle.
Below Methven Castle, 18th-century engraving, showing the 17th-century entrance forecourt and offices, now removed.

Methven Parish Church.

100 **Methven Castle**, 1664, possibly John Mylne
Beacon in the landscape, the bright harling visible for miles around. Built for Patrick Smythe of Braco, who bought the estate and substantial old house (where Margaret Tudor died in 1542) from Duke of Lennox in 1664. Replacement house, incorporating parts of earlier structure, curious hybrid of classical form with baronial corner towers, not far removed from William Bruce and Robert Mylne's remodelling of the Palace of Holyroodhouse or John Mylne's Panmure, Angus. The Mylnes, Bruce and James Smith may have had some involvement at Methven. Overall plan is rectangular but roof echoes popular 17th-century U-plan arrangement of principal rooms, in this case surrounding the grand staircase. More chaste classical tendencies of *c.*1800 resulted in the fanlight over the old entrance and remodelled interior. Spectacular scheme to gothicise the house prepared by James Gillespie (Graham) for Robert Smythe in 1813 (colour p.117), but only east drawing-room wing, west service wing (both now demolished) and possibly **lodge** were built. House derelict by 1986 when architect Ken Murdoch began valiant restoration. To west, a small outbuilding with enormous ogee-roofed cupola, from old Perth Academy extension.

Methven Parish Church, 1781,
Mr Smythe of Methven
Large and quite flash, by the standards of

neighbouring parishes, with pilastraded tower and spire. These and the north aisle were added 1825–6 to standard rectangle by Perth City Architect, William M Mackenzie, who also designed the Tudor **manse** of 1830. Good complete interior apparently also of this date. Detached **Methven Aisle**, earlier 15th century, was added to north side of an earlier church and probably housed the college of canons founded by Walter Stewart, Earl of Atholl, in 1433. Delicate tracery of blocked north window would certainly suggest a construction of this date, although the large crowsteps and tabernacle head may date from the expansion of the richly endowed college in 1510 and 1516. One of the most extraordinary and sophisticated buildings of its date in Scotland, the **Lynedoch Mausoleum**, 1792–3, James Playfair, was much influenced by French neoclassical architects such as Ledoux and Boullée. Playfair produced a miniature primitive temple of bulging rusticated masonry so monumental in design and archaeological in detail that it appears to have been excavated out of the earth, rather than built on it.

Top *Methven Aisle*. Above *Lynedoch Mausoleum*.

Former UP Church, 1867, John Honeyman
Understated mid-Pointed gothic by the celebrated Glasgow architect, enlivened internally by the 'wibble-wobble' of Daniel Cottier's stained glass.

Tippermallo, 1752
Quintessence of a small Scots classical house: beautifully proportioned, modestly sized at two storeys and three bays, employs local materials and restrained crafted stonework details such as the scrolled skewputts and cornice over door. Walled garden aligned on axis of house.

Balgowan House, early 18th century
Only one of the derelict pavilion wings of this Graham seat survives. Thomas Graham could no longer bear to live at Balgowan following the death of his mother, so purchased Lynedoch Cottage (see p.105). Main house gradually ruined, and knocked down, 1860s; its successor has also been demolished.

Keillour Castle, c.1877, Andrew Heiton Jr
Constructed on site of a tower house, Heiton's replacement also a tower, but Rhenish in character with tall pavilion roof, odd rubbly chimneys and canopied dormers.

The Lynedoch Estate was bought by Thomas Graham of Balgowan in 1787 as a retreat from his Leicestershire seat of Brooksby. Graham commissioned the **Lynedoch Mausoleum** for his wife, Catherine, the beautiful and talented second daughter of 9th Lord Cathcart, who died in 1791. Thomas Gainsborough's ravishing portrait of the Hon Mrs Graham hangs in the National Gallery of Scotland. Subsequently Graham distinguished himself as one of Wellington's generals in the Peninsular War, and was created Baron Lynedoch of Balgowan in 1814. Graham indulged his passion for agricultural improvements, planting, and stock-breeding at Lynedoch and Pitcairngreen (see p.105), employing W H Playfair to build the model farm at **Dalcrue**. He continued to make his regular autumn visits until his death in 1843 at the age of 95.

Tippermallo.

Madderty Parish Kirk.

Inchaffray Abbey, late 12th century
Very fragmentary remains of west range of
monastic buildings, *c*.1200. A 97ft long wall, now
coped, stands about 7ft high, and barrel vault and
rebuilt gable survive at north end of site.
Monastery was founded by Gilbert, Earl of
Strathearn and his wife, Matildis, before 1198.

101 Madderty Parish Kirk, 1689
Beautiful plain long low country kirk, retaining
17th-century proportions, rectangular plan, steep
crowstepped gables and birdcage bellcote.
Reputedly built using stone from ruins of
Inchaffray Abbey. G T Ewing gothicised the kirk,
1897, transforming the tripartite sash-and-case
windows into cusped lancet windows, adding rose
window to west gable, a lancet to east and porch
in north wall. Although inappropriately gothic,
alterations do not intrude too glaringly on solid
Presbyterian simplicity. **Session House**, *c*.1840.

*Williamston House by W F Lyon, mid-19th
century.*

Williamston House, from 16th century
Small T-plan house of great character and charm,
perhaps once the lodging to larger establishment.
Probable original entrance tower in centre of
north side, rounded at the base and corbelled to
square above with small upper stair corbelled in
re-entrant. Presumably a newel stair rose to hall
at principal floor – now accessed by straight
flight of stairs entered from south side, perhaps a
fashionable alteration by Laurence Oliphant of
Gask, who purchased the estate from Sir William
Blair of Kinfauns in 1650. Both gables have
straight skews (i.e. no crowsteps) and satisfyingly
substantial chimneys, the western stepped.
Enormous wallhead 'hospitality' chimney of hall
rises to left of centre on south front, and small
drawing-room wing *c*.1800 adjoins to east.

Woodend House, late 17th century
Impressive laird's house originally belonging to
the Oliphants of Gask. Long and predominantly
regular frontage, expanded from core at east end
to nine windows, mid-18th century, when house
sold to a Mr Watt. Two-storey bay window
replaced two western windows *c.*1860. Further
west addition, 1928.

Perth Museum & Art Gallery

Abercairny Abbey.

Abercairny Abbey, 1804–42, Richard Crichton and
R & R Dickson (demolished 1960)
Remarkable sprawling Gothick mansion begun by
Crichton for Charles Moray, set in the park
landscaped by Thomas White, 1790–5, for
previous house. Moray died in 1810 and Crichton
in 1817, leaving the completion to respective
successors, James and William Moray and R & R
Dickson. R Thornton Shiells added tower, 1869.
Externally, house was a red sandstone riot of
buttresses, traceried windows, pinnacles and
Tudor arches, probably becoming more
asymmetrical as the building evolved. Glory was
the interior, an exuberant display of the plasterer's
art from the mock hammerbeam ceiling of the hall,
through the gothic fantasy of the east corridor and
fan vaulting of the library, to the rib-vaulted
ceiling of the spectacular 115ft gallery.

Abercairny House, *c.*1960, Claude Phillimore
Neo-Georgian house on site of the Abbey.
Impressive Tudor-gothic **stable court**, 1841,
R & R Dickson, complete with towers, buttresses
and mullioned windows.

Newbigging Farmhouse, *c.*1835
Similar to Drummond Hall Farmhouse (see p.145),
a handsome Improvement farmhouse. Tall central
block with bay window, flanked by single-storey
wings, all with shallow-pitched roofs and
overhanging eaves.

Cross of Fowlis.

RCAHMS

FOWLIS WESTER
Small and attractive kirkton, mainly of early
19th-century date, centred around **Cross of
Fowlis**, early 9th century, a tall red sandstone
tapered cross-slab with hunting scene on reverse,
unique in Pictish art for projecting arms of cross (a
cast – original now inside St Bean's). New houses,
1990s, by James Denholm and Ulrik Lawson.

Below *St Bean's Parish Church.* Bottom
Cultoquhey House Hotel, late 19th century.

Stephen Stuart

102 **St Bean's Parish Church**, from 13th century
St Bean's appears to have escaped the early 19th-
century craze for kirk reconstruction. In fact the
old fabric was thoroughly 'repaired' in 1802.
Fashion was decidedly against the heritors' box
by 1927 when Jeffrey Waddell zealously re-
medievalised the building. Essential to the
beguiling 'old look' was removal of the harling,
rediscovering the kirkyard gate pediment (*Tak
heid to thy foot when tho entrest the House of God,
1644*), the aumbry, a leper squint and 9th-century
Pictish cross depicting Jonah and the whale.
Celtic motifs embellish replacement furnishings.
The Grange, 1820, with single-storey wings
*c.*1840, is the former manse.

Perth Museum & Art Gallery

Cultoquhey House Hotel, *c.*1820, Robert Smirke
Pronounced 'Cultoowhey'. Restrained,
asymmetrical Tudor-gothic mansion. Hoodmoulds
ornament entrance and west fronts. Tall, offset
chimneys enliven skyline. Terraces built using
stone from Balgowan House (see p.81). Offices
incorporate 16th-century doorway from the mint or
Cunzie House in the Cowgate, Edinburgh.

GILMERTON
Largely 19th-century settlement at junction of old
Crieff/Perth toll road and Wade's road through
the Sma' Glen to Aberfeldy. Landmark
crenellated Mid-Pointed tower and broached
spire of **Former Free Church**, 1869, J J Stevenson
of Campbell Douglas & Stevenson, built from
local red sandstone with contrasting dressings.

K D Farquharson

CRIEFF

Bustling holiday town set on the boundary of the
Highlands, second largest settlement in Perthshire
after Perth itself. In the 18th century, the town
hosted an important cattle 'tryst' and agricultural
market. East High Street, part of the old kirkton, is
the oldest area. King Street and Ferntower Road,
linked by James Square, formed part of General
Wade's military road to the Sma' Glen.
Commissioners of forfeited Drummond Estate
feued the broad street that bears their name
c.1774. A further major planned development was
Burrell Street and Square of 1809. Fashionable
villas, such as those in Victoria Terrace, followed
the establishment of the Academy and Crieff
Hydro further up Knock Hill. In the later 19th
century, the churches too deserted the town centre
for the genteel leafy suburbs.

James Square forms the heart of the town, set
out as a marketplace by George Drummond of
Milnab, 1685, but largely feued by James
Drummond, 3rd Duke of Perth, taking his name.
Retains much of its holiday atmosphere,
bequeathed by numerous late 19th-century
hotels, apart from the disastrous redevelopment
of the east side in the later 20th century. Focus is
103 the red and grey granite **Murray Fountain**, 1893,
capped with cavorting fish and weathervane,
commemorating the town's fresh water supply
provided by the Murrays of Ochtertyre. Matching
fishy lampposts. Pavilion roof of **Drummond
Arms Hotel**, 1871–2, a landmark on the north
side of the square, but neighbouring **Royal Bank
of Scotland**, 1874, probably David Rhind, is

Below *Murray Fountain.*
Bottom *Drummond Arms Hotel.*

Haynes

Haynes

85

better detailed with pediments and arcaded first floor. More late 19th-century hotels and shops adjoining, particularly good shopfront at **No 8**.

104 **Tourist Information Centre**, High Street, 1850
Stout red sandstone tower and crowstepped rectangle below. Built as Town Hall to replace 1685 Tolbooth. Old council chamber on first floor, lit by geometrically patterned windows. **Cross of the Regality of Drummond**, 17th-century, **jougs**, and **Cross of Crieff**, 10th century, a red sandstone interlaced Celtic cross, now housed below the Town Hall.

105 **The Bank Restaurant**, 32 High Street, 1900, George Washington Browne
Very handsome metropolitan sophistication in red Dumfriesshire sandstone by the architect of the Caledonian Hotel (see *Edinburgh* in this series) for the British Linen Bank. Sumptuously carved François Premier doorpiece at base of circular tower; large arched window to former banking hall; pilastered first floor and richly ornamented cornice; curvy dormers and spire roof to tower above. Compartmental ceiling inside.

Post Office, 45 High Street, 1906, Office of Works, has a decent Edwardian freestyle frontage, arcaded at ground floor, with bracketed canopy over door. On the corner with Church Street, **John Hooker Books**, earlier 20th century, former cinema, heavy inter-war classical. Fish-scale conical towers and crowstepped gable with thistle finial grace the tall narrow front above **The Pretoria**, late 19th century, corner of Mitchell Street.

Fine group of pilastered doorways and unusual
106 ribbed chimneypot to houses at **79-83 East High**
107 **Street**, later 19th century. **Tower Hotel**, East High Street, early 19th century, recessed from street to form small courtyard. Gothic hoodmoulds and lying-pane windows. Tower originally formed part of neighbouring buildings, now flatted, late 18th-century medical college, recast as girls' college for the Episcopal Church. Jacobean **Taylor's Institute**, Perth Road, 1842, established as school for the parish poor.

108 **Scrymgeour's Corner**, Comrie Street and West High Street, 1990–2, Nicoll Russell Studios
Mixed development of shops and flats on prominent corner site, described by *Prospect* magazine as designed to *reflect Crieff's heritage without vernacular reproduction*. Result is an uncomfortable hybrid, neither pure unfussy

Top Tourist Information Centre. Middle Cross of Crieff by James Giles, early 19th century. Above The Bank Restaurant.

modern, nor really grounded in vernacular. Where the local buildings use a limited palate and vocabulary, Scrymgeour's Corner (named after the previous department store on site) is busy with colours, materials and architectural features, such as the concrete stairtower balanced on a pylon. Saltire Award 1993, RIBA Regional Award 1994.

Cross of the Regality of Drummond, constructed sometime after 1687, when James VII erected parts of Crieff into a burgh of Regality in favour of James Drummond, Earl of Perth and Chancellor of Scotland. Drummond's charter was never ratified by the Scottish Parliament as he refused to recognise the claims of William and Mary, and the cross never saw active market service.

Left *Scrymgeour's Corner*. Below *Antiques Centre by J J Stevenson*. Middle *Cross of Crieff by James Giles, early 19th century*. Bottom *Morrison's Academy*.

109 **Antiques Centre**, Comrie Street and Coldwells Road, 1880–2, J J Stevenson
Powerful Scots Gothic Free Church erected in red sandstone on a difficult sloping site, designed to be viewed for maximum impact from Scrymgeour's Corner. Aisles, clerestory, and traceried windows. Gentle batter of tower and slated spire based on Dunblane Cathedral. Modestly detailed interior with arcade and three-sided gallery. Minor alterations, Robert Lorimer in his final year, 1929.

110 **War Memorial**, Comrie Street, early 20th century, Peter MacGregor Chalmers
Beautifully crafted. Panelled base, shaft banded with regimental emblems; delicately scrolled cross.

111 **Morrison's Academy**, Hill Street, 1860, Peddie & Kinnear
Main building symmetrical baronial with crowstepped gables and turreted centre block. Baronial Memorial Hall within, remodelled Scott Morton & Co., 1920. War Memorial window by Douglas Strachan. Founded on the fortune of Thomas Morrison, native of Muthill and master builder in Edinburgh (Morrison Street), who left £26,000 in 1826 to endow an academy.

Roundelwood Health Spa, Drummond Terrace, 1885, John Honeyman
Muscular baronial mansion, built in bull-faced red sandstone as Knock Castle for William Miller. Complete with turrets and towers to take in the view, and an instant lineage, recorded in heraldry and emblems over door and pedimented windows.

112 St Michael's Parish Church, Strathearn Terrace, 1882, G T Ewing
Striking First/Second Pointed gothic church. Tall central gable flanked by pinnacled buttresses and outer aisles. Tower almost a campanile, detached from main church, with open arcade below gabled top stage. Inside, impressive kingpost barrel roof and arcaded aisles with uncut capitals.

113 St Andrew's Church, Ferntower Road and Strathearn Terrace, 1883, T L Watson
Unusual design, entered through rounded apse, based on J J Stevenson's Kelvinside Church (see *Central Glasgow* in this series). Fine tower and spire.

*Above St Michael's Parish Church.
Right Crieff Hydro.*

Crieff Hydro was founded as Strathearn House by Thomas H Meikle, an Aberdeen doctor, who had succeeded his brother in a small hydropathic establishment there. With the aid of the Secretary of the Meteorological Society of Scotland, Meikle selected the site at Crieff as most suitable for the foundation of a new spa resort. The initial building cost £30,000, and used water drawn from springs north-west of Ochtertyre House.

114 Crieff Hydro, Ewanfield, 1867–8, R Ewan (Aberdeen)
Vast rambling Scots-Jacobean palace originally dedicated to the delights and mysteries of hydropathy. Lively skyline a profusion of towers, turrets, chimneys and gables. Entered from north, where six-storey tower dominates, building is strung out east/west with southern wings linked by later two-storey winter garden to take advantage of fantastic views across Strathearn. Light glazed extension to winter garden, 1991, James Denholm Associates.

St Ninian's Centre.

Crieff Bridge, 1866–8, leads via Gallowhill to **Burrell Street** and **Square** (originally the Octagon or Sexagon), laid out to a plan for the feuars Lord and Lady Gwydyr, 1809–10, continuing the expansiveness and formality of the avenue leading to Crieff from their estate at Drummond. Architectural unity of houses never achieved, although dominant form is two-storey, three-bay plain classical. However, the plan survives, focused on hilltop **St Ninian's Centre**, Comrie Road, 1836–8, the gawky former West Parish Church, further weakened by later insensitive alterations and additions.

Leading off Gallowhill, **King Street** is the old
military road. Good corner blocks at junction
with **Commissioner Street**, particularly **King
Street Carpets**, *c.*1900, tall gabled shop and
tenement with domed tower and horseshoe
window. **Weavers' Hall**, Commissioner Street,
1936, interesting pair of harled tenements;
piended roof and moderne doorways with
concrete canopies. Further along, **No 42**
belonging to the Factor to the Commissioners,
mid-18th century, with scrolled skewputts,
survives lower than modern street level.

Inchglas, Broich Terrace, 1850s, Frederick T
Pilkington
Wonderfully eccentric Rogue Gothic villa, full of
oddities, not least the almost Moorish carving of
ground-floor lintels. Built by the architect for
himself, but never occupied by him. Adjacent
Mardon, later 19th century, has flourishes of
Alexander 'Greek' Thomson's Italianate style,
including column mullions to windows, and
anthemion motifs to gableheads and gatepiers.

Crieff Community Hall, Church Street and Bank
Street, 1786
Former parish kirk. Protracted building history:
begun 1786 as large heritors' God box, but not
completed until 1827, and only then by order of
the Court of Session. Contractor abandoned work
when the congregation, who gathered in the
kirkyard during construction, occupied the
unfinished building to escape a rain shower.
William Stirling was responsible for repairs,
completion and upper parts of crenellated tower.

Broich House, 1770
Once-elegant three-bay villa with fine
balustraded T-plan porch and piended roof,
now much extended to sides and rear.

Dollerie House, early 18th century
Much-altered, central part of early 18th-century
origin, now distinguished by ogee-roofed tower
of 1840, possibly William Stirling or Alexander
MacGregor. **Witch's Bridge**, 1781, idiosyncratic
masonry footbridge, humped over the Pow
Water, with chicane in the approach.

Innerpeffray Castle, mid-15th century
Atmospheric ruinous tower house adjacent to the
Earn, probably built for John Drummond and wife
Margarete Stewart, remodelled and heightened for
James Drummond, 1st Lord Maddertie, 1610.

Top *Inchglas*. Above *Crieff Community Hall*.

Innerpeffray Castle.

89

L-plan with square stairtower in re-entrant, containing relatively spacious newel stair. Keyhole gunloops, mid-15th century, as are the window reveals. Ground-floor kitchens etc. are vaulted, and tall, probably enlarged, windows light first-floor hall. Massive wall and gablehead chimneys, and plain crowsteps, but no baronial trimmings on remodelled top. Remnants of courtyard wall and gateway at north-west corner.

Former Innerpeffray School, *c.*1845
Domestically scaled and nicely grouped with church and library. Curiously angled porch to old schoolroom.

119 **Innerpeffray Collegiate Church of the Blessed Virgin**, 1508
Long and low rectangle, on venerable and ancient site – a chapel for the Drummond family existed here from at least 1365. Entered and mainly lit from the south side; northern sacristy long-since demolished. Chapel survived the Reformation as burial place. Very little evidence of furnishings and fittings, other than defaced stone altar, stoup, corbels for chancel screen loft and fragments of painted decoration. Laird's loft was later installed at west end.
Historic Scotland; open to the public

Top *Innerpeffray Collegiate Church of the Blessed Virgin. Above Faichney Monument, 1707, moved from the churchyard; a touching artisan memorial to Jean Murray, James Faichney and 'OUR CHILDREN BELOW', depicting the couple with their ten children forming the pilasters.*

Innerpeffray Library, 1758–62, Charles Freebairn
First free lending library in Scotland, founded in 1680 by David Drummond, 3rd Lord Maddertie. Severe U-plan on two storeys, enlivened by elegant south-facing Venetian window overlooking the Earn. Bright white harling with sandstone margins and piended roof. Handsome panelled library and librarian's tiny office occupy entire first floor. Under patronage of Robert Hay Drummond, Archbishop of York, it moved from loft of Innerpeffray Collegiate Church to adjacent new building in 1762. A private trust, the Innerpeffray Mortification, was established to administer Maddertie's endowment in 1694. Library contains many rare books, particularly Bibles, the earliest dated 1530. Lending ceased 1968, although it continues as reference library (colour p.119).
Open to the public; guidebook

Innerpeffray Library.

Colquhalzie House, 1729
Charming small classical country house, set in idyllic grounds near the Earn. As originally built, the harled symmetrical house was of two storeys with visible basement, and five bays wide, all set under steep piended roof broken only by centre

pediment and four substantial chimneys. Mounded ramp led to fine architraved doorpiece. William Stirling added west wing for John Hepburn, 1826, and probably raised the entrance court to hide the basement, giving south side a very low-hung appearance. Present arrangement completed, 1929, by the addition of east wing, John Stewart of Stewart & Paterson. Classical **stable block**, 1834, incorporating west range dated 1697. Eyecatching **Duke's Tower**, 1811, circular with crenellated parapet.

Above *Colquhalzie House.* Left *Millearne House.*

Millearne House, 1821-35, possibly R & R Dickson (demolished 1969)

Apart from the beautiful setting gently rising from beside the River Earn, all that remains of the earlier 19th-century work at Millearne are the castellated stable court and a Puginesque cross of 1840 commemorating Janet Jardine, John Home Drummond's mother. Closely related to Abercairny Abbey (see p.83) in style and materials, and possibly by the same architects, Millearne was equally flamboyant, but rather more academically gothic.

Kinkell Bridge, *c.*1793

Elegant four-arched bridge, gently sweeping up over the Earn. Triangular cutwaters carried up as refuges for pedestrians. Built by subscription. Tollhouse survives alongside.

St Bean's Church, Kinkell, 16th century

Shell of the ancient parish kirk, abandoned on unification of Kinkell and Trinity Gask. Long and low in medieval tradition, formerly lit by four windows in south wall.

Kinkell Church, 1782

Harled Secession church of plain rectangular design.

The erratic and sporadic building progress at Millearne seems to have been governed by the income, rather than capital, of the owner, John George Home Drummond. As each increasingly lavish part of the great Tudor palace was completed in an anti-clockwise direction around the core of the service block, a date and the initials J G H D were added. The result was a plan and elevations more irregular than almost any house of its date in Scotland, finally breaking away from the symmetrical plan dictated by classically derived elevations, which had dominated the previous 150 years. The house presented an astonishing array of towers, battlements, moulded chimneys, and mullioned or traceried windows, those of the library (in the form of an early 16th-century chapel) and cloister being particularly elaborate. The interiors too were quite extraordinary, and very advanced for their date, many of the ceiling details derived from Augustus Pugin's archaeological publications *Specimens of Gothic Architecture* (1821) and *Examples of Gothic Architecture* (1828–31).

Kinkell Bridge

DRUMMOND CASTLE

Top *Drummond Castle from* Scotia Depicta, 1804. Above *Drummond Castle by Timothy Pont.*

120 Drummond Castle, from *c.*1490
The approach to Drummond from the Crieff/ Muthill road is via a very smart circular arrangement of walls and handsome 18th-century wrought-iron gates beside Italianate **East Lodge**, earlier 19th century. **West Lodge** and **Aldonie Cottage**, curiosities with rustic masonry and circular bottle-shaped chimneys.

Castle itself, a fantastic wonderland of towers, turrets and topiary, where almost nothing is quite what it seems. Although first three floors of the mighty **tower** built by John, 1st Lord Drummond, Steward of Strathearn and Justice-General to James IV, survive in remodelled state, it was much damaged by Cromwell mid-17th century, and upper third dismantled following 1745 Rebellion to prevent it being garrisoned by government troops. Only rebuilt mid-19th century with curious blocked arch on north side, and interiors remodelled to form an armoury (colour p.119). **Gatehouse**, 1630–6, John Mylne III, a sturdy accommodation block with large archway and original yetts, perhaps the least altered part of the complex, and, like gatehouse at Stobhall (see p.168) bears the insignia of the 2nd Earl and Countess of Perth.

Across circular paved courtyard stands what appears to be an L-plan 19th-century baronial country house. In fact the core of this is the mansion erected for the 4th Earl of Perth in 1689, extended twice in the 18th century, remodelled at least once in the early/mid-19th century, and finally achieving its present form at the hands of Crieff architect G T Ewing, who baronialised the exterior in 1878 and extended the east wing following a fire in the early 1900s.

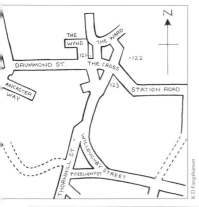

The **garden** is the glory of Drummond. A vast formal parterre, set below the house on the south side in classic 17th-century style, it is not the renaissance garden it appears (colour p.119). Survival of extraordinary multi-faceted obelisk **sundial**, 1630, John Mylne III, which tells the time in different capitals of the world, suggests there was a sophisticated garden at Drummond in the earlier 17th century. Basis of the present garden was not laid out until the late 1820s for Clementina Sarah Drummond and her husband 21st Baron Willoughby de Eresby, possibly by Charles Barry in conjunction with Lewis Kennedy (estate factor, and former gardener to the Empress Josephine at Malmaison). Geometric design centred around the sundial in an enormous saltire, replete with statuary, urns, planters, etc. Classical archway, the **Grimsthorpe Façade**, later 18th century, brought from Grimsthorpe in 1932, directs the eye beyond the later 18th-century kitchen garden to the avenue on hill behind. Following Second World War, the garden was overgrown. Largely replanted by Phylis Astor in simplified form, early 1950s.
Garden only open to the public, May-October; guidebook

MUTHILL
Pronounced 'Mew-thil'. Parish boundaries encompass rugged upland and deep glens around Creag-Bein-an-Ean in the west, wooded slopes in the north-east at Turleum Hill and fertile lowland surrounding Rivers Earn and Machany in the north and east. Roman road from Camelon to Bertha runs through, and archaeological evidence of a 1st-century watchtower and fort survive at Westerton and Strageath respectively.

The heart of village is adjacent to the Old Parish Kirk where roads widen to form **The Cross**, the former market place. From here **Drummond Street** (shown on General Roy's map of 1747–55) runs directly west in a straight line, largely comprising two-storey vernacular houses of apparently late 18th- to mid-19th-century date, perhaps incorporating earlier work. Similarly **Willoughby Street**, which serpentines southwards from The Cross, forms a triangular green, Highlandman's Park, with **Thornhill Street** and early 19th-century **Pitkellony Street**. **Little Culdees**, on the east side of Willoughby Street, stands out as an early 19th-century single-storey battlemented gothic villa, perhaps by the architect of the real Culdees Castle and local suitor, James Gillespie Graham?

Top Garden, Drummond Castle.
Above Sundial, Drummond Castle.

John Reid, author of the first Scottish gardening book *The Scots Gard'ner* was employed by the 4th Earl of Perth, himself a well-known improver and sylviculturalist. Roy's military map of 1747–55 shows a simple geometric arrangement of four plots, but this was erased by fashionable informal planting in the late 18th century.

Muthill is extremely picturesque and unspoilt; part planned, part evolved. Character largely derived from traditional houses feued by Drummond Castle Estate from earlier 18th to late 19th century, to replace village burnt by retreating Highlanders after Battle of Sheriffmuir (1715). Apart from agriculture, cotton weaving was main industry in 19th century.

Drummond Street.

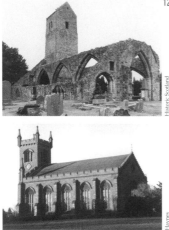

Top *Old Parish Kirk.* Above *New Parish Church.*

Below *St James Episcopal Church.* Bottom *Culdees Castle.*

121 **Old Parish Kirk**, 12th century
Plain square Romanesque tower in four narrowing stages, once free-standing with saddleback roof, but later incorporated into aisled church reputedly built or rebuilt by Michael Ochiltree, Dean (1419–29) and Bishop (1429–46) of Dunblane. Ruinous arcades of aisles remain, but only foundations of choir survive. James Gillespie (Graham) designed unexecuted addition in 1824, but kirk declared unfit by Presbytery in 1825, and new site chosen. Opposition to re-use by Episcopalian-leaning heritors left the building as a ruin. Clearly a major parish kirk and, even in its ruined state, a great rarity. Kirkyard contains particularly fine monument to John Erskine of Clathick, also designed by Gillespie Graham.
Historic Scotland; open to the public

122 **New Parish Church**, 1826–8,
James Gillespie Graham
Considered to be *unequalled by any country church in the land* (*New Statistical Account*, 1837), Muthill Church is certainly one of Gillespie Graham's most successful gothic designs, the warm red sandstone having tremendous picturesque presence in the landscape and on axis of Drummond Street. Square tower with pinnacles at each corner. Five buttressed bays with enormous perpendicular-traceried windows to body of church. Pinnacles, crowsteps and crenellations enliven skyline (colour p.119). Fine pulpit; simple interior bathed in light.

123 **St James Episcopal Church**, 1836, R & R Dickson
Having lost the use of the old kirk, Episcopalians secured a site opposite, and a comparatively pedestrian gothic design by the Dicksons, who were working nearby at Abercairny. Cruciform plan, with lancet windows and corbelled bellcote topped by octagonal pinnacle. Apse added 1904. Mid-20th-century repairs, including new ceiling by Frank W Hansell, Drummond Estate Factor. Plain interior with well-crafted fittings.

Culdees Castle, 1810, James Gillespie (Graham)
Sadly derelict. Originally a pretty Gothick castle in red sandstone for General Andrew John Drummond, re-oriented entrance from south to north, extended and severely baronialised by David Bryce, 1867. Full Bryce scheme, including a Fyvie-style entrance tower, never implemented, to its benefit. Restored after a fire in 1887. Robert Lorimer remodelled the interior, *c.*1910. Toy fort **stables** also by Graham, converted as housing.

K D Farquharson

Comrie and its surrounds are famed for earthquakes, usually modest tremors, but occasionally reaching six (out of 12) on the European MSK Intensity Scale. The 'Great Quake' of 23rd October 1839 was one such event. Shocks in the area were first recorded by James Melville in his diary of 1597, and continue to this day. Serious monitoring of the quakes began in 1840 with the installation of a 10ft inverted pendulum seismometer in the steeple of the White Church. A Mallet Seismometer was set up in the newly built Earthquake House in 1874 to measure both the direction and intensity of the shocks.

Below *Comrie from* The Beauties of Upper Strathearn, *1870.* Middle *The White Church.* Bottom *Lintmill Knitwear.*

RCAHMS

Haynes

COMRIE
Known as the 'Shakey Toun' on account of earth tremors, Comrie is really three Highland villages informally linked together: Comrie proper, Z-plan, north of the River Earn; Dalginross, an earlier 18th-century linear planned crofting settlement, south of the Earn; and The Ross, a weaving clachan, between the Earn and Water of Ruchill. Leisurely and expansive in layout and ambience, Comrie contrasts with its wild Highland backdrop of steep hills and narrow glens. Famed for annual torchlight Flambeaux Procession on 31st December.

124 **The White Church**, Dunira Street, 1805, John Stewart
Built as the parish kirk on an ancient site to fashionable boxy pattern favoured by the heritors (i.e. as big and inexpensive as possible). Generous clear gothic windows light the two long sides and east gable, and original doorways remain on the south side. Landmark battlemented tower and stone steeple are later additions. Restored 2000, James Denholm Partnership. Now a community centre (colour p.118).

125 **Lintmill Knitwear**, Dunira Street, 1903–4, Charles Rennie Mackintosh of Honeyman, Keppie & Mackintosh
Very easy to overlook this white harled shop and tenement, so subtle in its play on the traditional building etiquette of the village. On closer examination, oddities become apparent: oversized turret bulges over the corner with Melville Square next to a tall, gently tapering, wallhead chimney; dormerheads are windowless; roof is unusually high with large skylights; sash

Haynes

95

Top Interior, Lintmill Knitwear.
Above Comrie Primary School.

Comrie Parish Church.

windows are painted black; and most tellingly, doors are panelled in grids. Inside, distinctive Mackintosh style is more apparent in the heart motifs on the counter, and slender panelled doors. Mackintosh reconstructed the draper's shop, flat and workshop for his friend Peter Macpherson following fire. Restored 1986, Stewart Tod & Partners.
Landmark Trust; flat available for holiday let

Baronial **St Kessog's**, late 19th century, is the best of the remaining neat run of **Dunira Street** shops and tenements. **Smiddy House**, Dunira Street, late 18th-century, traditional two-storey, three-bay house with steps and railings to front door, smiddy surviving behind, forms elegant terminal to Dundas Street. **Schoolhouse**, Dundas Street, 1832, Peter Comrie, same format but more sophisticated whinstone ashlar, pilastered doorpiece, umbrella fanlight and piended roof.
126 **Painted Heart**, the old United Free Church, Dundas Street, 1866, John Melvin, has plate tracery, gablehead bellcote, unfinished tower with fish-scale pavilion roof and good cast-iron
127 railings. **Comrie Primary School**, 1908, School Road, G T Ewing, a pretty Edwardian renaissance block with domed cupola.

Dundas Street continues in regiments of late 18th- and 19th-century, two-storey houses built hard against the street. Beyond, footpaths lead from Monument Road to dramatic waterfall of **Slocha'n Donish**, or De'il's Cauldron, and
128 **Melville Monument**, Dunmore Hill, 1812, James Gillespie (Graham), a 72ft granite obelisk to Henry Dundas, Viscount Melville.

129 **Comrie Parish Church**, Burrell Street, 1879–81, G T Ewing
Impressive French Gothic former Free Church of dark local stone and contrasting cream-coloured dressings and spire. Interior complete, but restrained to the point of barn-like appearance. Built to replace nearby **Comrie Hall**, 1843, a plain rectangle with Gothick windows, constructed in the first throes of the Disruption.

At the centre of the village, **Melville Square** is home to the **Royal Hotel**, *c*.1800. Opposite, pedimented doorway of **Clydesdale Bank**, early 20th century, and corner dome of **Royal Bank of Scotland**, *c*.1900, mark the start of **Drummond Street**, laid out in linear plan by James Drummond of Strageath, and largely constructed between 1782 and 1800 with some later 19th-

Interior, St Serf's Episcopal Church.

century incomers. Quirkily named back lanes
lead off: Back o' Toon Lane, Pudding Lane and
130 Nurse's Lane. **Library**, later 19th century, an
unusual clapboarded structure with bracketed
canopy porch. Attractive former miller's house,
Millside, Nurse's Lane, late 18th century. Simple
low lines to white-harled **St Serf's Episcopal**
131 **Church**, late 19th century; pleasing open timber
roof inside.

Comrie House, 1803, William Stirling
Low two-storey harled mansion incorporating
the arms of Dundas of Beechwood over door
(from Dunira House see p.98). Bowed bays to
outer ends of main west frontage.

South of the bridge opposite Melville Square,
Dalginross, a planned development on old
Dalginross Muir, laid out from the 1740s in a grid
pattern with two small squares, **Upper** and **Mid**,
on the main axis. Early feuing conditions stipulated
the houses faced south. Beatrix Potter stayed for a
period and wrote at **Four Hollies**, Barrack Road,
*c.*1805, later 19th-century remodelling.

Bridge of Ross.

The Ross
West of Burrell Street on the St Fillan's Road the
first left leads over picturesque humpbacked
Bridge of Ross, 1792. Beyond, **House of Ross**,
1908, G T & C Ewing, 18th-century Scots

97

vernacular, low and rambling with near symmetrical main block, pedimented at centre. Ewings also restored the house after fire in 1914. **Bobbin Mill**, *c.*1830, three-storey T-plan mill with half-piended roofs, carefully restored and converted to house and flat, 2000, Gareth Hoskins Architects. New cedar-clad lobby continues and exaggerates sweep of roof. Bright, light-filled interior.

Two major houses are **Drumearn**, later 19th century, Andrew Heiton Sr & Son, large Italianate distinguished by slim entrance campanile, and **Auchenross**, *c.*1910, Foster Lovell & Lodge, gabled Arts & Crafts in Voysey manner. Contemporary London import.

315 **Earthquake House**, The Ross, 1874
Small square instrument house with a pyramid roof, built for the British Association's Committee for the Investigation of Scottish and Irish Earthquakes. Inside, a model of the original Mallet seismometer, and modern seismological equipment installed by the British Geological Survey.

Tulliechettle, 1784
Former manse. Smart new piend-roofed symmetrical front, 1818–20, William Stirling.

Aberuchill, late 16th century
Colin, second son of Campbell of Lawers, was granted a Crown charter to build a *fortalicio* here in 1596. Presumably this is the three-storey L-plan laird's house with angle turrets that stands at the centre of the current mansion. Early part of house unusual in that roof of the north jamb runs parallel with main south range, forming pair of gables to the east. Now partly obscured by early 19th-century toy gothic wing. Porch and low-key baronial additions to north-west, 1869 and 1874, perhaps David Bryce.

Dalchonzie House, 18th century
Long two-storey harled house with splendid fanlight over door and early 19th-century bow-fronted drawing-room wing.

Dunira House, 1851–2, William Burn (demolished)
Medium-sized Jacobean-Baronial house for Sir David Dundas, replacing Viscount Melville's mansion, extended by William Stirling to designs by Henry Holland, 1798. **Sawmill**, in place by mid-19th century, later extended; 14ft waterwheel transferred from Comrie Cornmill. Refurbished 1995.

Top Bobbin Mill. *Middle* Earthquake House. *Above* Aberuchill before 1869.

Dunira House.

ST FILLAN'S

An unrivalled scenic location, set at the eastern end of Loch Earn. The 18th-century village, known as Port of Lochearn, was refounded as St Fillan's in 1817 by Lord Gwydyr, husband of Clementina Drummond, heiress to the

316 Drummond Estate. **Drummond Arms Hotel**, *c.*1872, Andrew Heiton Jr, the most flamboyant building with its Italianate tower after the manner of 'Greek' Thomson. Heiton, or his father, was probably also responsible for little gothic **Free Church**, 1856, now converted to house. Rubble-built **St Fillan's Bridge**, 18th century, over River Earn has one broad arch and smaller span beside. Ruinous rectangular remains of pre-Reformation **St Fillan's Old Kirk** lie between the village and ancient hillfort of Dunfillan.

Dalveich Castle

Ruins of an unusually narrow and elongated tower house with a round tower at the north-east corner and possibly a further tower at the south-west corner forming a Z-plan.

Above *Drummond Arms Hotel.*
Left *Ardvorlich House.*

Ardvorlich House, 1790, Robert Ferguson, master mason
Originally modest symmetrical three-bay house with gabled Venetian window to attic, half-heartedly baronialised by turrets and a tower, 1890, C & L Ower. Late 18th-century **McDonald Stone** at the haugh on the public road over Ardvorlich Burn records: *Near this spot were interred the bodies of seven McDonalds of Glencoe killed when attempting to harry Ardvorlich Anno Domini 1620.*

The Milton, early 19th century
Former miller's house. Low pitched roofs, broad eaves, similar in detail to West Lodge at Lawers House.

RCAHMS

RCAHMS

Lawers House: top from north; above from south-east; right from Vitruvius Scoticus.

Lawers House was built for Colonel, later General, Sir James Campbell, 3rd son of 2nd Earl of Loudon, a distinguished soldier who fought at battles of Malplaquet (1709), Dettingen (1743), and Fontenoy (1745), where he died.

317 **Lawers House**, 1724–6 and 1737–44, William Adam

Seen from south, the impact of Lawers on its eminence above the main road is dissipated by an over-extended horizontal composition. This is not the gutsy medium-sized country seat reconstructed by Adam for Col Sir James Campbell, rather the result of early 19th-century remodelling and re-orientation by Richard Crichton, and subsequent enlargements. South-facing entrance front of Adam's house was just five bays wide with slightly advanced pedimented centre, and lower two-bay wings. Re-using the pediment, Crichton created a portico linked to new single-storey wings by a long colonnade across the garden front, and added a stable court in linear plan to west. Adam wings raised to height of main block and unifying balustrade added, c.1840.

RCAHMS

Adam's house more clearly visible from north, now the entrance, where two curved gables survive. Crichton's beautiful stables with their entrance tower also face north. Fine panelled interiors retaining numerous florid overdoors and overmantles and bold classical plasterwork. Of particular note is the ballroom, originally the saloon, which maintains coved ceiling, despite later extension into portico. Unusual V-shaped **walled garden** and 'mount' feature are probably earlier 18th century, approached by rustic bridge and arched gateway of early 19th-century vintage.

Clathick House, 1827
Small mansion for W L Colquhoun. Asymmetrical
picturesque composition with overhanging eaves.

MONZIEVAIRD & STROWAN

Pronounced 'Monnyvaird'. Wild and grand
mountainous parish taking in Ben Chonzie,
Auchnafree, Upper Glen Almond, Glen Turret,
and the more populous lands of old Strowan
straddling the Earn between Crieff and Comrie.
The battle of Monzievaird was fought in 1005 on
the south side of Loch Monzievaird, where
Kenneth III, King of Alba, was killed.

Monzievaird, 1837, probably William Stirling
Only a wall monument of 1804 church survives in
kirkyard, but the former manse remains a little
distance away, rightly described as *the best
planned and finished manse in this district of the
country* (*New Statistical Account*, 1842). **War
Memorial**, 1919, Reginald Fairlie, a panelled
pedestal topped with sculpted emblem and
polygonal shaft to metal cross.

Sir David Baird's Monument, Tom a'Chaisteil,
1832, William Stirling
Landmark 84ft Aberdeen granite obelisk, built
on site of old castle of the Malises or Grahams.
Commemorates Sir David Baird of Ferntower,
1757–1829, leader of British forces in Egypt and
at Seringapatam.

Bridge of Strowan, River Earn, early 18th century
Once stately, three segmental arches on triangular
cutwaters. Steeply ramped approaches kept, but
now ruinous with one arch missing.

318 **Kirk of Strowan**, earlier 17th century?
Ruinous crowstepped gable and remains of the
old parish kirk of Strowan. Appears to have been
a long low rectangular kirk of traditional design,
perhaps incorporating earlier fabric. Skewputt
inscribed 32, and panel dated 1684.

Lochlane House, 1710
Remarkably complete small harled classical
mansion of great charm. Central doorway with
sculpted pediment, flanked by two small
windows. Remaining windows to two floors and
four bays regularly sized and spaced. In place of
pediment, curious sculpted gablet and window
protrude above wallhead at centre. Panelled piers
and low wall form small courtyard in front.

Below *War Memorial*. Bottom *Lochlane House*.

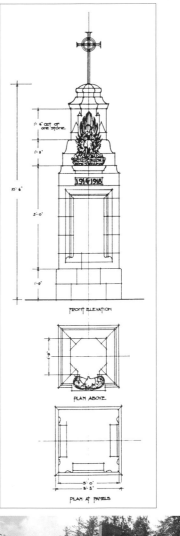

Top *Locherlour Steading*. Above *Roof detail, Ochtertyre House*. Right *Ochtertyre House*.

Below *Mausoleum, Ochtertyre House*. Bottom *Glenturret Distillery*.

319 Locherlour Steading, 1832
Impressive Improvement steading on sloping site, originally symmetrical with two broken pedimented ranges. Extensive additions, 1872.

Ochtertyre House, 1784–90, James McLeran
Lovely plain classical mansion of whinstone, set in commanding position above Loch Monzievaird. Entered from two-storey north side, with centre pediment and porch. Pediment also to three-storey south side; centre bowed at basement and principal floor with Venetian window above. Cast-iron balcony runs across front of all main south-facing rooms. Venetian windows to single-storey wings. Interior boasts magnificent staircase dome, decorated with delicate Adamesque plasterwork. Built for Sir William Murray, Bart. Contemporary fan tracery to arches of U-plan **stable**.

Mausoleum, 1809, Charles Heathcote Tatham, now a roofless ruin, a miniature perpendicular chapel, exquisitely detailed, employed arcaded recesses instead of aisles, little clerestory and richly coloured stained glass. Built for Sir Patrick Murray on ancient site of Monzievaird Parish Church to house family remains. Older gravestones surround. **Granite Lodge**, unusual Aberdeen-bond red granite gatehouse with Tudor-gothic windows, may also be of the same date by Tatham.

Castle Cluggy, Dry Isle, Loch Monzievaird
Ruinous three-storey remains of stout unvaulted tower of indeterminate date. Described as ancient in a charter of 1467, it was reduced from a rectangle to square plan, probably for Sir William Murray, mid-17th century.

Glenturret Distillery, The Hosh, 1775
Claimed as Scotland's oldest distillery, the complex grew out of a number of early 18th-century bothies housing illicit stills. Thriving visitor attraction incorporating kilnhouses, restaurant and shop.
Regular guided tours

Monzie Castle.

John Paterson was also working at Taymouth Castle at this time. The intention must surely have been to demolish the old house at Monzie on completion of the new, but somehow it survived, probably as service quarters rather than for sentimental reasons.

Monzie Castle, from 1634

Set in beautiful mature grounds beside the Shaggie Burn, Monzie is really two houses back-to-back, one a gem-like L-plan laird's house built for James Graeme, 1634, joined to the other, a colossal Gothick castle with corner towers and bowed centrepiece *c.*1795–1800 by John Paterson for General Alexander Campbell, rebuilt following fire in 1817. Interiors of both houses reworked by Robert Lorimer, 1908–12, after second fire, transforming castle into a lavish Edwardian entertaining suite and house into a more intimate living space. Although beautifully embellished in late 17th-century classical style, and superbly crafted by Scott Morton & Co., the sheer scale of the castle's set-piece rooms overwhelms details. Fine castellated and crowstepped **stables** and good collection of lodges: **East Lodge**, 1812, William Stirling, circular crenellated tower after the manner of main house, but better detailed and scaled with Tudor-arched gateway; **Mid Lodge**, probably contemporary with East Lodge, a splendid fortlet and bridge (colour p.120); and finally little polygonal-ended **West Lodge**, *c.*1830, probably also William Stirling.

Monzie Parish Kirk.

320 **Monzie Parish Kirk**, 1830–1, William Stirling
Sparkling white-harled box on an older site, nicely finished with earthy red sandstone dressings to windows and corners, corbelled octagonal bellcote with 1692 Meikle Bell and elegant classical gatepiers. Plain galleried interior with wonderful glowing west window by William Morris (swirling foliate panels) and Edward Burne-Jones (figurative work). **Old Manse**, 1779, probably reconstructed by Stirling at the same time as church.

Connachan Lodge.

Connachan Lodge, early 19th century
Outstanding *cottage-ornée* of fantastic rubble masonry and log-built arcaded veranda.

Bridge of Buchanty, River Almond, 19th century
Originally built by the Earl of Tullibardine, 1639, reconstructed 19th century as single large segmental arch.

Tulchan Gardens, *c.*1830
Unusual single-storey house with a central tower, swept roof and octagonal porch.

Right and below *Trinity College*.

321 **Trinity College**, Glenalmond, 1843, John Henderson
Fantastic collegiate gothic vision in deep red local sandstone. Founded by Sir John Gladstone as a theological college of the Scottish Episcopal Church. Stung by criticisms of dogmatic *Ecclesiologist* magazine, the Edinburgh architect altered the style of the chapel windows from perpendicular (regarded as too late and tainted by the classical renaissance) to Decorated (seen as earlier, purer gothic). Tower and spire never built, chapel richly furnished with glass by Powell, 1851, War and Neish Memorials by Sir J Ninian Comper, 1922 and 1939, and west screen by Sir Basil Spence, 1960. Main collegiate buildings developed sporadically throughout the 19th and early 20th century. Sir George Gilbert Scott redesigned John Henderson's planned hall, 1861; A G Heiton added the gym, 1889, and library, 1904–6; George Henderson made additions and rebuilt the entrance range after fire, 1894, and Mills & Shepherd of Dundee added the Matheson Building, New Cloister and new Warden's House between 1926 and 1932.

Old Bridge of Ardittie, *c.*1786
Replacing an earlier structure of 1619, this steeply humpbacked bridge has single arch of 60ft span and circular hollows in the spandrels to decrease weight and distribute load.

Dalcrue House, 1832, William Henry Playfair
Model farm and Italianate farmhouse built for Lord
Lynedoch. House was designed with integral dairy.
132 **Dalcrue Bridge**, 1832–7, also by Playfair, a
magnificent single arch of 80ft span across the
River Almond, *an object of general attraction, both for
elegance of design and workmanship, and for its
singularly romantic situation* (*New Statistical Account*,
1837), for which the architect sought inspiration
from Old Master paintings.

Lynedoch Cottage, *c.*1790, possibly James Playfair
Confusingly, this cottage with three rustic arches
is actually the lodge to old Lynedoch Cottage – an
ultra-picturesque thatched farmhouse set in
spectacular romantic scenery overlooking the
River Almond, probably extended by James
Playfair as a rustic retreat or 'hut' for Thomas
Graham. Playfair's son, William Henry, added
similarly thatched dining room in 1832; now all
demolished. Also by W H Playfair, the
contemporary **Dry Bridge** over the Dalcrue/
Moneydie road, part of a long private drive from
Lynedoch to Bertha.

PITCAIRNGREEN

Laid out around a bucolic circular green in 1786
by the Duke of Atholl's factor, James Stobie, for
Thomas Graham. The predicted rivalry with
Manchester still has some way to go. The **Inn**
and **East End** houses are earliest parts of the
picturesque scheme. Corner blocks were erected
(**Knockerb**, **Old Manse** and **Old Schoolhouse**
survive), but little of the intervening housing,
intended for the bleachfield and mill workers of
Cromwell Park, was built. **Former St Serf's
Manse**, 1847, Andrew Heiton Sr & Son, on west
side of the green, designed as a restrained
classical manse for the Free Church. To the west,
Pitcairn Cottage, earlier 19th century, a
miniature variant on Playfair's Dalcrue
farmhouse for Thomas Graham.

BRIDGETON

Guardian of the steep north approach to
Almond Bridge, the old part of the village
comprises a row of traditional two-storey, three-
bay houses, *c.*1800.

133 **St Serf's Almondbank Church**, Bridgeton, 1905,
Hippolyte J Blanc
Solid neo-perpendicular design for United Free
Church. Touches of Glasgow stylism in tracery
and domed ventilator. Steep roof enveloping

Top *Lynedoch Cottage*. Middle *Dry Bridge*.

Lynedoch Cottage, for all its beautifully
crafted classical details, was intended to
be picturesque, after the manner of the
18th-century engraver Piranesi (who
depicted Roman ruins, particularly
great arches and bridges, in decay): *Ivy
is beginning to cover it and will soon bring
it into harmony with the rugged woods
which surround it.* (W H Playfair).

East end, Pitcairngreen.

*Go Manchester and weep thy slighted loom
Its arts are cherished now in Pitcairne
Green …
Thus blest, this village shall some unborn aye
Behold a city grac'd with many a dome;
Of note in commerce, and of arts the stage.*
Hannah Cowley, 1786

Top *St Serf's Almondbank Church.*
Above *Redgorton Parish Church.*

The Romans constructed a fort at Bertha, where the Almond and the Tay meet, as part of their Gask Ridge frontier road in the early 80s AD. Impressive Pictish burial site south of Cairnton Farm gave rise to Pitcairn, which prefixes several place names in the parish. Kenneth III won a notable victory over the Danes at the Battle of Luncarty *c.*990, still commemorated by the King's Stone at Denmarkfield. The parish was at the heart of the Perthshire textile industry from the mid-18th century with its cotton/flax mills and vast bleachfields at Luncarty, Pitcairnfield and Cromwell Park.

aisles. Sadly, tower went no further than first stage. Plain but beautifully crafted interior with arcaded aisles, amply lit by clear glass windows.

Almond Bridge, 1827, James Jardine (Civil Engineer)
Now redundant, this elegant bridge of three semi-elliptical arches once carried the Great North Road across the River Almond parallel to the A9 just north of the Inveralmond roundabout.

Belvedere House, 1847-8, probably Andrew Heiton Sr & Son
Sandwiched between the A9 and railway below, house a stocky Italianate tower of three storeys, as befits its name. Almost certainly designed for Scottish Midland Junction Railway by their architect, but with windows firmly focused on views not the track.

Redgorton Parish Church, 1776
Plain rubble rectangle possibly incorporating parts of its *c.*1690 predecessor. Minimal expenditure and maximum capacity (focused on the pulpit) were standard demands at a time of rapidly increasing rural population. Addition of the north arm and galleries, 1841, Andrew Heiton Sr & Son, to form a T-plan. Churchyard dates from earlier building and contains mort-house, 1832, for the safe-keeping of bodies until burial. Doorstep to **manse**, 1866, Andrew Heiton Jr, was the setting for Sir John Millais' famous 1886 painting *Bubbles*, later used for advertising Pears' Soap.

Right *Battleby House.* Below *Graham coat of arms, Battleby House.*

134 **Battleby House**, 1861–3, David Smart
Perthshire picturesque with shallow-pitched roofs and overhanging eaves, rambling in plan. Graham **coat of arms**, salvaged from *c.*1730 pediment of Balgowan House (see p.81), built into south-west front. Inside, fine pedimented doorways were retained on conversion to offices for Scottish Natural Heritage.

Scottish Natural Heritage Visitors' Centre.

Scottish Natural Heritage Visitors' Centre, 1974,
Morris & Steedman
Converted barns and new-build circular
auditorium with splendid latticed steel and
timber to wood-lined dome. RIBA Award 1974.

LUNCARTY

Now swamped by modern housing as dormitory
village to Perth, old Luncarty was established in
1752 by William Sandeman to house workers at
his bleachfields. Some of the single-storey
workshops survive from this enterprise, which
grew to be the largest of its kind in 19th-century
Scotland. Early in the history of **Luncarty House**,
an early 19th-century classical box, the main
entrance was moved to the side elevation, and
has remained there augmented by an Ionic porch.
Pedimented front much altered by late 19th-
century bay windows.

Former Moneydie Parish Church, 1813,
Thomas Graham of Balgowan
Displays eccentric traits, such as squat tower and
circular crenellated porch, suggesting its amateur
design by principal heritor, later Lord Lynedoch.

Blackpark Lodge, mid-19th century
Harled patternbook Italianate house, probably
taking its tone from Dalcrue (see p.105), also once
part of Lynedoch Estate.

Tullybelton House, *c.*1850
Classical mansion remodelled with swept roof
1911–12 by Andrew Grainger Heiton, following
fire. Good early 19th-century symmetrical **stable
block** with doocot tower.

Nicoll Monument, Little Tullybelton, 1857
50ft banded stone obelisk to local poet, Robert
Nicoll (1814–37).

Below *Luncarty House.* Middle *Former
Moneydie Parish Church.* Bottom *East
elevation, Tullybelton House.*

*Happy, happy be their dwellin's
By the burn and in the glen –
Cheerie lasses, cantie callans
Are they a' in Ochtergaen.*
Robert Nicoll

House of Nairne.

Lady Margaret Nairne, said to have studied architecture with Sir William Bruce at Kinross, is credited as the first woman architect in Scotland. Works included additions to Blair Castle and the Hall of the Court of Regality at Logierait, much praised as one of the finest buildings in Perthshire, unfortunately demolished before end of 18th century. Lady Nairne died in exile at Versailles.

Below *Main Street, Bankfoot, late 19th century*. Bottom *Auchtergaven Parish Church*.

House of Nairne, Loak, 1710 (demolished) *'The Glory of Strathord'*, built for William and Margaret, 2nd Lord and Lady Nairne, with advice from some of the major architectural forces of the time, William Bruce, Alexander MacGill and the Earl of Mar. Tall, closely grouped centre block had unusual segmental-headed pediment and full-height channelled pilasters. Other peculiar features were pyramid-roofed towers between *corps-de-logis* and wings. Ground floor was entirely vaulted, each floor above contained 13 large rooms. There were also *'cellars, kitchens, pantrys, bakehouse, brewhouse, dairy and other conveniences'*. Estate forfeited following the 1745 rebellion and bought by the Duke of Atholl, who presented the cupola to James VI's Hospital in Perth (see p.23) when he demolished the house in 1764.

BANKFOOT
Largely developed along the Dunkeld Road on ground feued by James Wylie of Airleywight, early 19th century. Double-glazing men have done their worst with the regular rows of vernacular houses. Notable exception, **Bankfoot Hotel**, with nepus gable and porch constructed *c.*1911 from the columns of Tullybelton House. On pre-Reformation site to south-east, **Auchtergaven Parish Church**, 1812–13, by John Stewart of Dunkeld, a shotgun marriage of standard preaching box and battlemented gothic tower, the latter built at the insistence and expense of the Duke of Atholl. Interior recast 1899.

Airleywight House, *c.*1810
Built for the laird, James Wylie, in unusual classical manner with coarse pilasters, circular domed porch, and domed circular towers to north front. Piended roof and low gables at **Airleywight Mains** are from same stable.

Muirheadston Farm, early 19th century
Interesting Improvement farm based on courtyard plan, entered through pend. Circular horse-mill and farmhouse attached.

Rohallion Lodge, Birnam Wood, *c.*1835, probably James Gillespie Graham
Quirky mansion in Murthly Estate style, romantically sited in Birnam Wood on edge of Robin's Dam. Dominated by candle-snuffer tower like Graham's own house at Orchill (see p.73).

Bee Cottage, Pass of Birnam, *c.*1840
Picturesque by name and design, again in Murthly Estate manner with overhanging eaves and bay window. Diamond pattern borders to glazing.

BIRNAM

Douce terraces, villas, hotels and lodgings at the foot of Birnam Hill owe their existence to the arrival of the railway in 1856. For seven years the line from Perth terminated at Birnam, bringing tourists to marvel at spectacular scenery and enjoy the modern comforts of Perthshire's first Highland resort. Growth dropped away quickly after 1863 when railway reached Pitlochry. To this day there is the spaciousness and genteel baronial grandeur of a village built for leisure, not commerce or industry.

Best approach is by the beautifully detailed
136 Jacobethan **Dunkeld & Birnam Station**, 1856, Andrew Heiton Jr, now unfortunately bisected from the village by the A9. **Station Road** largely later 19th century: mildly baronial **Merryburn Hotel**, long row of single-storey houses and gabled dormers in **Birnam Terrace**, two blocks of lodgings with corner turret at **Parkview**, and
137 **Birnam Institute**, 1883, C S Robertson, containing inset panels by Beatrix Potter, extended 2000, Morgan & McLauchlin.
138 **Birnam Hotel**, Perth Road, *c.*1850, built for Sir William Stewart in Murthly Estate style, the largest and most prominent of the village hotels, with pagoda roof to corner tower. Interior lavishly remodelled after fire, 1912. Twin-towered stables. Adjacent, colossal gatepiers and former **lodge**, *c.*1870, to Murthly Castle. Granite bowl to

Airleywight House.

The western half of Auchtergaven parish is formed from the rugged foothills of the Grampians, rising to about 1500ft at Creag na Criche, while fertile eastern lands bound the tight bend in the River Tay at Stanley. Stone circles at Strath-head and standing stones on lower ground at Staredam, Meikle Obney, Pitsundrie and Court Hill.

Below *Birnam Hotel.* Bottom *Beatrix Potter Garden (colour p.120).*

109

Thomas Ormsby and Mary Newham
139 **Underwood Fountain**, *c.*1914. **Tower Buildings**,
140 1859, and **Murthly Terrace**, 1862–5, with corner
towers and lively baronial skylines framing
western entrance to Perth Road, were the main
141 lodgings. Further east, **post office**, early 20th
century, has Wild West veranda finished in rustic
timber. Opposite, **Armoury House**, 1895, more
conventionally picturesque with bracketed eaves.
Macbeth Cottage, *c.*1845, elaborate bargeboards
and Jacobethan porch.

142 **St Mary's Episcopal Church**, Perth Road, 1856–7,
Richard Cromwell Carpenter
Sadly the soaring tower and spire planned by
Carpenter were never completed by his successor
William Slater, and pumped up muscularity of
lower tower buttresses fizzles out in feeble
battlemented top stage added later. North aisle,
1883, Norman & Beddoe. Rich interior including
east window by Kempe, and other windows by
William Morris to designs by Edward Burne-Jones.

At bosky **Torr Hill**, between Perth Road and the
River Tay, several mansions were laid out in their
own substantial grounds off **St Mary's Road**.
143 **Torwood**, *c.*1850, probably Andrew Heiton Sr &
Son, after the Jacobethan manner of his master,
William Burn, for P Wallace of Perth. Baronial at
Dunnaird House, 1865, for David Brodie, and
Birchwood House, 1858, for Miss McLagan.
144 **Ladyhill House Hotel**, *c.*1860, eccentric Scots
Jacobean with French pavilion roof and ironwork
cresting to entrance tower, built for Revd John
MacMillan of St Mary's Episcopal Church. The
best, **St Mary's Tower**, *c.*1860, John Carver, a
bristling baronial extravaganza, has been
145 demolished, but the biggest, **Erigmore**, 1862 and
1867, David Smart for Captain Napier Campbell,
survives in calmer Franco-Scottish baronial style.
Let to Sir John Millais in 1880.

Smaller and more regimented schemes of large
villas grew up at **Oak Road**, and south of the
station at **Birnam Bank** from 1859. Best here are
The Lodge, 1859, and **Craigmore**, *c.*1865, in the
Murthly Estate style.

LITTLE DUNKELD
Barely more than a hamlet standing to the west of
the bridge road on Wood's map of 1823, Little
Dunkeld remained largely untouched by the
19th-century development of its close neighbour,
Birnam. The mid-20th-century decline of housing
conditions in Dunkeld added the school and

From top *Post office; St Mary's Episcopal
Church; Torwood; Dunnaird House;
Ladyhill House Hotel.*

housing estates of Kirkfield and Willowbank
around the old kirk.

Little Dunkeld Parish Kirk.

146 **Little Dunkeld Parish Kirk**, 1798, John Stewart
of Dunkeld
Even a standard heritors' design cannot fail to
impress in such a wonderful setting. Sparkling
white harled box with round-headed windows
and blocked doorways on south front, small
classical urns on corners and pyramid cap to
balusters of the bellcote. Inside, horseshoe gallery
and splendid original pulpit. Interesting 'Adam
and Eve' stones of 1744 and 1762, and Niel Gow
and Charles Mackintosh memorials, in kirkyard.
Overhanging eaves and later bay windows to
147 **manse**, 1819–24, Archibald Elliot.

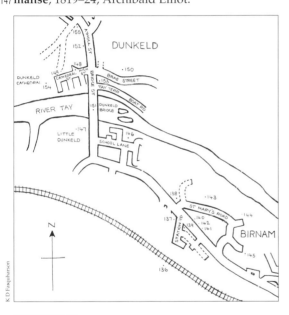

DUNKELD

Dramatically sited in the punch-bowl formed by
Craig a Barns, Crief Hill, Newtyle Hill, Birnam
Hill and Craig Vinean, Dunkeld is blessed with
surroundings of great natural beauty, particularly
when the leaves turn in autumn. Followers of
Columba are thought to have established a
monastery here in the 6th century. Kenneth mac
Alpin is reputed to have brought the relics of the
saint from Iona to his new church in Dunkeld for
safekeeping in 849. A new cathedral was
constructed from the middle of the 13th century,
and unroofed during the Reformation. The
original town, which lay mainly to the north and
west of the cathedral, was almost completely

John Slezer's view is dedicated to Lord James Murray, published 1693, but probably engraved 20 years previously, before the burning: heightened drama in the scenery, and artistic licence with Dunkeld House, certainly in terms of size. Ruins of Bishop's Palace tower can be seen to the left.

*Above Public sculpture, Craig Vinean.
Right High Street.*

By 1953 numbers of the 18th-century houses at the heart of **Dunkeld** were crumbling, and a local poll voted in favour of large-scale demolition. A last minute rescue package co-ordinated by the National Trust for Scotland saved many of the houses in Cathedral Street and The Cross from the bulldozer, and restored them to domestic use. Repair materials were scarce, and improvement grants demanded strict compliance with contemporary housing standards. To modern eyes, the Saltire Award winning repairs, 1954–64, by Ian Lindsay were highly interventionist, replacing much original fabric and imposing a uniform aesthetic of bright white harling and painted concrete margins – extremelybeguiling in its own way, and perhaps a necessary antidote to the drabness of the post-war years, but not authentic.

Beechwood House.

destroyed by Viscount Dundee's victorious Jacobite Highlanders after the Battle of Killiecrankie in 1689. The new town to the east of the cathedral, comprising a single east/west street on a slope widening to a market place, was built from 1690, and bisected by a north/south street as a consequence of Thomas Telford's bridge over the River Tay, 1809.

The broad market place of **The Cross** forms the heart of the town rebuilt from 1690. At the centre of the traditional 18th-century houses, spiky gothic 148 **drinking fountain**, 1866, a memorial to the 6th Duke of Atholl (colour p.118). **Ell's Shop**, 1757, which takes its name from the ell or weaver's measure fixed to the wall outside, was built as St George's Hospital to house seven bedesmen. At the north-east corner, built across the old entrance avenue to Dunkeld House, the former **Duchess of Atholl Girls' Industrial School**, 1853, R & R Dickson, Tudor gothic with polygonal spirelet, incongruous ashlar (re-used from demolished Dunkeld Palace) among the gleaming white harling. Oldest surviving part of town, **Cathedral Street**, 1690–1730, leads off to south west. Possible medieval work surviving here in rear stairtower of 149 **No 19** and at **Rectory House** nearest the cathedral. Facing the river, **The Manse**, a handsome house of 18th- and 19th-century origin reconstructed 1887 by J McIntyre Henry. Between The Cross and the Tay, harled and slated housing and facilities in conservation idiom, built for the Scottish Horse Regiment, c.1960.

Much of **High Street** is mid-18th-century vernacular (colour p.156), with notable exceptions of renaissance palazzo of the **Bank of Scotland**, mid-19th century, Andrew Heiton Sr, originally the Central Bank, and its eastern neighbour, c.1809. **Brae Street**, which winds steeply up Sunny Brae, formed the tail of High

Street until bisected by the new road from the bridge in 1809, and much rebuilt in the early to mid-19th century. At Hillhead of Dunkeld, 150 **Beechwood House**, *c.*1840, a gabled Jacobean mansion after the style of William Burn, bristling with tall offset chimneys.

151 **Dunkeld Bridge and Tollhouse**, 1809, Thomas Telford

Mock-fortified road bridge over the Tay, seven spans and 208m in length, an outstanding engineering feat in a wonderfully romantic setting. Bridge cost £33,978, and linked the new town at Dunkeld to Little Dunkeld and Birnam. Arch voussoirs are channelled, each pier supports a mock half-round tower with blind arrow slits (colour p.117). Accompanying tollhouse survives at south-east end, the town lock-up was located inside the north land arch. Telford was engineer to the Commission for Highland Roads and Bridges, who funded the bridge, along with the Duke of Atholl. Toll riots in 1868 led to county council ownership.

Dunkeld Bridge.

A very ambitious classical palace block scheme for **Bridge Street** and **Atholl Street** was drawn up by Robert Reid, King's Architect, in 1806. Eventually the present reduced scheme was laid out in 1809 as a broad single street. The measured blocks of Atholl Street came first, and Bridge Street built largely to designs of Perth-based architect W M 152 Mackenzie in the late 1820s and early 1830s. **Royal Hotel**, with four-storey main building and fine Roman Doric frontage, the major exception to the two-storey norm. Nearest the bridge, the 153 competing **Atholl Arms Hotel**, Bridge Street and Boat Road, 1833, three-storey with smart Greek Doric entrance to Bridge Street, sadly blocked to form a window. Opposite, an elegant bow starts the Bridge Street run of shops and tenements.

Boat Road, facing the Tay, was made possible by the construction of an embankment in the late 1820s. Although plain, the tower of the former Free Church, now **Dunkeld Antiques**, 1874–5, David Smart, is a distinctive part of the townscape. Neighbouring three-storey ashlar house, *c.*1830, with Ionic-columned porch, is severe but grand in scale and aspect.

Below Bridge Street. *Bottom* Dunkeld Antiques.

Gavin Douglas, 1476–1522, Bishop of Dunkeld, is renowned for his remarkably early, vivid and scholarly translation of Virgil's *Aeneid* to: *the language of Scottis natioun – kepand na sudroun* [English] *bot awin language* (Prologue 1).

RCAHMS

Right Engraving of Dunkeld by T Prion, early 19th century. **Below** *Dunkeld Cathedral.* **Middle** *Wall painting, north wall of tower, Dunkeld Cathedral.* **Bottom** *Earl of Buchan's Tomb, Dunkeld Cathedral.*

Crown copyright Historic Scotland

Crown copyright Historic Scotland

Crown copyright Historic Scotland

154 **Dunkeld Cathedral**, mid-13th century
Hauntingly romantic setting of trees and lawns beside the broad, dark and deceptively tranquil Tay. In its ruinous state the cathedral was incorporated into the 18th-century landscape garden of Dunkeld House, which stood just to the north. Nave ruinous, choir in use as a church (colour p.117).

The earliest part is the choir, probably constructed from mid-13th century and finished by Bishop William Sinclair (1309–37). Following the Reformation, choir was derelict until partly repaired as private chapel by the Marquess of Atholl *c.*1691. One of the first government repair grants for an historic building was made for the choir in 1762, and a further grant was made in 1814 for extensive restoration by Archibald Elliot, including replacement of tracery and construction of imitation stone-vaulted roof. Scholar and architect Peter MacGregor Chalmers prepared a more sympathetic scheme in 1900, but it was not until 1908 that the choir was altered to its present arrangement and beautifully crafted furnishing by the London firm Dunn & Watson, under the patronage of Sir Donald Currie of Glenlyon (see p.128).

Three-tiered nave started by Bishop Robert Cardeny, 1406, and consecrated 1464 by Bishop Thomas Lauder, also responsible for south porch, chapter house (1457), enlarging the spectacular west window (similar tracery design to south transept window of Linlithgow Parish Church – see *West Lothian* in this series) and start of the great west tower in 1467. Nave unusual for cylindrical piers and curvilinear tracery, drawing both on Scottish tradition and continental European influences, particularly from the Low Countries. Vaults of grand four-stage tower retain extensive fragments of original painted decoration, including scenes of the judgement of

Solomon and of the women taken in adultery, reflecting its use as a consistory court for matrimonial and other church matters.

Exceptionally fine collection of monuments dating from the 8th century: south aisle chapel, magnificent effigy and tomb of **Bishop Cardeny** (1398–1437); Chapter House, **'Apostles' Stone'**, fragment of 8th- or 9th-century cross-slab carved with 12 standing figures and on south wall the splendid classical **1st Marquess of Atholl Monument**, 1704, Alexander Edward; choir, **Black Watch Memorial**, 1872, Sir John Steell, and recumbent effigies of **Bishop William Sinclair** (1309–37) and **Earl of Buchan** ('Wolf of Badenoch', d.1405). **Gates**, 18th century, re-used from Dunkeld House c.1832.

Nave and tower: Historic Scotland; open to the public; guidebook

Dunkeld House, 1676–84, Sir William Bruce (demolished 1827)
Built as a winter retreat from Blair Castle for the 1st Marquess of Atholl, to replace house destroyed by English troops in 1654. Dunkeld was the first house in Bruce's oeuvre to be built from scratch, and he used this freedom to design a dignified two-storey classical box of seven by five bays with attic, basement, swept piended roof and cupola, and incorporated a convenient enfiladed plan around a central hall. House faced east towards the town and along Strathtay, and was extended by pavilions to form Palladian arrangement in 1758. Uniquely, it appears to have been built of rendered brick. See also House of Nairne, p.108.

155 **Dunkeld Lodge**, Atholl Street, 1809, Archibald Elliot
Pretty toy-fort gothic. Along with huge stable court which once stood to east, an early sign of the 4th Duke's gothic mania which was to result in Dunkeld Palace. Elliots also worked at Taymouth Castle in similar vein (see p.123).

Dunkeld Palace, 1828, Thomas Hopper (demolished)
As if a major gothic cathedral was not enough in the Dunkeld landscape, the 4th Duke of Atholl commissioned a fantastical gothic palace on a rival scale from London-based architect Thomas Hopper. Only the ground floor, including 96ft gallery, was completed before the death of the Duke in 1830 put an end to work, after which it survived as an aptly gothic folly for at least another dozen years.

The gardens at **Dunkeld House** were initially quite contained and semi-formal. 2nd Duke of Atholl initiated a major scheme in the 1730s, including new avenues, woodland walks, and Stanley Hill, which was raised as a viewing platform. First of the famous Dunkeld Larch arrived from the Austrian Tyrol in 1738. The **Fort**, c.1756, **Giant Steps** (terraces still visible on the drive to Dunkeld House Hotel), and the now demolished **Chinese Temple**, 1753, were also undertaken for the 2nd Duke. Planting of 3rd Duke continued enthusiastically and in less contrived manner by his son, 'Planter John', who fired tree seeds to the higher reaches of Craig a Barns from a cannon, on the advice of Alexander Nasmyth.

For his winter retreat, the 2nd Duke of Atholl travelled from Blair to Dunkeld in a sedan chair, a journey which took 13 hours, even following the construction of General Wade's military road in 1739.

Below *Design for Chinese Temple, Dunkeld House.* Middle *Dunkeld Lodge.* Bottom *Dunkeld Palace.*

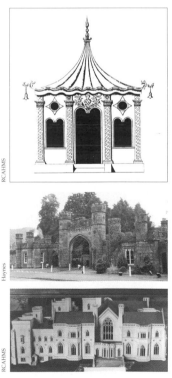

RCAHMS

Haynes

RCAHMS

South elevation, Hilton Dunkeld House.

The first of **Beatrix Potter**'s picture letters to the son of her former governess, *The Tale of Peter Rabbit*, was written from Eastwood House on 4th September 1893. The following day she began work on another letter, relating *The Tale of Jeremy Fisher*, based on Sir William Brown, a friend of her father's, whose comical boasts of his fishing exploits far outweighed his catch.

Hilton Dunkeld House, 1898–1900, J McIntyre Henry
Modest and belated replacement for Dunkeld Palace on a new riverside site. Originally a near-symmetrical design with generous bay windows of dining and smoking rooms facing the Tay, and dumpy entrance tower. Much extended as hotel.

Eastwood House, *c.*1835
Uninspired by his father's grandiose scheme for Dunkeld Palace, the 5th Duke of Atholl abandoned Dunkeld in favour of this modest two-storey country mansion with broad eaves, half-piended gables and semi-octagonal bays facing the river. Extended 1861–2 by Lord James Murray.

Amulree Bridge, River Braan, earlier 18th century
Two substantial arches, a smaller flood arch and triangular cutwater. Probably constructed in the 1730s as part of Wade's Crieff/Dalnacardoch military road, but widened in shuttered concrete.

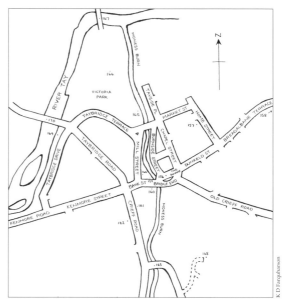

ABERFELDY
Described as a village in 1842, Aberfeldy had grown and prospered on its strategic position as a crossing of the Tay, and was to grow further throughout the 19th century to become a police burgh in 1887. The old village formed a linear plan east of the Moness Burn. Robert Burns' famous song 'The Birks [birches] o' Aberfeldy' (1787) was written at the beauty spot of the Falls of Moness, just to the south.

Haynes

RCAHMS

V & A Picture Library

Historic Scotland

Haynes

Top *Huntingtower.* Middle *Ceiling, Large Drawing Room, Taymouth Castle.* Above left *Scheme for Methven Castle, 1813.* Left *Dunkeld Bridge.* Above *Dunkeld Cathedral.*

117

Top *Tibbermore Church.* Above right
Ecclesiamagirdle. Middle *Fountain, The
Cross, Dunkeld.* Right *White Kirk,
Comrie.* Above *Coll-Earn, Auchterarder.*

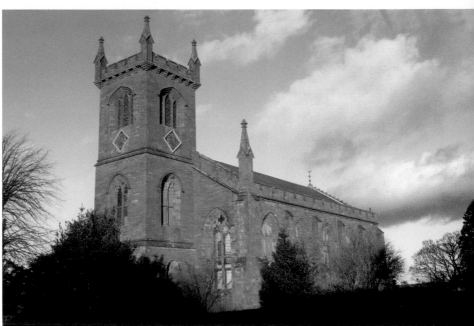

Top *New Parish Church, Muthill*. Above left *South view of a design for Drummond Castle by Sir Charles Barry, 1828.* Middle *Innerpeffray Library.* Left *Montrose Mausoleum.* Above *Drummond Castle Gardens.*

119

Top *Dron Parish Church*. Above right *Straw Bale Shed, Upper Granco Street, Dunning*. Above *Beatrix Potter Garden, Birnam*. Right *Mid Lodge, Monzie Castle*. Below *Aberfeldy Bridge*.

The heart of modern Aberfeldy is **The Square**, laid out 1806, but largely redeveloped for

156 commercial use, such as the **Royal Bank**, 1885–6, A G Sydney Mitchell, on the west side, the 1898 cast-iron shopfronts below the former Temperance Hotel on the east side, now the **Co-op**, and the late 19th-century Dutch gabled buildings on corner with Old Crieff Road. Modestly anchoring the north-west corner, the spire of the former Congregational Church, later 19th century, now **Tourist Information Centre**.

On the north-east corner with Dunkeld Street, the lumpy Art Deco former **Birk's Cinema**, 1939, and at **32 Dunkeld Street** the late 19th-century baronial premises of tweed manufacturers,

157 Haggarts. **Roman Catholic Chapel**, Home Street, an interesting surviving example of a 'tin tabernacle', timber and corrugated-iron clad structures cheaply and hastily erected in the frenzied competition of later 19th-century church-building. On the outskirts, the pagoda ventilator of the kiln block distinguishes the late

158 19th-century core of **Aberfeldy Distillery**. Later 20th-century still-house and red-brick chimney continues the linear plan of original buildings. Large bonds and cooperage behind.

159 West of The Square, **2-6 Bank Street**, 1910, E Simpson (Stirling), sumptuous red sandstone tenements and shops in Flemish renaissance style.

160 Opposite, **Bank of Scotland**, c.1865, originally Central Bank of Scotland, built in cottagey villa style after the manner of David Bryce. More cottagey bargeboards and gabled dormers at **Ivybank**, **Rosemount**, et al., c.1840, on south-west corner of Kenmore Street and Crieff Road. **Kenmore Street** starts as an impressive regiment of mid-19th-century, two-storey, three-bay houses, built on site of flax spinners' cottages, then transforms to villadom further west.

161 **Aberfeldy Town Hall**, Crieff Road, 1887, James M Maclaren

Presented in honour of newly achieved burghal status by the 3rd Marquess of Breadalbane, an exceptionally avant-garde piece of Free Style, surely influenced in its rubbly Romanesque arcade by published designs of great American architect H H Richardson. Strong horizontal emphasis, harling, broad sweeping gables and bold geometric forms favoured by emerging Arts & Crafts architects such as C F A Voysey (who built his first house in the following year). Art Nouveau, which dominated the architecture of Glasgow at turn of century, also presaged in eccentrically exaggerated ventilator.

From top *Roman Catholic Chapel; Aberfeldy Distillery; Bank Street; Kenmore Street; Aberfeldy Town Hall.*

Top *St Andrew's Church of Scotland*.
Middle *Meal mill*. Above *Victoria Park
Pavilion*.

Black Watch Monument.

162 St Andrew's Church of Scotland, Crieff Road,
1884, John and G P K Young
Plain gothic Established Chapel of Ease for Dull
Parish, within which the burgh stands. Tall
slated flèche serving in place of unexecuted
tower over porch.

Further south on Crieff Road, an elegant early 19th-
163 century **bridge** over Moness Burn, incorporating
voussoirs from earlier Wade bridge. North of
Kenmore Street on Taybridge Road, only the tower
remains of former Breadalbane Free Church of
164 1857. **Meal mill**, Mill Street, 1826, in Breadalbane
Estate gothic, has 6.1m cast-iron overshot
waterwheel and two pairs of 1.5 ton burr stones.
Further downstream, later 19th-century M-gabled
165 **tweed mill** with shallow arched windows also
operated from Moness Burn. **Victoria Park**
166 Pavilion, early 20th century, pretty timber structure
with broad swept roof and rustic timber columns.
167 Plastic **footbridge**, *c.*1986, University of Dundee.

168 Moness House, 1758
Plain classical five-bay mansion with piended and
platformed roof, built for the Flemyng family. Long
flight of steps over archway leads to entrance on
the principal floor. Three bays added to east,
probably *c.*1808, and single-storey wing, *c.*1845.

169 Black Watch Monument, Taybridge Drive, 1887,
John & William Birnie Rhind
Powerful memorial to Royal Highland Regiment in
the form of a cairn surmounted by an heroic statue
of a soldier, Private Farquhar Shaw, drawing his
sword. Split by lightning in 1910, the tall boulder
cairn much rebuilt in cement, incorporates the
figure of a climbing soldier. Inscriptions record the
first gathering of the regiment in Aberfeldy in 1839,
and first muster of 1840.

170 Tay Bridge, 1733, William Adam
Finest and least military of the 40 bridges built at
the order of Lt Gen. George Wade for the Board
of Ordnance, Adam's Tay Bridge would not look
out of place in the pleasure grounds of a country
house. Wonderfully robust classical details adorn
the arches and piers. Parapets are swept up over
steep humpback of the 60ft central arch, and
capped with four panelled obelisks at the refuges.
Inscribed panels boast of Wade's road-building
achievements and the paltry nine months taken
to complete the bridge (not strictly accurate, as
the parapets and obelisks had to await next
building season). Forming part of the vast

network of roads and bridges constructed for the government following the Jacobite risings of 1715, the Tay Bridge lies on the road built from Crieff to Dalnacardoch via Aberfeldy and Tummel Bridge (colour p.120).

Bolfracks, 18th century
On the main approach to Taymouth Castle from Aberfeldy, the modest 18th-century farmhouse was given an impressive castellated front *c*.1830, probably by James Gillespie Graham, as part of gothic makeover of Taymouth Estate for the 2nd Marquess of Breadalbane. Extensively altered, 1872, Peddie & Kinnear.

The baroque theatricality of the Tay Bridge has not always been admired. Dorothy Wordsworth described it as *'ambitious and ugly architecture'* (1803), and Robert Southey doubted its structural soundness: *At a distance it looks well but makes a wretched appearance on close inspection. There are four unnecessary obelisks upon the central arch and the parapet is so high you cannot see over it. The foundations are very insecure, for we [Southey and Thomas Telford] went to the bed of the river to examine them. Journal of a Tour in Scotland*, 1819

Haynes

171 **Taymouth Castle**, 1802–42, J Elliot, W Atkinson, James Gillespie Graham
Superlatives apply in almost every respect to this quite extraordinary powerhouse of the Campbells of Breadalbane. Not least is the romantic fairy-tale setting at the head of Loch Tay. The progress of the Gothic Revival, from mock gothic to archaeological gothic, is reflected in the building's intermittent construction over 40 years. At the heart of the building is the 4th Earl of Breadalbane's great castellated *'Tea Cadie'* with round towers at the corners and square lantern at centre, 1802–10, James Elliot, possibly based on a design by Alexander Nasmyth, and incorporating a half-built scheme by John Paterson. All executed in local Bolfracks grey-green chlorite slate and consciously in the manner of, and surpassing, the senior Campbell seat of Inveraray Castle, Argyll. Perhaps the least successful addition is low rambling east wing, 1818–21, William Atkinson. Last major flurry of building activity, this time by James Gillespie Graham for the 2nd Marquess, added 'cloisters', re-cased and heightened old William Adam west pavilion and linked it to the main block by a fantastic 'chapel' with enormous perpendicular window (the Banner Hall) – details reputedly derived from house in Normandy.

Right Taymouth Castle. Below Corner detail. Bottom Taymouth Castle, marked as Ballach, by Timothy Pont.

Haynes

National Library of Scotland

RIAS Collection

Even lacking their original furnishings, interiors are still some of the most staggeringly opulent spaces of their time. Although Sir John Soane prepared plans for the interior of Elliot's centrepiece, the work was eventually designed and executed by James Wyatt's celebrated collaborator, the Italian plasterer Francis Bernasconi. Much of his work survives, the most spectacular the soaring gothic fan-vaulting of the Great Staircase and groined work of Baron's Hall. More seriously antiquarian, perhaps fired by Lord Breadalbane's preparations for attending the 1839 re-enacted medieval tournament at Eglinton, are sumptuously baronial Banner Hall (colour p.156) and intricate gilded carving of the jewel-like **Library**. These were designed by Gillespie Graham, 1838–42, probably with considerable assistance from A W N Pugin, and executed by Edinburgh firm Trotter & Co. Baron's Hall re-fitted with a dado of antique carved panels, and redecorated in magnificent style by Thomas Bonnar. Final completion of interiors for Queen Victoria's visit in 1842 was undertaken by famous London decorators, Frederick and J G Crace, who supplied much of the furniture, down to reproduction suits of armour, and painted the vibrant gothic Arabesque ceilings of the Large and Small Drawing Rooms (colour p.117). They even transformed the boats for Victoria's excursion on Loch Tay.

Landscape has an even more complicated evolution than the house, incorporating features dating from early 17th century, such as riverside Berceau and Bow-Shaped Walks, and is sadly neglected in parts or pitted with golf bunkers. Like most major gardens, Taymouth followed the fashion for formality at the beginning of the 18th century in a scheme possibly by William Boutcher, and uprooted everything in pursuit of informality by the 1750s (Thomas Winter and others). The legacy of 18th-century classical garden structures would have been impressive, had fashion not caught up again in 19th-century

Haynes

Top *Taymouth Castle from* Vitruvius Scoticus. *Sir Colin Campbell, 6th Laird of Glenorchy built magnificent Balloch Castle on the site, 1559. William Adam's work of c.1742 balanced it into something approaching a symmetrical house with pavilion wings, now re-named Taymouth. The central arcade was never built.* Above *Library.*

Taymouth Castle
The firing of the guns, the cheering of the great crowd, the picturesqueness of the dresses, the beauty of the surrounding country, with its rich background of wooded hills, altogether formed one of the finest scenes imaginable. It seemed as if a great chieftain in olden feudal times was receiving his sovereign. It was princely and romantic … A small fort, which is up in the wood, was illuminated, and bonfires were burning on the tops of the hills. I never saw anything so fairy-like.
Queen Victoria's Journal, 7th Sept 1842

rusticity and gothicism. Again, exceptional range and quality of structures, transforming the policies into something of a battlefield of mock forts, ramparts and lookout towers.

Approaching the house from Kenmore, the main West Drive winds around Tom More and **dairy**, c.1838, an astonishing rustic concoction of gleaming white local quartz and log-columned porticos with central belvedere and bowed wing, now private house. South Drive from Kenmore passes crushed remains of circular gazebo with ogee roof, known as **Apollo's Temple**, c.1774, probably John Baxter, and continues beyond picturesque **dairy byre**, **curling pond**, **sawmill**, over two early 19th-century castellated **bridges**. Further up on Braes of Taymouth, **The Fort**, a castellated sham fort comprising central tower linked by screen walls to drum towers, also thought to be of 1774 by Baxter, was part vantage point and part banqueting house, originally complete with mock-defensive cannons. On main Aberfeldy road, **Fort Lodge**, 1830s, another outstanding rustic creation, in particular the log-columned portico with undulating eaves, wooden arches and vaulting. Behind, bright white landmark of **Kennels Tower**, mid-18th-century battlemented prospect tower with screen walls.

Entering the policies from Aberfeldy, **Main Gate Lodge**, c.1810, James Elliot, presents a bristling array of battlemented square, round and octagonal towers, incorporating 16th- and 17th-century armorial panels from demolished Balloch Castle. Also at this end of the estate, the ruinous Gothick stable court of **Newhall**, c.1800, possibly by John Paterson, who had begun an abortive attempt to build the new centre block of the main house at this time. Graceful lattice ironwork of dilapidated **Newhall Bridge** spans the Tay to Inchadney **Star Battery**, 1829, a mock military battery of half-star plan at eastern end of the North Terrace, on the site of the old parish kirk.

At the centre of the Bow-Shaped Walk behind the house, the outstandingly picturesque cast-iron **Chinese Bridge**, c.1829, more Tudor gothic than oriental – it appears to have inherited the name from its timber predecessor. On the north side of the Tay, **Rock Lodge**, early 19th century, a once habitable two-storey circular tower built to look ruinous has now thoroughly achieved that state. Further west towards Kenmore is the remarkable **Maxwell's Temple**, 1831, William Atkinson, designed in the form of a 'Queen Eleanor' market cross, dedicated to Mary, Countess of Breadalbane.

'Slippery John', the 1st Earl of Breadalbane, founded the family fortunes by appropriation of royal funds intended to buy the pacification of the clans in the late 17th century. Other rewards resulting from the 1707 Act of Union followed.

From top *Dairy; Main Gate Lodge; Chinese Bridge; Rock Lodge.*

Kenmore.

Kenmore is derived from the Gaelic *ceann*, head, and *mór*, great. Located at the heart of Highland Perthshire, the parish topography is dominated by the sinuous 16 miles of Loch Tay, fed by the Rivers Lochay and Dochart and innumerable burns from the surrounding mountains. The greatest of these is Ben Lawers on the northern boundary of the parish, at 3,984ft. From the 18th century until 1920, the whole parish was owned by the earls and marquesses of Breadalbane, who left their mark most spectacularly at Taymouth Castle, but also influenced virtually every structure down to the distinctive jagged coping of the estate walls.

KENMORE

Planned estate village, *c.*1755, designed on a T-plan to the east of Kenmore Church. Initially single storey, the houses were raised half a storey and given rustic porches and dormers, mid-19th century. **Kenmore Parish Church**, 1760, William Baker, incorporates remains of 1669 kirk. Remodelled again in 1869, the pinnacled tower heightened for maximum effect. Another outstanding scenic structure is **Kenmore Bridge**, 1774, John Baxter Jr George III gave £1,000 from the Annexed Estates for the construction of this beautifully cambered seven-arch bridge over the River Tay. On the north side, polygonal-ended **The Beeches**, mid-19th century, a former lodge to Taymouth Castle. So too is the restored **Delarb Lodge**, early 19th century, a splendidly rugged crenellated tower built of rough rubble to encourage moss and ivy growth, which even has branches overlaying the window frames for extra rusticity. **Mains of Taymouth**, *c.*1880, a suitably magnificent home farm complex, all smartly painted in estate red, with grand archway to courtyard and decorative iron cresting to Italianate chimney. Separate ruinous **gasworks** also has decorative chimney. Following re-routing of the West Drive to Taymouth Castle, spiky gothic **West Gate**, *c.*1838, probably by the Clerk of Works, James Smith, was built on axis of the church and village, and a similar arch erected at the **walled garden** beside the loch.

Below *Kenmore Parish Church.* Middle *Mains of Taymouth.* Bottom *The Scottish Crannog Centre.*

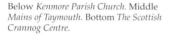

The Scottish Crannog Centre, Kenmore, 1996, Scottish Trust for Underwater Archaeology Thatched teepee with wattle walls, built on timber stilts off the shore of Loch Tay. Fascinating reconstruction of prehistoric defensive homestead, based on Oakbank Crannog, off Fearnan Village, one of the many artificial islands created up to 5,000 years ago along the length of the loch (colour p.155).

172 **Acharn Hermitage**, *c.*1760

Visitors to Taymouth in search of the Sublime were guided through the woods south of Acharn village to the 3rd Earl of Breadalbane's small octagonal 'hermit's cave', entered from two tunnels. Here the wild untamed beauty of nature, in the spectacular 240ft Falls of Acharn and Loch Tay, could be admired from the safety of the window. Sadly now a consolidated ruin and denuded of its romantic wooded setting.

ACHARN

Estate village above south bank of Loch Tay. Best groups of picturesque workers' housing with log-columned porches at **Haugh Cottages** and **Fernbank**, *c.*1860.

LAWERS

Hamlet on main Kenmore to Killin road. **Old**
173 **Lawers Church**, 1669, once with galleries to each arm of T-plan, now ruinous. **Lawers Church**, 1833, John Murray (Clerk of Works to William Atkinson at Taymouth Castle), dour rectangle built for 1st Earl of Breadalbane under patronage of the Society for Propagating Christian Knowledge – economy evangelism at £685. Pyramid finials to bellcote. Old **grain mill** and **smithy** both survive from early 19th century.

174 **Morenish Chapel**, 1902

Built by Aline White Todd in memory of her daughter, Elvira, who died in childbirth. Wonderful heavily leaded east window by Tiffany & Co. of New York depicting Moses receiving the ten commandments.

Morenish Lodge Hotel, earlier 19th century Overgrown picturesque cottage, whitewashed with lying-pane windows, tall corniced chimneys and cusped bargeboards to gables and dormers.

GLEN LYON

Bridge of Lyon, 1793, Archibald Ballantyne On the Fortingall/Fearnan road, this majestic bridge is gently cambered with three wide segmental arches and heavy cutwaters. Panel records: *ARCHIBALD BALLANTYNE HIS WORK 1793*. To north, **Culdaremore**, unusual late 18th-century farm with symmetrical piend-roofed blocks (north block is farmhouse), flanking pedimented tower and side arches.

Cathy Orton

Acharn Hermitage.

Our guide opened a door*, and we entered a dungeon-like passage, and, after walking some yards in total darkness found ourselves in a quaint apartment stuck over with moss, hung about with stuffed foxes and other wild animals, and ornamented with a library of wooden books covered with old leather backs, and mock furniture of a hermit's cell. At the end of the room, through a large bow window, we saw the waterfall ... a very beautiful prospect.* Dorothy Wordsworth, 1803

Below *Lawers Church.* Bottom *Morenish Chapel.*

RCAHMS

John Freeman

Meggernie Castle, Glen Lyon, late 16th century
Gleaming white in spectacular mountainous
setting. Prominent original tower house with
richly moulded doorway, square corner turrets
and dormers dated 1673. Long east wing
probably added at this time by Robert Campbell
(infamous leader of Glencoe massacre) and later
remodelled by insertion of mini tower, 1848.
Early 19th-century service court.

Glenlyon House, from 1694
Major remodelling of old mansion of
Tullichmhuilinn by Dunn & Watson as shooting
lodge for Sir Donald Currie from 1891 (colour
p.154). Oldest part of L-plan house lies in west
wing, followed by long north-west wing, c.1728,
and south wing. Perhaps based on ideas by James
MacLaren, Dunn & Watson responded sensitively
to the 17th-century model in like style. Entrance
tower, service quarters, entrance court and interiors
belong to this phase of works, but **laundry** and
garages by the same firm are slightly later (1913).

Glenlyon Farmhouse and Steading, 1889,
James MacLaren
Perhaps the most revolutionary of MacLaren's
designs for Sir Donald Currie, the farmhouse
experiments with geometric form in proto-
modernist manner. Eastern wing largely traditional
in gabled appearance, apart from enormous
stylised renaissance panel and dormer in red
sandstone on east elevation, the west entrance
wing and large northern lean-to boldly juxtapose
rectilinear, triangular and rounded forms. Massive
wallhead chimneys break the horizontal emphasis.
Steading too, a mix of harling and red sandstone,
with dominant vertical feature in its polygonal
corner tower/doocot. Beautifully crafted ogee
dormers and shutters pierced with heart motifs in
Arts & Crafts style.

From top *Meggernie Castle from
Mackenzie and Moncur Electric
Lighting Catalogue; Glenlyon Farmhouse;
Glenlyon Steading; steading window.*

Balnald, 1886, probably James MacLaren
Rambling L-plan group of farmhouse and
steading. Odd combination of traditional rubble
and slate with English vernacular details in tile-
hung gables, casement windows and half-timbered
features. Tile-hung **sawmill** incorporates earlier
grain mill. Mid-19th-century cottage to west.

Popular tradition ascribes Fortingall as
the birthplace of Pontius Pilate, son of an
Augustan emissary and a local woman.
The famous yew tree in the kirkyard is
said to be 2,000–3,000 years old.

FORTINGALL
Although an ancient kirkton, current layout and
appearance of village owes much to the patronage
of shipping magnate, Sir Donald Currie, and his
London-based (but Stirling born) estate architect, J

M Maclaren, and successors, Dunn & Watson and W Curtis Green. Maclaren began transformation of village in 1889 with **Kirkton Cottages**, a Z-plan arrangement of estate workers' cottages forming a square with the hotel. Diverse vernacular sources from Scotland and England are synthesised to produce an extremely picturesque composition: harled walls, reed-thatched roofs, crowstepped gables, dominant red sandstone angle chimney, eyebrow dormers, leaded casement windows and rosemary-tiled porch. Immediate inspiration may have been repairs, probably by Maclaren, at nearby fermtoun of **Drumcharry** (now largely derelict), where genuine vernacular cottages and farm buildings refurbished using thatch and rosemary tiles. Former policeman's cottage, **Cairn** and **Menzies Cottages**, 1889, also thatched and harled with projecting wing, by Maclaren; **New Cottages**, 1914, now slated, are by Dunn &Watson. **Village hall**, 1936, W Curtis Green, continues vernacular crowstepped theme with vigour and contains an impressive scissor-braced roof.

Kirkton Cottages

The Dial House, 2000, Roger Wilson
Unusual bookend to village, interpreting Maclaren idiom in thoroughly contemporary manner: strong tower and tapered chimney elements anchor the radiating plan, dominant sweeping angular roof and triangular 'eyebrow' dormers.

Following Maclaren's premature death in 1890, Dunn & Watson took over his commission for rebuilding the inn as **Fortingall Hotel**, 1891. More

Left and below *Fortingall Hotel.*
Bottom *Fortingall Parish Church.*

the domestic end of baronial tradition, employing harling with stone crowsteps, dormerheads and door surrounds, and massive ingleneuk chimneys. Fine Arts & Crafts lettering over entrance.

175 Fortingall Parish Church, 1900–2, Dunn & Watson
First church on the site was probably built end of
the 7th century in memory of St Cedd, patron saint
of the parish. Its pre-Reformation successor was
replaced by current structure, a beautifully detailed
Scots country kirk by Dunn & Watson. Long and
low in medieval fashion, with crowstepped gables
and 18th-century style bellcote placed over chancel
arch. Crisply moulded sandstone dressings and
ambitious traceried windows reveal this as a clever
piece of historicism. Tranquil interior equally well-
crafted with plain oak pews and adzed timbers to
barrel-vaulted roof. Celtic handbell and 1765 bell
by Johannes Specht of Rotterdam remain from
predecessors. In the kirkyard, **Stewart of Garth
Burial Enclosure** surrounds bellcote of previous
kirk and famous Fortingall Yew. Unusual jerkin-
roofed **manse**, 1835, I Marshall of Perth.

Garth House.

Hansia Santimano

Garth House, 1838, Andrew Heiton Sr
Delightfully spiky cream-painted gothic
mansion by the elder Heiton, extended in
similar style by his son *c.*1880, possibly in
pioneering mass concrete. Symmetrical front
with *porte-cochère* and corner tourelles.

RCAHMS

RCAHMS

Above *Garth Castle before restoration.*
Right *Tower, Garth House.*

176 Garth Castle, 15th century
Extraordinarily stark tower house perched above
precipitous west side of the Strath of Appin.
Ruinous since 18th century, partially rebuilt by
Andrew Heiton Jr for Sir Donald Currie, *c.*1890,
and gained ruthless boxy profile and fashionably
flat roof on conversion to house in 1963. Almost
square in plan and devoid of ornament, the four-
storey tower was originally furnished with gabled
cap-house and vaulting to principal floors. Straight
narrow flights of stairs within the wall thickness.

Alexander Stewart, the notorious Wolf
of Badenoch, is reputed to have died at
Garth in 1396, probably in a
predecessor building.

KELTNEYBURN

Picturesque hamlet with extensive group of corn and woollen mills, dye works, smithy and cottages. Arts & Crafts **village hall**, *c.*1895, probably Dunn & Watson for Sir Donald Currie – delicate thistle motifs in leaded clear glass windows; nicely restored Blairish Restorations/Stephen & Boyle Partnership, 1994. Kilted figure of **David Stewart Monument**, 1925, commemorates the historian of the Highlands and Highland regiments.

Village hall, built as reading room.

From top *Engraving of Comrie Castle by T Watt; St Adamnan's Parish Kirk; Camserney Longhouse; Castle Menzies Home Farm.*

Carnbane Castle, later 16th century
Sited above the River Lyon. Ruinous remains of rectangular-plan tower house with corner circular stairtower, possibly 'Duninglas in Glenlyon' described as under construction in 1564. According to tradition, destroyed *c.*1580 by cattle reivers who shot a burning arrow into the thatched roof.

Comrie Castle, by Coshieville, later 16th century
Ruins of characteristic L-plan tower house. Vaulted kitchen at ground floor. From roll-moulded and round-headed doorway in re-entrant, a broad square staircase leads to the great hall on the principal floor. Narrow spiral stair, corbelled out over the entrance, leads to upper storeys.

DULL

A rough-hewn **cross** with missing arm stands at the centre of the village, one of four markers to the extent of sanctuary of the former Dull Abbey. **St Adamnan's Parish Kirk**, a long rubble rectangle incorporating fine birdcage belfry, 1819, Charles Sim. Pretty broad-eaved **manse**, 1842, James Laing, based on Weem manse.

CAMSERNEY

Remarkable collection of vernacular structures. **Camserney Longhouse**, 18th century, restored 1992 and 1997, James F Stephen Architects, has six pairs of crucks or couples to support turfed and rye-thatched roof (reinstated by Duncan Matheson) and hanging lum (colour p.156). **Redgorton/Milton Cottage**, perhaps most complete, retaining original roof structure intact. Another corrugated-iron roofed longhouse at **Nether Tullicro**.

Castle Menzies Home Farm,
from late 18th century
White harled farmhouse with single-storey wings is earliest part. Model steading constructed round quirky gothic tower with doocot under broad eaves of Italianate pyramid roof. Sensitive, stylish conversion to gallery and restaurant, 2000, M Gray.

Right *Castle Menzies.* Above *Castle Menzies from Timothy Pont's late 16th-century map, showing the house at its full five storeys, surrounded by woodland and perhaps a formal garden to the east and a garden building to the north. This is one of the most detailed depictions shown on any of the Pont maps. The pavilion to the north may be the hermitage created in the 16th century as a retreat for the Menzies laird.*

Opposite from top *Menzies tomb; Bourne House; Killiechassie Doocot; Derculich.*

Below *The Weem.* Middle *New Kirk.* Bottom *Old Parish Kirk.*

177 Castle Menzies, 1571–7

Sumptuous mansion built by James Menzies and Barbara Stewart (daughter of the Earl of Atholl) incorporating old Place of Weem, burnt in clan feud by the Stewarts of Garth in 1502. Stonework at attic level, and Timothy Pont's late 16th-century sketch, appear to suggest that whole Z-plan edifice, originally a storey taller, and that beautifully carved dormers dated 1577 have been re-used from demolished upper storey. This interpretation may be over-reliant on accuracy of Pont. Without doubt, the main door was moved from re-entrant to centre of south elevation, large stairtower was added to north and much internal remodelling took place. William Burn designed large west drawing-room wing and new entrance porch in sympathetic style, 1839–40, for Sir Neil Menzies. Inside, ground floor vaulted, and only stair rises in south-west tower to fine hall and chambers above. Good panelled interior. Practically derelict by 1960s when rescued by Clan Menzies Society (colour p.156).
Open to the public

WEEM

At west end of village, fine late 18th-century gatepiers and **East Lodge** to Castle Menzies. Pretty grouping of dormered cottages and farmhouse/U-plan steading, dominated by gleaming whitewashed bulk of **The Weem**. Original two-storey inn to right, adjoined by huge three-storey addition *c.*1800. Pear tree at entrance planted 1832. To east of Old Kirk, **New Kirk**, 1870, gothic replacement with lancet windows, gabled bellcote and steeply pitched roofs, swept at eaves.

Old Parish Kirk, 1609

Beautifully sited in ancient kirkyard at foot of Weem Hill, Old Kirk now forms Menzies Mausoleum. One of a handful of surviving churches built between 1560 and 1620. Although T-plan expresses no ecclesiastical hierarchy, inscriptions over doors and rear laird's loft

indicate social order of patrons, Sir Alexander
Menzies of Castle Menzies and his wife, Margaret
Campbell (colour p.155). Long south entrance
elevation punctuated by rectangular door and
window openings, but east and west gables
contain the only known pointed-arched windows
of this period in Scotland. Inside, galleries and
furnishings gone, but magnificent **Menzies tomb**,
1616 remains a riot of carved stone statuary and
decoration, along with sombre painted
hatchments. Plain classical, piend-roofed former
manse, 1829–30, Charles Sim of Pitnacree.

Bourne House, Weem, 1992, Gaia Architects
Environmentally friendly house, employing all
timber construction and breathable walls,
constructed by local builder for less than
equivalent kit house. Distinctive Scandinavian
roof, pinched up to steep pitch at ridge. Stairwell
forms solar-gain atrium to reduce heating energy.
Interesting internal spaces with spectacular views.
UK House of the Year 1993.

Killiechassie Doocot, *c*.1850
Ornamental pigeon house of unusual Gothick
design. Pagoda roof to central tower, set into
ground-floor room with gothic windows. Fine
horse-mill at steading.

Cluny House, *c*.1825
Splendid plantsman's woodland garden setting,
laid out 1950, with views to Ben More, Ben
Lawers and Strathtay. House itself has entrance
tower dated 1880, but this is presumably the date
of alteration, rather than of the Gothick
hoodmoulds and tracery of main structure, which
appears to be earlier 19th century.

Derculich, early 19th century
Probably a fairly modest traditional farmhouse
improbably transformed into fairy-tale castle by
addition of conical-roofed round towers at each
corner, mid-19th century. Gillespie & Scott
extended the house westwards in super-baronial
manner *c*.1930, losing much of the tautness of
earlier symmetrical design.

Former Daniel Stewart's Free School,
Clochfoldich, 1819
Manse-like in its three-bay form, only panel over
door indicates it was established as a school near
his birthplace by Daniel Stewart, founder of more
famous and long-lived school in Edinburgh. Built
on a massive artificial D-plan platform.

Clochfoldich House, Strath Tay, 1828
Refined five-bay classical sandstone mansion.
Greek Doric porch to advanced centre and giant
order pilasters to outer ends. Slightly eccentric
use of oculi in east elevation. Contrasting Gothick
stable in rubble; pyramid roofs to centre and
pavilion blocks.

Findynate House, Strath Tay, 1876, W F Lyon
Baronial. Remodelling extensive to the point of
virtually constructing a new house, 1909,
F W Deas, in his usual Arts & Craftsy manner.

*Above W F Lyon's 1874 RSA presentation
drawing of Findynate, before reconstruction.
Right Silvia Simon Studio.*

Silvia Simon Studio, 1998,
Douglas Forrest Architects
Award-winning custom-built house and studio
designed as a pair of interlocking canopied cubes
floating on a timber deck. Walls a combination of
local stone, bright blue painted concrete panels,
slatted timber and gridded Calwall – a white,
opaque and light-diffusing composite. Few
windows but huge studio flooded with light from
skylights and translucent Calwall (colour p.153).

Pitnacree House, Strath Tay, 18th century
Remodelled early 19th century, probably Charles
Sim. Fine broad symmetrical frontage taking
advantage of views. Pedimented centre, Roman
Doric doorpiece; canted windows in outer bays.

Grandtully Castle from Picturesque
Scotland.

Grandtully Castle, from 15th century
Pronounced 'Grantly'. Extremely beautiful setting
south of the Tay. Enormous addition, *c.*1890,
Leadbetter & Fairley, transformed old tower house
into a small citadel of towers and chimneys. Square
proportions and massive core walls suggest tower
of 15th-century origin. By end of 16th century,
building transformed by addition of two towers
and circular stairtower to Z-plan. In 1626 Sir
William Stewart raised stairtower and capped it
with distinctive ogee roof and curious east-facing
dormer. Robert Lorimer designed wrought-iron

gates for remnants of courtyard walls, 1895.

178 **St Mary's Church**, Grandtully, 1533
Founded by Alexander Stewart of Grandtully to
serve township of Pitcairn. Exceptionally fine and
rare survival of pre-Reformation chapel, long, low
and plain in the tradition of most medieval rural
parish churches. Such external austerity suggests
nothing of extravagant and sophisticated painted
ceiling inside, added along with western extension
in 1636 by Sir William Stewart and Dame Agnes
Moncreiff: a riot of colourful biblical and heraldic
panels set in *trompe-l'oeil* coffers and strapwork. St
Mary's and the contemporary Montgomery Aisle
at Skelmorlie are principal surviving ecclesiastical
painted ceilings in Scotland (colour p.153).
Historic Scotland; open to the public

Kinnaird House, *c*.1770
Originally a compact classical house of three
bays, pedimented at centre, and Venetian
windows to either side of entrance. Large
addition of 1840 was further extended *c*.1900, and
again by billiard/smoking-room wing to north-
west, 1928–9, Forsyth & Maule (London) – all
fairly plain with occasional bay windows.
Drawing room painted, *c*.1870, with panels of
delicate arabesques and Highland scenes in
French rococo style, very similar to now lost
scheme at Glenormiston House in Peeblesshire.

179 **Dalguise Railway Viaduct**, 1861–3,
Joseph Mitchell
Probably the finest of the toy-fort viaducts on the
Inverness line, reflected in its cost at nearly four
times that of the masonry viaduct at Killiecrankie.
Virtuoso main span of the latticed structure a
massive 210ft; landward span is 141ft. Fairbairn &
Sons, Manchester, provided the ironwork.

From top *St Mary's Church; Painted
ceiling, St Mary's Church; Kinnaird
House; Dalguise Railway Viaduct.*

Dalguise House, 1753
Clumsy architectural witticism by Andrew
Heiton Sr attempted to make this look like an
ancient rubbly tower with harled Georgian
extensions. In fact a rather fine mid-18th-century
classical house, extended west, *c*.1825, and east
with a bow front, *c*.1835; finally Heiton's keep
loomed behind in 1885. Quadrangular **stables**.

Charleston, Dalguise, late 18th century
Pretty whitewashed estate cottages laid out in
symmetrical arrangement with two-storey end
houses and gap at centre. Piend-roofed sheds at
right angles to houses complete elongated U-plan.

For eleven summers between 1871 and
1881 Dalguise was rented by Rupert
Potter, father of **Beatrix Potter**, 1866–1943.
The experience of Perthshire people,
countryside, wildlife and folklore fired
Beatrix's imagination. Figures such as
Katie Macdonald, the washerwoman, Sir
William Brown, a friend of her father's,
and Mr McGregor, the gardener who
waged war on marauding bunnies, later
emerged as the basis for Mrs Tiggy-
Winkle, Jeremy Fisher, and Mr McGregor
in her children's stories. Charles
Mackintosh (see p.137), the postman, was
also a great favourite, who encouraged
her botanical sketches of fungi. Rupert
Potter and his daughter shared a love of
photography expeditions from Dalguise.

Dalguise Church, 1843
Picturesque rubble rectangle with pyramid bellcote, built frugally as Free Church in the year of the Disruption. Church reconstructed as Chapel of Ease, 1878, C S Robertson, presumably emulating the mother church at Little Dunkeld in its simple rounded tracery pattern. Converted to house, 2000.

180 **The Hermitage**
Although divided from Dunkeld by the Tay, the Hermitage once formed part of the pleasure grounds of Dunkeld House.

Above *Dalguise Church*. Right *Ossian's Hall, engraving by W Byrne, late 18th century.*

The Hermitage
We were conducted into a small apartment, where the gardener desired us to look at a painting of the figure of Ossian, which, while he was telling us a story of the young artist who performed the work, disappeared, parting in the middle, flying asunder as if by the touch of magic and lo! we are at the entrance of a splendid room, which was almost dizzy and alive with waterfalls, that tumbled in all directions, the great cascade, which was opposite to the window that faced us being reflected in innumerable mirrors upon the ceiling and against the walls. We both laughed heartily which no doubt, the gardener considered as high commendation.
Dorothy Wordsworth, *Recollections of a Tour made in Scotland*, 1803

Ossian's Hall, 1757–8
Even in its simplified restored state of 1951, Ossian's Hall still sparks excitement as a precipitous open viewing platform for the dramatic roaring falls of the River Braan. First built as The Hermitage by John Murray, later 3rd Duke of Atholl, the folly stood in a barren landscape, and the falls were viewed through green and red glazing, creating a *cataract of fire* or a *cascade of liquid verdigrease*. In 1782, surrounded by exotic trees and renamed Ossian's Hall, the 3rd Duke transformed the two chambers to provide a much more elaborate theatrical experience, as mirthfully described by the later eyes of Dorothy Wordsworth. It was partly blown up in 1869 by a barrel of gunpowder, probably in protest at the levying of road tolls on the Dunkeld Bridge, and vandalised in 1930, when the extraordinary mirrored interior was lost.
Hermitage Bridge and **Ossian's Cave**, *c.*1785, probably George Steuart, respectively a precarious rustic arch over the gorge and a man-made elliptical domed cave, both forming part of the 3rd Duke's second scheme to heighten the visitor's thrill and imbue the area with a mythical history. *National Trust for Scotland; open to the public*

INVER

Once a weaving village and ferry crossing set on a small tongue of land between the rivers Tay and Braan, Inver still retains a pretty core of cottages. East approach crosses solid mid-18th-century arches of **Inver Bridge** over the Braan. On the brow of the hill overlooking the village, **Niel Gow's Cottage**, perhaps incorporating earlier 18th-century fabric of traditional longhouse. **Inver Square**, mid-18th century, a planned U-plan development of two storeys, incorporating one of the former village inns at the centre. East of the square, a more informal arrangement of cottages, including that of Charles Mackintosh, the 'Perthshire Naturalist'. **Inver Railway Viaduct**, 1861–3, Joseph Mitchell, elegant single arch over River Braan with battlemented refuges and end piers, carefully designed to avoid injury to the scenery.

Cardney House, from 18th century
Carefully extended in near-symmetrical design of bow-fronted additions enclosing an elevated courtyard, *c.*1910, J M Dick Peddie. Fine broken pedimented doorway of same date.

Forneth House, *c.*1785
Gleaming white on wooded hillside above Loch of Clunie. Original three-bay house, arcaded at basement with corniced windows at principal floor, stands to right of large west-facing addition by Lake Falconer, 1904. Pedimented front with canopied metal porch facing north. Immaculate crisp white restoration and extension, 1978–84, Ian Begg. **Stars of Forneth**, late 18th century, steadings forming symmetrical wings to farmhouse.

The Long Row, Craigie, *c.*1800
Picturesque 80m long row of limestone quarry-workers' cottages, each of three bays with door at centre and solid mutual chimneys.

181 **Clunie Parish Kirk**, 1840, William Mackenzie
Supremely beautiful setting on west side of Loch of Clunie beside great motte of Castle Hill, site of a castle established, 1141, as hunting lodge for royal forest of Clunie (colour p.154). Kirk itself, a pretty Tudor-gothic box with crowstepped gables and pinnacled tower by Perth City Architect. Good quality interior fitting, panelling and pulpit. Very beautiful early 13th-century arched doorway forms entrance to little detached building south-west of church. Piend-roofed former **manse**, 1803, part of the group, which stands apart from any settlement.

Niel Gow, 1727–1807, the '*Highland Orpheus*', was head of a great dynasty of fiddlers and composers, famed for reels and Strathspeys. Gow was born in Strathbraan, but spent much of his life at Inver. Under the patronage of the Duke of Atholl, Gow achieved fame in Edinburgh and London, and attracted many admiring visitors including Robert Burns. Sir Henry Raeburn's celebrated portrait of Gow in tartan breeches hangs in the Scottish National Portrait Gallery.

From top Inver Square; Cardney House; Forneth House; Clunie Parish Kirk.

Right *Clunie Castle and St Catherine's Chapel*. Below *Clunie Castle from south east*.

Clunie Castle, Loch of Clunie, *c.*1500
Ruinous tower house of Bishop Brown of Dunkeld set in unsurpassed romantic location on wooded artificial island. Rare surviving example of ecclesiastical estate architecture, well-documented in accounts of *Dunkeld Rentale*. Much of the stonework for the L-plan tower plundered from remains of old royal castle on the shores of the loch. Plan is standard, with the exception of possible **chapel** dedicated to St Catherine adjoining the hall. Remodelling, including new fireplaces and pedimented half-dormers on west front, took place in mid to late 16th century. House remained in use throughout 18th and 19th centuries, with sporadic phases of repair, alteration and addition, including fine panelled interior, *c.*1700, and lochside features such as ruinous boathouse and now derelict formal garden and summerhouse. Vandals took advantage of the frozen loch in 1963 to wreck the building.

Kincairney House, *c.*1835
Handsome plain classical house with piended roof, broad eaves and Ionic porch, added to older house at rear.

Old Snaigow House, 1824–7, William Burn
Probably the best of Burn's 'cottage houses', designed for Mrs Keay in simple vernacular Tudor idiom. Not particularly attractive in dark

red sandstone, but in terms of style and planning (east entrance, L-plan suite of principal rooms, north service wing) it formed the prototype for numerous other houses. Dry rot and demolished, 1960.

Snaigow House, 1960–1, Basil Hughes
Quiet neo-Georgian house, long and low, harled, with small pane sash windows. Informally planned, and built on footprint of demolished Burn house, utilising old staircase. Interesting shuttered concrete **Snaigow Steading**, 1884, William Cox, engineer of Camperdown Works, Dundee (see *Dundee* in this series), employing traditional clay technology to raise the building in 0.5m courses; sparse renaissance details.

Kinloch House Hotel, *c.*1850, probably James MacLaren
Attractive ivy-clad house with big canted bay in centre. Nice contemporary ensemble of stables, lodge and walled garden. Entrance wing and internal remodelling, 1908–10, by MacLaren's successor, C G Soutar.

Top *Old Snaigow House.* Above *Kinloch House Hotel.*

Kinloch Parish Kirk, 1793–4
Harled with stone margins, attractively plain heritors' kirk, only adorned by two round-headed windows in south wall and little birdcage bellcote. Similar restraint inside to three-sided gallery and original pulpit. Fine old **manse**, *c.*1842, overlooking Marlee Loch, probably bigger than the kirk and certainly more generously lit, with three big tripartite windows.

Below *Marlee House.* Bottom *Glasclune Castle.*

Marlee House, 17th century
Pont's late 16th-century map depicts a substantial tower house, 'Kean Loch' or Kinloch, remains of which are incorporated into 17th-century main block of present house. Four wings and connecting passages added to this five-bay *corps-de-logis* between 1754 and 1760 to form dramatic white-harled Palladian arrangement. A J Meacher remodelled the interiors, 1890 and 1909. **John Brown of Marlee Tomb**, 1858, impressive columned canopy enclosing small sarcophagus on raised platform.

Glasclune Castle, 1584
Two ruinous detached blocks stand prominently on hillside to south-east of Mains of Glasclune on the Middleton road. Northern block built, 1584, to form Z-plan with existing L-plan tower house, and walled courtyard extended to west.

182 Ardblair Castle, late 16th century
Approached by broad avenue, miniature L-plan tower house of great charm extended to palace arrangement by addition of 17th-century and later ranges on three sides of courtyard. Screen wall with splendid gateway and pediment dated 1688 on north side. Harled white. Exceptional renaissance doorpiece and armorial niche, carved with grotesques and animals, in re-entrant angle. Although much remodelled, 1908, house retains simple 18th-century interiors.

Cleaven Dyke, early to mid-Neolithic
Long thought to be related to construction of nearby Roman fort at Inchtuthil, recent archaeological investigation proved conclusively that the massive straight parallel banks of Cleaven Dyke are an incredibly well-preserved Neolithic linear ceremonial/ritual monument, some 2.3km long. As such, one of the finest structures of its type and date in mainland Britain.

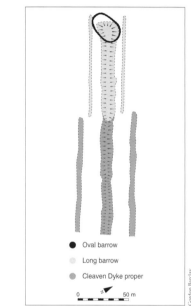

- ● Oval barrow
- ○ Long barrow
- ● Cleaven Dyke proper

0 ────────── 50 m

Top *Ardblair Castle*. Above *Cleaven Dyke*. Below *Meikleour House, c.1870, before reconstruction by Bryce*. Bottom *Entrance front, Meikleour House*.

MEIKLEOUR

Picturesque settlement, once the centre of several local fairs for hiring farm workers and selling produce. The **Cross**, 1698, is more sophisticated than it first appears: a carved stone column is set into recess in the shaft, and stars and crosses form the decoration. Probably of similar date is the **Tron**, roughly hewn stone with tall spike weathervane, and the jougs, or metal collar for miscreants, attached. **Brick House**, *c.*1790, unusual for its harled brick and timber Doric-columned porch. Former **Meikleour Hotel**, 1820, has tall offset chimneys and log-columned porch. Other houses, mainly early to late 19th century, characterised by gables and overhanging eaves.

183 Meikleour House, 1734
Fairly substantial houses marked 'Monklowyr' and 'Mekle Ouyr' are depicted on two of Pont's late 16th-century maps, but main core of present house dates from 1734 when fine new classical house constructed. It had a curved pediment over centre three of seven bays and linear links to Venetian-windowed pavilions. In 1869 David Bryce prepared two schemes for the Dowager Marchioness of Lansdowne, daughter of the Comte de Flahault, to re-orient and radically remodel the house into spectacular French renaissance *château*. Compared to the proposals, built scheme is rather underpowered, omitting the more lavish decorative treatment and the high pavilion

David Bryce, early in his seventies, when returning from an inspection of work at Meikleour, slipped and broke his leg on an icy platform at Cargill Station; an accident from which he never fully recovered before his death from bronchitis in May 1876.

Meikleour Beech Hedge, believed to have been planted in autumn 1745 by Jean Mercer of Meikleour and her husband Robert Murray Nairne, is now the tallest in the world, at an average height of 100ft over a distance of 580yds (colour p.154).

Left Meikleour House, presentation drawing of speculative reconstruction by Bryce. Below Bridge of Isla.

roofs. Internally, fireworks reserved for the opulent oak staircase, French 18th-century gallery and saloon. Pedimented doorway from the classical mansion, dated *17RMR34*, inserted at stables.

Bridge of Isla, A93, 1794–6
Majestic sweep of five arches spanning River Isla at its broadest point before joining the Tay (colour p.153).

Lethendy Bank Farmhouse, 18th century
Attractive farmhouse of traditional harled design, with widely spaced windows and earlier 19th-century rear wing forming T-plan.

184 **Lethendy Kirk**, Kirkton of Lethendy
Abandoned after the union of churches, 1929, Lethendy is a ruinous narrow rectangle of uncertain date – certainly an ancient site, as testified by 17th-century stones in kirkyard. South wall rebuilt with shouldered openings, and new ogee-roofed bellcote provided, 1847, John Ramsay (colour p.154).

Lethendy Tower, from *c.*1570
Beautiful setting of mature lime trees, beeches, Douglas Firs and sycamores. L-plan tower house of local rich red sandstone, notable for huge buttresses, built for Sir David Herring (Heron) of Drumlochy. Re-used principal doorway in the middle of the old east wall, now inside the new house. South wing partly refaced to provide continuity with new super-baronial mansion added to form the front, 1884, Andrew Heiton Jr. Built from same local stone, new work includes mock tower and cap-house with corbelled turrets and full range of baronial trimmings. Restored, Douglas Forrest Architects. Simplified **lodges** to match.

Below and bottom Lethendy Tower.

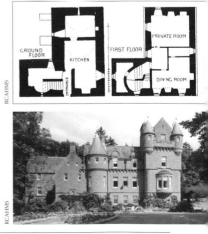

Gourdie House, 1765
Exceptionally attractive classical laird's house set in beautiful wooded countryside. Two-storey-and-basement, five-window, white harled with exposed sandstone quoins and margins, gabled roof. Flyover stair to Gibbsian doorpiece.

Old Delvine House, 1714, James Smith (demolished 1961)
Smith, former Surveyor of the Royal Works, provided architectural advice to William Mackenzie on this prototype of the classic early 18th-century laird's house.

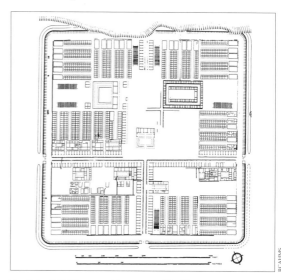

Inchtuthil Roman Fortress, 83–88AD
Exceptional archaeological remains of unfinished legionary fortress for at least 5,500 troops, and temporary camps used during construction. Fascinating evidence survives from almost every aspect of the complex, from ditches and turf ramparts, and their later stone facing, to gravelled streets, tribunes' houses, granaries, hospital, barracks and *principia* or headquarters. *Lavarium*, bath house, probably first brick structure in Scotland. Abandoned before completion 87/88AD.

SPITTALFIELD
Attractive planned weaving village, from 1766 designed around large green. High piend-roofed **Weigh House**, 1767, now converted for housing, stands at centre of symmetrical rows of single-storey cottages on north side. Other sides of the square continued to be built into early 19th

Right *Inchtuthil Roman Fortress*. Below *Spittalfield Weigh House, late 19th century.*

century, followed by former **school**, *c.*1845, with central gable and ventilator.

185 **Caputh Parish Kirk**, 1798–1800,
Alexander Thomson
Perched above River Isla at the heart of the tiny picturesque village of Caputh. Initially a heritors' barn to seat 800 people, a southern aisle, laird's loft and little spired tower added, 1865. Whole building beautifully re-ordered and re-furnished, 1912–22, Andrew Grainger Heiton, adding chancel and further south aisle, removing side galleries, rebuilding the roof as half-round timber structure and replacing pews in oak. **Mural monument** to Graham Murray, 1912, Robert Lorimer. Colourful apse glazing, 1922, John Jennings. **Church hall**, 1909, gifted by Lyle of Glendelvine (colour p.155).

Old Kirkyard, Mute Hill, 1798
Old kirk chancel of 1500 said to have been incorporated into **Delvine Vault** when new church built on fresh site. West wall refaced in ashlar with Norman arch and wrought-iron gates, 1879. Marble tablets to Mackenzies. Vaults reputedly lined with Roman tiles from Inchtuthil. Particularly grand pedimented **Monument to John Hagart of Glendelvine**, 1816, strangely detailed with rose motifs in frieze.

Top Caputh Parish Kirk. Above Delvine Vault.

Kinclaven is a rich farming and woodland parish without major settlement, beautifully situated in the crook of the Tay north of Stanley.

Murthly Asylum, 1871, David Smart
Impressive in scale rather than plain renaissance detailing. Administration block distinguished by large timber cupola. Ward blocks, 1864, by Edward & Robertson. Convalescent house, 1895, also Smart.

186 **Kinclaven Parish Church**, 1848
Preaching box barely disguised by addition of mid-wall gables; the style a curious blend of Tudor and Romanesque with a dash of exotic thrown in at the pinnacled bellcote (contains 1656 Burgherhuis bell). Interior warmly lit by stained glass. **Alexander Cabel**, Bishop of Brechin, is commemorated in the churchyard wall by a virtuoso display of carved heraldic devices, modelled heads, momenti mori and inscriptions, completed sometime after 1608, and salvaged from the old kirk. Reginald Fairlie's beautifully detailed **War Memorial Lych Gate**, 1919, forms an attractive approach to this peaceful spot.

Below Murthly Asylum. Bottom Kinclaven Parish Church and lych gate.

Kinclaven Castle, early 13th century
In woodland above the Tay, opposite the mouth of the River Isla, stand the ruinous remains of the

Ballathie House Hotel.

massive square-plan curtain wall to this royal castle, favoured by Alexander II and thought to have been built between 1210 and 1236. Similar in plan to Tarbert, Argyllshire, and Kincardine, Mearns. Harry the Minstrel's metrical chronicle *The Wallace* (late 15th century) relates how William Wallace won the castle from an English garrison in 1296.

Kinclaven Bridge, 1903-5, J E Harrison, Engineer, with Foreman & McCall
The Tay is at its most majestic here: broad, smooth-flowing and powerful. The last road bridge before Perth with six Tudor arches, narrow deck and masonry finishes belies its modern shuttered concrete construction, costing £7,577.

Ballathie House Hotel, mid-19th century
Built for Major General Richardson of Tullybelton. Low and rambling with lots of chimneys, gables and frilly bargeboards, in shooting lodge style. Three pepperpot towers provide slightly unexpected baronial seasoning. Good collection of **lodges** and **gardeners' cottages**.

Stanley Mills
Urbe-in-rus. Founded adjacent to an existing 1729 corn mill by Perth MP George Dempster of Dunnichen and other investors including the wig-maker turned inventor and entrepreneur, Richard Arkwright, who was also a prime mover at the contemporary New Lanark development. The cotton mills were re-founded in 1802 by a group including another New Lanark investor, David Dale, and overseen by his son-in-law, Robert Owen. The mills were salvaged yet again by the Glasgow firm of Denniston, Buchanan & Co in 1823, who invested a massive £160,000 in their expansion.

187 **Stanley Mills**, 1785–1850
Once Perthshire's single largest industrial concern, rescued by Historic Scotland and the Phoenix Trust from the brink of demolition in 1995. At the heart of the complex are three large mill buildings, informally arranged in a U-plan around a courtyard which contains the enormous early 19th-century waterwheel-pit and earliest extant gasworks chimney (before 1833) in Scotland. **Bell Mill**, largely designed by Richard Arkwright after his earlier Cromford Mills, and complete by 1790, was the first and finest. Basement and ground floor are of stone, four storeys of brick above, amply lit by segmental-arched windows, and crowned with hexagonal bellcote. Interior exceptional for early use of cast-iron columns –

Right Stanley Mills. *Below* Bell Mill.

probably to support the drive system rather than structural. **East Mill** was next, but rebuilt 1802–13 after a fire in 1799, and much enlarged 1823–9 at the same time as fireproof construction (cast-iron columns carrying brick arches on iron beams) of **Mid Mill**, and the building of the north and east ranges of associated warehouses and workshops. **East Lodge**, Gothick in the Scone Estate style, while main **West Lodge**, late 19th century, and mass-concrete **hydro-electric station**, 1921, are both circular with ogee roofs like garden pavilions.

Mill-workers' housing was laid out on a grid-plan of 1784 by Atholl Estate factor, James Stobie. The plan was dominated by two long parallel streets, **King Street** and **Percy/Store Street**, but never completed systematically and seems to have petered out west of the main Dunkeld Road. Once grand three-bay brick houses on **Store Street**, 1820s, now ruthlessly modernised and shorn of chimneys, were actually small tenements. Pinnacled gothic **Stanley Parish Church**, a chapel of ease of 1828 (a *quoad sacra* parish church from 1877), built for £4,000 by mill owners Denniston Buchanan & Co., on the Charlotte Street axis of the scheme. Pendulum clock by Richard Roberts of Manchester for the Great Exhibition of 1851. **Duchess Street**, leading west from Duke Square, starts with late 18th-century tenements and inn, but soon informalises to villas opposite the mill manager's **Craig House**. Outside the plan, **St Columba's Episcopal Church**, 1898, Speirs & Co. of Glasgow, a kit church in English half-timbered style, notable for its timber construction, tall flèche and cusped windows. Stone-built hall added, 1907.

Drummond Hall Farmhouse, *c.*1838

The feel of a Palladian villa, suggested by the tall gabled central block and lower symmetrical wings, enhanced by the fertile rolling fields of Perth's 'Veneto'.

Kirk o' the Muir, 1744

Virtually nothing now remains of this exceptionally early and long-dilapidated seat of the Secession Church. Barn-like in external appearance, the interior was galleried. Revd James Fisher, who led his parishioners to their new church, was the son-in-law of Secession founder, Ebenezer Erskine (see p.227 – Cleish).

Stewart Tower Farm, *c.*1840

Large and idiosyncratic farmhouse, U-plan with arched windows and candle-snuffer top to tapering

Top *West Lodge*. Middle *Store Street*. Above St *Columba's Episcopal Church*.

On the boundary of Redgorton, Auchtergaven and Kinclaven, the old lands of Inchbervis Castle were re-named after the 1st Marquess of Atholl's wife, Lady Amelia Stanley, through whom the family acquired sovereign Lordship of the Isle of Man. Stanley owes its existence to the complex of cotton mills sited to exploit the immense water power drawn through an 800ft tunnel from the north side of this dramatic loop in the Tay. In spite of its population of almost 2,000 in 1841, the perceived threat of workers' influence ensured the village never gained burghal status.

Kirk o' the Muir.

Murthly Castle.

Sir William Stewart, 'William the Ruthless', of Grandtully bought the Murthly estate in 1615. His son, Sir Thomas built the Garden House, and is credited with laying out the magnificent Dutch Garden, remodelled in simplified form, 1977, Russell & Greer. The policies and pleasure grounds, long famous for their woodlands, were much augmented from 1828, John Wallace. Perhaps the most colourful laird was Sir William Drummond Stewart, who inherited in 1838. He travelled extensively in the Wild West of America, returning with two native Indians, who lived in the Garden House for several years, and a herd of buffalo, which grazed on Duncan's Hill. A specimen American Garden, south of the east drive was established at this time, but abandoned in 1936.

Below *Front elevation, New Murthly Castle, later 19th century.* Bottom *Garden House.*

folly tower. Magnificent classical steading and horse-mill opposite also part of Sir W D Stewart's extensive improvements to the Airntully estate.

Murthly Castle, from 15th century
Long and low, Murthly is an agglomeration of many periods, resulting in an F-plan. Oldest part is the tower at south-west corner, turreted on diagonally opposite sides, with quatrefoil gunloops and odd decorative mini-turret. One of Pont's two late 16th-century depictions of the house shows two towers apparently linked by an arch. Arch has gone, but presumably the second tower is that on the south front. Very sophisticated classical entrance hall, earlier 18th century in the manner of William Adam, was added to the 17th-century ranges. Following fire in 1850, fitments designed by Pugin for great hall and drawing room of New Murthly Castle were installed in the old house. Middle wing rebuilt, 1893, A Duncan. **Colryden** and **Lantern Lodges**, *c.*1840, pyramid-roofed towers of similar design.

New Murthly Castle, 1827–32, James Gillespie Graham and A W N Pugin (demolished)
Jacobean palace built to immediate south of the old house for Sir John Stewart, but never fitted out internally. Graham studied Hatfield, Burleigh and other English houses of the early 17th century as his model. Pugin claimed authorship of designs for the interiors, all early 17th-century style, apart from the Louis XIV drawing room. Blown up 1949, along with the axial **Malakoff Arch**, 1868, and stone carted away to build the dam and hydro-electric station at Pitlochry.

Garden House, Murthly Castle, 1669
Delightful 17th-century Scots garden house of the sort much admired and emulated by Sir Robert Lorimer. Square-plan, forming part of walled

garden. Great flowing ogee roof with scalloped lead flashings. Little gabled dormers and forestair. Later 19th-century porch.

Chapel of St Anthony the Eremite, Murthly Castle, 1846, James Gillespie Graham and A W N Pugin
Romantic woodland setting appropriate to the dedicatee. Sumptuous private Roman Catholic chapel added to original 16th-century mortuary chapel of Stewarts of Grandtully for Sir William Drummond Stewart, probably in collaboration with Pugin. Romanesque rectangular-plan design of five buttressed bays with tower. Astonishing interior including hammerbeam roof, richly painted decorative scheme by Alexander Christie RSA and students, lavish gilding, marbling, woodwork and huge mural depicting the Vision of Constantine. Furnishings supplied by Trotter of Edinburgh. Stained glass by Ballantine's. First Roman Catholic place of worship to be opened after the Reformation. Carefully restored mid-1990s.

Chapel of St Anthony the Eremite.

Roman Bridge, Birnam Burn, mid-19th century
Fantastical estate bridge in the style of a Roman aqueduct. Five massive pylons of rustic masonry carry the bridge over a deep ravine, with refuges corbelled out above each spandrel and battlemented parapet.

Rotmell Farm, 1790, probably George Steuart
Perched above the Tay, Rotmell, originally St Colme's, is a planned classical steading of the first calibre. Grand arcades of cart-arches link two pavilions to central tower over entrance arch. Smaller version of same scheme exists at Blairuachdar (see p.164).

George Steuart, c.1730–1806, native Atholl Gaelic speaker, started his career as a house-painter, but by 1770 was practising as an architect in London, where he designed a house for his patron, the 3rd Duke of Atholl, in Grosvenor Place. His country houses, mainly in Shopshire, were characterised by severe neoclassical restraint. Steuart died in Douglas, Isle of Man, where he had worked for the Governors (also the dukes of Atholl).

DOWALLY
Formed as an independent parish in 1500, encompassing the lands on the north bank of the Tay above Dunkeld, Dowally subsequently merged with Dunkeld at an unknown date.
Dowally Kirk, 1818, standard rubble preaching box, remodelled c.1880, replaced an earlier structure on same site. Distinctive birdcage belfry, and good gothic timberwork inside, probably by Archibald Elliot, removed from Dunkeld Cathedral in 1908. Ugly porch of 1946.

Cuil-An-Duin, 1925–7, Reginald Fairlie
Two-storey mansion in Scots 17th-century vernacular revival.

Below *Dowally Kirk.* Bottom *Cuil-An-Duin.*

Tulliemet House.

Westhaugh of Tulliemet, mid-19th century
Distinctive farm grouping beside the A9,
particularly notable for its surviving circular
horse-mill.

Tulliemet House, *c.*1800
Small classical mansion with bowed and
crenellated centre, probably built for Dr William
Dick of the East India Company. Porch added to
left side.

Laird's House, Pitcastle, 17th century
Picturesque ruins of single-storey-and-attic laird's
house, rare for its cruck-framed construction.
Rubble masonry set in clay mortar. Remains of
winding stair and stone fireplaces inside.

Moulinearn *(right)* was famed for its
Atholl brose:
*To make a quart, take four dessertspoonfuls
of run honey and four sherry glassfuls of
prepared oatmeal; stir these well together
and put in a quart bottle; fill up with
whisky; shake well before serving.*
*To prepare the oatmeal, put it into a
basin and mix with cold water to the
consistency of thick paste. Leave for about
half an hour, pass through a fine strainer,
pressing with the back of a wooden spoon
so as to leave the oatmeal as dry as possible.
Discard the meal and use the creamy liquor
for the brose.*
Early 19th-century recipe.

189 **Moulinearn**, by Ballinluig, mid-18th century
Barrack-like former 'King's House', or
government-backed inn, of 10 regularly spaced
bays. Established for sustenance and safety of
travellers on the military road. Explorer of
northern Canada, Sir Alexander Mackenzie, died
here, 1820.

Adam Ferguson, 1723–1816, son of the
minister of Logierait, went on to study
in Perth and at St Andrews University,
before becoming Professor of Natural
Philosophy, and then Moral Philosophy
at Edinburgh University at the height of
the Enlightenment. Known as the *'father
of sociology'*. Ferguson's *A History of Civil
Society* (1767) influenced Hegel and
Schiller, and sparked a renewed interest
in ancient Greece.

Logierait Parish encompasses many
ancient sites, including tumuli,
earthworks, cup and ring marks,
standing stones and the notable stone
circle at Tynreich, north of Ballinluig.
From early times the parish was
associated with the administration of
laws and justice in the ancient province
of Atholl. Unfortunately the much-
admired Hall of the Court of Regality,
designed by Lady Margaret Nairne in
the early 18th century, has not survived;
the Regality itself was abolished after
the 1745 Rebellion; remains of prison in
outbuilding of **Logierait Hotel**.

LOGIERAIT
Large, exceptionally scenic highland parish
stretching from near Dunkeld in the south to
Pitlochry in the north, Aberfeldy in the west and
Creag nam Mial in the east. The broad straths of
rivers Tay and Tummel, both peppered with farms
and lairds' houses, meet just below Logierait.

Logierait Parish Kirk, 1804–6, John Stewart
Enormous heritors' box designed to seat 1000 by
Stewart 'wright and undertaker in Perth'. Porch
and vestry added and interior remodelled 1929;
Pictish cross behind pulpit. Three mortsafes, fine
18th-century gravestones and unusual, broken
Pictish cross in kirkyard.

6th Duke of Atholl Memorial, Logierait, 1866,
Robert Rowand Anderson
Early work by Anderson in form of richly sculpted
Celtic cross. David Bryce, consulted by memorial
committee, may have recommended Anderson.

190 **Logierait Viaduct**, 1861–5, Joseph Mitchell
Long and impressive latticed iron railway
viaduct built across the Tay on stone piers with
clustered columns above, for now defunct branch
line to Aberfeldy.

Cuil-an-Daraich, by Logierait, 1864,
James Campbell Walker
Spare but imposing 110-bed poorhouse for
parochial boards of Atholl and Breadalbane.
Symmetrical gabled design overlooking the Tay,
large, but much reduced from colossal 1858
competition entries. Edinburgh-based Walker,
pupil of Burn and Bryce, a poorhouse specialist,
completed those at Auchterarder, Dysart,
Galashiels and Dumbarton.
Museum

Top *6th Duke of Atholl Memorial*. Above
Logierait Viaduct. Left *Cuil-an-Daraich*.

Dunfallandy House, 1818
Severe classical arrangement of three-storey,
three-bay main house and single-storey wings.
Slightly bellcast piended roof. Once the seat of
the Fergusons, now hotel. Smart contemporary
former stables in symmetrical arrangement with
pedimented centre and pavilions.

Cross-slab, Dunfallandy.

Cross-slab, Dunfallandy, 8th century
Signposted from the Pitlochry/Logierait road.
Splendid Pictish red sandstone cross-slab in
amazingly good condition, now protected by
glazed shelter. Cross itself intricately patterned,
and surrounded by winged figures and animals
in relief. Reverse also has figures and symbols.
Historic Scotland; public access
Here also large gothic **memorial** to General
Archibald Fergusson, 1755–1834.

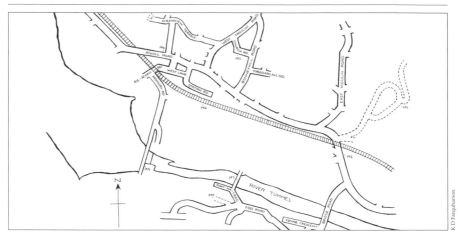

PITLOCHRY

Pitlochry's rise over its neighbour Moulin (see p.176) began with General Wade's new military road of 1728, which bypassed the ancient kirkton. Nestled below Ben Vrackie, Pitlochry thrived as a crossroads into the 19th century, attracting mills, distilleries and even its first banks in 1836. However, the recommendations of Sir James Clark, Queen Victoria's physician, and the arrival of the railway in 1863, saw an explosion in visitors and their attendant need for facilities. In spite of its role as a bustling tourist centre, maintained to this day, the town only achieved burghal status in 1947 at the second wind of the vast Tummel-Garry hydro-electric project.

Below Atholl Palace Hotel. Bottom Pitlochry West Church, c.1885.

Atholl Palace Hotel

191 **Atholl Palace Hotel**, 1875–8, Andrew Heiton Jr
Built as a hydropathic, no visitor to Pitlochry can fail to notice this colossal H-plan French *château* with its great circular towers and formidable pavilion-roofed wings, perched on a spectacular elevated site. Wonderful from a distance; tough early French details close up. Public rooms characterised by enormous scale and theatrical opulence. Original cost a then prodigious £100,000. Matching lodge.

Perth Museum & Art Gallery

192 **Pitlochry West Church**, Church Road, 1884, Charles & Leslie Ower
Eccentric Romanesque confection sited on a knoll, quickly nicknamed 'Mount Zion'. After the heritors refused to relocate the parish church from Moulin village, West Church was built to serve the town and summer visitors. Seating forms part circle around communion table. Porch 1995.

Atholl Road and its eastern continuation, **Perth Road**, form the main thoroughfare. **Holy Trinity**
193 **Episcopal Church**, Perth Road, 1858,
E Buckridge, enlarged 1890, good interior with open timber roof and Minton tiled floor, and ecclesiological fittings including candelabras and reredos. In the centre of town a frilly cast-iron canopy survives at the **Arcade**. **Smithy Cottage** and neighbours, **146-152 Atholl Road**, typical Perthshire picturesque, with overhanging eaves
194 to lots of gables and dormers. **156 Atholl Road**, late 18th-century vernacular cottage incongruously surviving in a suburban context. Corrugated-iron roof hid and protected earlier thatched roof throughout the 20th century.
Now in the care of Historic Scotland

Top *Arcade, Atholl Road.* Above *156 Atholl Road.* Left *Loch Faskally Dam, Pitlochry Power Station.*

Tummel/Garry Hydro-Electric Scheme, Perthshire's largest civil engineering project, was much criticised during construction for its huge environmental impact, but is now a tourist attraction in itself. The potential for hydro-electric power in the county was first promoted in the 1899 Highland Water Power Bill, but it was not until 1927 that large-scale development by the Scottish Power Company began at Rannoch. From 1943, the North of Scotland Hydro-Electric Board assumed responsibility for the scheme, which had become intimately bound up in social and economic policies for the Highlands. Rannoch Power Station opened in November 1930 to be followed by further stations generating a total of 241.3MW: Tummel Bridge (1933), Pitlochry (1950), Clunie (1950), Gaur (1950), Errochty (1955), Cuaich (1959), and Loch Ericht (1963). Major dams were constructed to form reservoirs at Lochs Cuaich, Ericht, Eigheach, Rannoch, Dunalastair, Tummel, and Faskally.

195 **Pitlochry Power Station, Bridge, Dam and Fish Ladder**, 1947–50, H O Tarbolton
Ingenious linear amalgamation of power station, bridge and dam across lower end of Loch Faskally, the man-made reservoir. Power station in monumental cubic style, faced in granite for extra muscularity. *Neart nan Gleann* (Power of the Glens) reads the Hydro-Electric Board's motto on the north elevation, in case of doubt. Reservoir levels controlled by massive automatic drum gates, and fish ladder enables salmon to return to spawning grounds. Completed posthumously.

196 **Pitlochry Station**, *c.*1890
Rebuilt in H-plan with canopy infilling space between wings on the platform side. Nicely detailed in typical Highland Railway style with crowstepped gables, tall chimneys and decorative ridging.

Pitlochry Station.

151

197 Suspension Bridge, Port-na-Craig, 1913
Bouncy public footbridge of lattice-girder pylons,
wire-rope cables, rod suspenders, lattice truss span
and wooden deck, to replace the ferry (associated
U-plan arrangement of early 19th-century cottages
remain). Erected in memory of Lt Col George Glas
Sandeman of Fonab, opened by the Marchioness
of Tullibardine on Empire Day 1913.

198 Port-na-Craig House, Foss Road, 1892,
Andrew Heiton Jr
Wonderful red sandstone baronial mansion, now
offices. Lively skyline of towers, bartizans,
chimneys and crowsteps. Very grand and
beautifully crafted panelled interior with suitably
baronial stone fireplaces and circular stair.

199 Pine Trees Hotel, Strathview Terrace, 1892,
Andrew Heiton Jr
Surprising bright white mansion with
proliferation of half-timbered gables mixed with
Dutch-style crowstepped gables on low, rambling
plan. Panelled entrance hall and drawing room.
More conventional picturesque gothic, including
pavilion-roofed entrance tower with decorative
fish-scale slates and iron cresting at **Craigard**,
Strathview Terrace, late 19th century.

Above *Foyer, Pitlochry Festival Theatre.*
Right *Pitlochry Festival Theatre.*

200 Pitlochry Festival Theatre, 1976–81,
Graham Law of Law & Dunbar-Nasmith
Carefully sited and designed to echo form of
surrounding landscape. Almost square-plan, built
into hillside using brown brick, profiled steel roof
and glazed walls to foyer. Small £2m budget was
maximised to provide light and airy public spaces
and functional backstage facilities for the May to
October season of the Pitlochry Festival Society.
Tented aluminium ceiling of foyer reflects 1951
origins of Festival Theatre in a tent at
Knockendarroch. Open staircases, wonderful
views through the glazed wall. Dressing rooms
below. Excellent 540-seat raked auditorium. Scene
stores flank the stage, which has no fly-tower.
Refurbished and extended, 1992.

Haynes

Historic Scotland

Charles McKean

David Taylor

Eric Ellington

A S Welch

Clockwise from top *Bridge of Isla; Schiehallion; Rannoch Station; Silvia Simon Studio; Scone Palace, 1783, by Charles McKean after the Hutton Collection; Detail, St Mary's Church, Grandtully.*

153

Top left *Lethendy Kirk*. Top right
Glenlyon House. Middle *Matthew Gloag
Headquarters*. Right *Clunie*. Above *Beech
Hedge, Meikleour*.

Cathy Orton

© Keith Hunter

Hanisa Santimano

Haynes

David Taylor

Haynes

Clockwise from top *Loch Errochty Dam; glazed foyer to ballroom, Blair Castle; The Scottish Crannog Centre; Detail, Weem Parish Church; Blair Castle; Caputh Church Hall.*

Top *Castle Menzies*. Middle *Dunkeld*. Above right *Banner Hall, Taymouth Castle*. Right *Balvarran House*. Above *Camserney Longhouse*.

Faskally House, 1829–31, William Burn
Earliest surviving house by Burn in Scots-Jacobean style – a mixture of crowstepped gables, towers, broad mullioned windows and tall chimneys – forerunner to full-blown Scots Baronial. Exceptionally for Burn, porch is located on the south front allowing visitors to glimpse into adjacent principal rooms. Also unusual, the white sandstone with buff micaceous quartz dressings. Built for gentleman-soldier, Archibald Butter. Altered and extended by Burn, 1837.

Faskally House.

201 **Clunie Power Station**, Loch Faskally, 1950
Striking and simple design for North of Scotland Hydro-Electric Board, clean modern lines, flat roof and pale granite aggregate, but classical symmetry and articulation through vertical units of tall keystoned windows and massive buttresses. Hydro-electric headquarters adjoin.

Tenandry Church, Glen Garry, 1836
T-plan Tudor Gothic *quoad sacra* church with spired bellcote.

Coille Brochain Cottage, Strath Tummel, mid-19th century
Picturesque *cottage-ornée* with round-headed dormers extending up into thatched roof. Rustic log-columned porch and single-storey wings. Woods behind are the supposed resting place of Robert the Bruce after the Battle of Methven, as recorded on the remains of a chimney gable.

Below *Bonskeid House, 1930s.*
Bottom *Balavoulin.*

Bonskeid House, Strath Tummel, 1881, Andrew Heiton Jr
Beautifully sited in terraced gardens and woodland above the River Tummel. Offices *c.*1805, completed as a long low classical house, and largely remodelled as new baronial tower house by Heiton (much in the style of his master, David Bryce). Further remodelled in 1909 and 1970s. Now YMCA. Heiton also responsible for **East** & **West Lodges**, *c.*1881.

Balavoulin, Glen Fincastle, 1905, Ramsay Traquair
Charming Scots 17th-century remodelling of former Milton Lodge. Largely symmetrical with ogee-roofed front tower and off-centre wallhead chimney.

Old Fincastle House, Glen Fincastle, from 17th century
Dated 1640 on window lintel, probably largely remodelled to long horizontal form and near-

157

STRATHTUMMEL

A wild affair! The storm howls, rushes, and whistles, doors are banging and the window-shutters are bursting open. Whether the watery noise is from the driving rain or the foaming stream there's no telling, as both rage together; we are sitting here quietly by the fire, which I poke from time to time to make it flare up. The room is large and empty, from one of the walls wet trickles down, the floor is so thin that the conversation from the servants' room below penetrates up to us: they are singing drunken songs and laughing; dogs are barking. We have two beds with crimson curtains; on our feet, instead of English slippers, are Scotch wooden shoes; tea with honey and potato cakes; there is a wooden winding staircase, on which the servant girl came to meet us with whisky, a desperate cloud-procession in the sky, and in spite of the servants' noise and door-banging there is repose. It is quiet and very lonely here! I might say that the stillness rings through the noise. Just now the door opened of itself. This is a Highland inn. The little boys with their kilts and bare knees and gay-coloured bonnets, the waiter in his tartan, old people with pigtails, talk helter-skelter in their unintelligible Gaelic.
Felix Mendelssohn-Bartholdy, letter from Tummel Bridge, 3 August 1829

Below *Old Tummel Bridge.* Right *Power Station.* Bottom *Foss & Tummel Parish Church.*

symmetrical arrangement, 1702 (date above door). Single-storey-and-attic wing, bearing marriage lintels of 1751 and 1754 and a remodelling date of 1807, projects at south-west corner.

Chamberbhan Cruck Cottage, Strathtummel, 18th century
Interesting vernacular survival now in use as store. Traditional three-bay cottage with openings grouped closely at centre, further single-bay room to west. Boulder rubble walls. Thatched roof supported on four couples or crucks, covered with corrugated-iron. Masonry central ridge chimney; metal chimney at east end probably replacing hanging lum. Timber-lined interior.

202 **Old Tummel Bridge**, *c.*1734
Constructed in rubble to carry Lt Gen. George Wade's military road, the now bypassed bridge comprises one very large humpbacked span, with smaller northern arch.

203 **Power Station**, Tummel Bridge, 1933
Muscular inter-war classicism, painted bright white. Built for the Scottish Power Company as part of Tummel Valley hydro-electric scheme, the station fed by a catchment area of 381 square miles, gathered into Loch Rannoch and a smaller reservoir at Dunalastair, and delivered from an aqueduct. Two generating sets, producing a total of 34MW, are unusual in that each turbine has two horizontal runners and spiral casings.

Foss & Tummel Parish Church, Foss, 1824
Plain, but prettily sited *quoad sacra* parish church with birdcage bellcote. Crenellated burial enclosure to the *Progeniter of the Old Stewarts of Kinnichan and Kinneard.*

Dunalastair, 1852, Andrew Heiton Sr & Son
Ruinous baronial pile, detailed in manner of
Heiton's master, David Bryce. Symmetrically
planned around French-looking circular entrance
tower with tall candle-snuffer roof. Truncated
from house by raised water levels required for
1930s' hydro-electric scheme, **East Lodge**, 1893,
Thomas G Leadbetter of Leadbetter & Fairley, an
impressive rubbly round tower adjoining
tripartite arched gateway.

Old Rannoch Church of Scotland,
Kinloch Rannoch, 1829, William Thomson
Second of Fortingall Parish's Parliamentary kirks,
built by contractor William Minto for £1,473
including manse and byre. Much altered, 1893.

204 **Kinloch Rannoch Bridge**, 1764
*THIS BUILDING ERECTED A.D.1764 AT THE
SOLE EXPENSE OF HIS MAJESTY OUT OF THE
ANNEXED ESTATES* reads the inscription, a
piece of propaganda intended to demonstrate the
personal generosity of George III and improved
stewardship of the estates forfeited after the '45.

St Blane's Chapel, Lassintullich
Small rubble rectangle of ancient but uncertain
date, transformed into burial enclosure for the
Stewarts of Innerhadden, 18th century. Tenth-
century **cross-slab** in south-west corner of
burial ground.

Crossmount, mid-18th century
Harled classical house with pavilions,
superficially gothicised by crenellated entrance
tower and timber perpendicular tracery fitted to
windows, *c* 1825.

205 **Tower**, Eilean Nam Faoileag, Loch Rannoch,
early 19th century
Two-stage crenellated tower set on tiny artificial
island in Loch Rannoch, erected by Baron Grantly
as reconstruction of island prison of the
Robertsons of Struan.

From top *Dunalastair; Old Rannoch
Church of Scotland; Kinloch Rannoch
Bridge; Tower, Eilean Nam Faoileag.*

Bridge of Gaur, 1838
Built in granite at west end of Loch Rannoch,
this elegant three-arched bridge was built by Sir
Neil Menzies to commemorate the accession of
Queen Victoria.

Braes of Rannoch Church, Bridge of Gaur, South
Loch Road, 1907, Peter MacGregor Chalmers
Plain harled exterior with round-arched Norman

Above *Rannoch School, Dall House, 1854, Thomas Mackenzie, harled baronial mansion, nicely composed. Lively skyline.* Right *Rannoch Station.*

Falls of Bruar are a spectacular series of five waterfalls, dropping some 60ft through a narrow chasm. Robert Burns famously criticised the lack of surrounding trees in his 1787 poem 'The Humble Petition of the Bruar Water'. In memory of Burns, the Duke of Atholl planted the area as a wild garden with 60,000 larch and 60,000 'Scotch firs', laid out paths, and erected the two bridges in 1796–7. Purist seekers of the wild and sublime, such as Elizabeth Grant of Rothiemurchus were disturbed that '*so many summer houses and hermitages and peep-bo places of one sort or another had been planted on favourite situations that the proper character of the torrent was completely lost*' (1815). The rustic summer houses eventually disappeared, and the trees were replanted after the Second World War felling, returning the scene to that envisaged by Burns.

Below *Loch Errochty Dam.*
Bottom *Auchleeks House.*

windows, apse and birdcage bellcote probably re-used from predecessor buildings of 1855 and 1776. Simple interior of granite and timberwork. Organ came from Urquhart Parish Church, Moray, 1991.

206 **Rannoch Station**, *c.*1890, James Miller
Dramatically isolated island-platformed station, variant of standard design for West Highland Railway. Long and low with deep swept roof carried over veranda either side. Red brick base on stone plinth, timber-framed above with scalloped shingle walling, astragaled windows, tall brick ridge stacks. Free-standing small control signal box similarly detailed. At north end of platform, cut by railway workers, is sculptured head of Mr Renton, director of the West Highland Railway who saved the line from bankruptcy when financial crisis hit in summer 1893 (colour p.153).

207 **Loch Errochty Dam**, 1955, North of Scotland Hydro-Electric Board
Spectacular diamond-headed buttress structure, 354m long and 49m high, built across the River Errochty to form man-made reservoir of Loch Errochty (colour p.155). Water fed to the loch from the River Garry and upper tributaries by 19km of tunnels; further 9.6km tunnel supplies **Errochty Power Station**, 1955, monumental cubic turbine house at head of Loch Tummel.

Auchleeks House, Glen Errochty, earlier 19th century
Built for Robert Robertson, possibly by builder Charles Sim with some James Gillespie Graham involvement. Notable classical house of five bays. Central pedimented bay and outer bays advanced and articulated by long and short quoins. Roman Doric doorpiece with tripartite window above. More expensive variant of Balnakeilly House (see p.177). House is set on a terrace enclosed by a hemicycle of railings with walled garden on an axis below. Contemporary courtyard **stables** entered by archway in small pyramid-roofed tower and doocot.

Dalnacardoch Lodge, Glen Garry, 1774
Built as inn by order of George III, according to
the inscription. The *New Statistical Account* of 1838
praised it as: *where every accommodation in the way
of posting and lodging is found, equal to that of any
inn in Scotland*. Original three-bay inn later
extended by large north wing and court of offices.

Clunes Lodge, Glen Garry, 1866
Plain neo-Tudor shooting lodge with corner
tower and gabled dormers.

Struan Church and Churchyard, Glen Garry,
1828, Charles Sim
Plain gothic heritors' box with birdcage bellcote,
on site of the old Struan or Strowan Parish
Church; remodelled internally, 1938. Pretty
former **manse** of 1828 at Baluain, midway
between churches at Blair and Struan, by Sim,
with 1862 wing by Robertson of Pitlochry.

BRUAR
House of Bruar, Glen Bruar, 1995
Upmarket shopping emporium, itself dressed in
Perthshire country casual style: harled, slated
roofs, anchored by a round tower.

BLAIR ATHOLL
Vast and spectacularly scenic highland parish, 30
miles long and 18 miles wide, encompassing Glen
Garry and its many tributaries at northernmost
limit of the county. Ancient heartland of the
Atholl estate. Blair Castle and the main settlement
of Blair Atholl sit at the junction of glens Banvie,
Tilt, Fender and Garry, beside the key strategic
north/south route from the Pass of Drumochter to
Killiecrankie. The four peaks of Beinn A' Ghlo,
rising to 1,120m, are the most dramatic.

Picturesque estate village, established in 1823
following construction of new **Bridge of Tilt**
and re-routing of Perth/Inverness road by
208 engineer John Mitchell. **Parish Church**, first of
the new village buildings, built posthumously to
a severe boxy design by Archibald Elliot, 1823–5;
recast internally 1950. Mildly Scots-Jacobean
Atholl Arms Hotel, 1832, probably R & R
Dickson, dominates village centre. **Blair
Cottages**, 1840, R & R Dickson, neatly planned
as eight dwellings, in stolid Scots Tudor with
two dumpy towers to central block. **Village hall**,
1907, by Edinburgh architect J McIntyre Henry,
restrained baronial, built as drill hall for the
Scottish Horse. Behind the main road,
picturesque **station** with latticed footbridge, and

Top *Dalnacardoch Lodge.* Middle *Struan
Church.* Above *House of Bruar.*

Below *Parish Church.* Bottom *Atholl
Arms Hotel.*

meal **mill**, 1833, built by Lord Glenlyon to replace 'five wretched mills' for drying and grinding corn; now converted to house. Cottage development at **Garryside**, 1856, also by R & R Dickson, this time in more picturesque style with overhanging eaves and gables. Further east, **Railway Viaduct**, 1861–2, Joseph Mitchell, a serious piece of engineering crossing the River Tilt in a single latticed span, jollified by toy-fort portals. Splendid renaissance gates and gatepiers at **Blair Castle Front Lodge**, 1869, represent some of the finest work of David Bryce.

Blair Castle: top Front Lodge; above drawing room; right by David Bryce.

Blair Castle is home of Europe's last surviving private army, the Atholl Highlanders (granted right to bear arms on Queen Victoria's visit to Blair in 1844).

Katherine, 8th Duchess of Atholl, 1874–1960, known as Red Katie, first Scottish woman MP and first Conservative woman minister was of formidable intellect and relentless energy. Outspoken opponent of fascism and appeasement policy, she lost the party whip and resigned her seat in 1938.

One of two depictions of 'Blair Castel' on maps by the late 16th-century cartographer, Timothy Pont. The plan of a building (unique on Pont's maps) in the bottom right hand corner may be the remains of the Black Castle of Moulin.

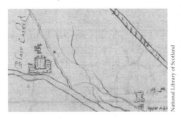

209 **Blair Castle**, from 1269

Ancestral seat of the dukes of Atholl: Highland romanticism at its most spectacular. An agglomeration of periods and styles unified for the 7th Duke by David Bryce, 1869–71, into a gleaming white-harled baronial pile, bristling with Fyvie-style bartizans, gables and battlements on entrance front (colour p.155). At north-west corner, six-storey Cumming's (or Comyn's) Tower, partly genuine baronial relic of 1269. The 3rd Earl of Atholl's 1530 Great Hall (now dining room) and vaulted kitchen range adjoins to south. Enlarged again by the time of Pont's 1590s' maps, further additions were constructed in the early 17th century, and more followed throughout that century. John Douglas began to heighten the southern block in 1736, as prelude to fine unexecuted scheme to Palladianise the house. James Winter built the two-storey south-east wing, 1743–5, 'clipped' the old towers, and completed an austere classical re-modelling as Atholl House after the '45 for the 2nd Duke. James Campbell Walker baronialised south-east wing, 1886. Discreet but stylish glazed foyer to ballroom, restaurant and shop, J Troughton & H Broughton, 1999 (colour p.155). Accretive nature of the building more readily apparent inside, where parts survive from most periods. David Bryce's most successful baronial interiors are the entrance hall and ballroom. The former boasts a ferocious array of weaponry gathered by the 7th Duke; the latter was built to house the annual gathering of the Atholl Highlanders, finished by John Bryce, 1876, complete with hammerbeam ceiling and forest of antler trophies. In contrast to the severity of Winter's external regularisation, interior work of the mid-18th century was lavish, in particular the extraordinary plasterwork by Thomas Clayton for the picture staircase, dining room and drawing room. The roles of these last two rooms were swapped during construction, marking new primacy in size and importance of the drawing room over eating and sleeping rooms in the great houses of Scotland. Despite its diminished status, dining room of 1751 is a riot of rococo plasterwork, and contains a superb marble fireplace and Trophies of War overmantle (perhaps a rather triumphalist Hanoverian jibe at the Jacobites, including the 2nd Duke's brothers). Abraham Swan designed equally resplendent front staircase, 1757, which serves as the family portrait gallery.

Open to the public, April-October; guidebooks

The designed layout of the gardens around Blair Castle extends to some 2,500 acres. In the 17th century, formal beds within a walled enclosure to the west side of the house. However, it was largely the 2nd Duke's activities, always impressive, but never quite at the cutting edge of fashion, that shaped the gardens we see today. The core, a semi-formal pattern of radiating avenues and walks, is contemporary with the 2nd Duke's regularisation of the house. Diana's Grove, or Wilderness, 1737, the first feature of the garden, focused on a statue of Diana the Huntress and Actaeon. Planting here was augmented, 1871, by magnificent exotic conifers, and the statue replaced in 1895, but unfortunately **Temple of Fame**, 1744, replete with lead statues and busts by John Cheere, has not survived. **Hercules Garden**, 1741–54, recently restored, an exceptional survival of a grand water garden, comprising pond and canal linked under a Chinese bridge, surrounded by strips of vegetable and fruit planting, and enclosed by high rubble walls. In the east wall, **Goraich nic Griogair**, or McGregor's Folly, 1888, an ogee-roofed gazebo, named after Miss Murray McGregor, companion to Duchess Louisa.

Dining room, Blair Castle.

Lead statuary formed an important component of the 2nd Duke's garden. Much of it was purchased in 1740 and 1754 from the London workshops of John Cheere, including the replica Farnese **Hercules** at the focus of Hercules Walk, **Time** supporting a sundial, and **Flora**. **Obelisk**, carved with Atholl emblems, was also supplied by Cheere in 1742.

Below *Hercules Garden.* Bottom *Goraich nic Griogair.*

Blair Castle has many royal connections; Edward II came in 1336; Robert II owned Blair following the Wars of Independence; the ancestor of the present Atholl family was Sir John Stewart of Balvenie, half-brother of James II, on whom the earldom was granted in 1457; James V and his mother, Margaret Tudor were entertained in a temporary hunting palace *'of greine tymmer wond witht birkis* (birches)', during a three day visit in 1531; Mary, Queen of Scots, and Bonnie Prince Charlie also visited.

From top *Blairuachdar; West Lodge; Former coaching inn, Old Blair; St Bride's Kirk; Tirinie House.*

Atholl Estates

David Taylor

Haynes

Haynes

Knight Frank

Further north, as an eye-catcher for the house, **The Whim**, 1762, two pyramid-roofed pavilions with Gothick triple archway. More Gothick arches at **Lady Jean's Well**, domed elliptical grotto rebuilt in 1899 as a reduced version of the West Grotto at Dunkeld. Perhaps the garden building most tailored to the wild romantic scenery of the estate is the splendid rustic **Grotto**, 1758, a large circular viewpoint with semi-dome roof opposite York Cascade on the River Tilt.

Two of the most impressive steadings on the estate are at **Blairuachdar**, 1790, George Steuart, and **Bailanloan**, 1867, possibly David Bryce. The former is classical with pavilions and centre block linked by arcades; the latter takes similar form, but is castellated at centre and crowstepped at pavilions.

The 1867 baronial **West Lodge** and pepperpot gateway on the B8079, may also have been designed by David Bryce, but were constructed along with a bridge over the track by the Highland Railway Company, presumably to maintain the western access and in partial recompense for building the line through the estate. The remaining compensation of £33,000 greatly assisted Bryce's transformation of the main house.

OLD BLAIR

The village straddled the old Perth to Inverness road, which was re-routed outside the castle policies on construction of the new Bridge of Tilt, 1823. **Former coaching inn** remains, converted to house, possibly by David Bryce, along with L-plan group of cottages. **St Bride's Kirk**, on a 12th-century site, probably reconstructed after the Reformation, now ruinous. Two ogee panels adorn groin-vaulted south aisle, altered, 1865 by David Bryce to house fine marble monument to the 6th Duke of Atholl (1814–64) by Queen's Sculptor for Scotland, Sir John Steell. John Graham of Claverhouse, 'Bonnie Dundee', is buried in the kirk vault.

Tirinie House, Glen Fender, 1934, Oswald Milne Perhaps the most spectacularly located house in the county, at 1,100ft on the slopes of Meall Dail Min above Blair Atholl, surveying the mountain landscape as far as Schiehallion (colour p.153). The 57 acres of land were sold by the 7th Duke of Atholl to his daughter, Lady Helen, and her new husband, David Tod, to build their home. Sensitive Scots vernacular design the work of fashionable London architect Oswald Milne, former assistant to Edwin Lutyens and Mayor of

Hampstead. Beautifully crafted interiors for entertaining on a grand scale, employing oak and Glen Tilt marble. **Farmhouse**, **steading**, **cottages** and **lodge** also by Milne.

Kilmaveonaig Episcopal Chapel, Bridge of Tilt, 1794, John Stewart
Opposite Tilt Hotel. Initialled and dated 'AR AG 1591' from the old parish kirk of Kilmaveonaig (Gaelic *Cille-Eonaig*, the chapel of St Eonaig), but rebuilt end 18th century as plain rectangular chapel with birdcage belfry and bell of 1629 from Little Dunkeld. Small crenellated narthex added, 1899, and Sir Robert Lorimer designed the reredos in 1912. Unbroken Episcopal worship on this site since the 1688 Revolution.

Lude House, Glen Tilt, 1837–9, William Burn
Classic Burn house of mid-1830s for J J McInroy. Comfortable in size, Scots-Jacobean in style, beautifully planned with symmetrical arrangement of south-facing principal rooms, the entrance, stairs and service wing to the north. Bridge of Tilt **Lodge** and gateway, also by Burn, 1839, in crenellated Tudor gothic. Similarly styled **stables**, dated 1824.

Top *Kilmaveonaig Episcopal Chapel.* Middle *Lude House.* Above *Lude stables.*

House of Urrard, 1831, William Burn
Extension of older house for Alston Stewart. Dutch curvilinear gables perhaps an architectural reference to the part played by House of Urrard, or Renrory, in support of William and Mary during the Battle of Killiecrankie – the bullet which killed Jacobite Viscount Dundee was reputedly fired from the old house. Lord Cockburn described the house as in Burn's '*gimcrack cottage style*'.

Killiecrankie Viaduct.

210 **Killiecrankie Viaduct**, 1864, Joseph Mitchell
Dramatic curving viaduct of 10 arches, costing £5,730 for the Inverness and Perth Junction Railway. Crenellated parapets and refuges in keeping with other structures along the line on its heroic ascent to 1,484ft at Drumochter.

Pass of Killiecrankie is a spectacular gorge carved by the River Garry, occupying a strategic position on the north/south route through the Highlands. The Battle of Killiecrankie took place in the pass on 27th July 1689 between government troops and Jacobites led by John Graham of Claverhouse, Viscount Dundee. Although Dundee was mortally wounded in the battle, General Hugh Mackay's government troops were heavily defeated, and fled over the hills. Donald MacBean survived only by jumping the 18ft distance over the River Garry, giving rise to the name Soldier's Leap.

Returning to Perth, the route of the guide now continues along the A93 to Blairgowrie and north.

Little is known of the composer **Robert Carver**, *c.*1484– *c.*1568, other than that he trained as an Augustinian canon at Scone Abbey. The extraordinary five masses and two motets of the *Carver Choirbook* are almost the only surviving examples of pre-Reformation Scottish polyphonic music, the manuscripts of which are preserved in the National Library of Scotland. His Mass *Dum Sacrum Mysterium*, in 10 parts representing the nine angelic orders joined by mankind, was used at the coronation of James V in 1513.

Scone Abbey, from 1114 (demolished 1559) Augustinian priory founded by Alexander I, and elevated to abbey status, 1164, probably stood south-east of present palace. Appearance not recorded, but architectural fragments suggest that building continued into 16th century. Burnt during Reformation.

Old Scone Palace, *c.*1580 (largely demolished/ remodelled 1803)
William, Lord Ruthven began a courtyard palace here after the grant of a temporal lordship of the former monastic lands, probably incorporating parts of the Bishop's Palace. James VI confiscated the estate following the Gowrie Conspiracy of 1600 (see p.15), and gave it to Sir David Murray of Gospetrie, created Lord Scone, 1605, and Viscount Stormont, 1621. Sir David began a magnificent building scheme, adding lavish 157ft gallery range to the east, forming another courtyard with precocious symmetrical E-plan southern range (colour p.153). On inheriting Mansfield earldom, 1793, David Murray, 7th Viscount Stormont commissioned George Saunders to improve the palace, removing old Gowrie buildings, remodelling east and south ranges. Saunders' unexecuted designs, 1802, are earliest-known revival of Scots Jacobean, some 30 years before William Burn and David Hamilton turned to the style in earnest.

Top *Old Scone Palace by A Rutherford, 1775.* Right *Scone Palace.* Above *Long Gallery, reproduced by kind permission of the Earl of Mansfield.*

'*So, thanks to all at once, and to each one whom we invite to see us crowned at Scone.*' Malcolm's final speech in Shakespeare's *Macbeth*

211 **Scone Palace**, 1803–12, William Atkinson
Castellated toy fort gothic won the day when the 3rd Earl of Mansfield decided to proceed with remodelling the palace, perhaps in the medieval spirit of the former abbey. Even though principal southern block has marked symmetrical tendencies, overall scheme is an early break from rigid symmetry of Adam castles. On main east entrance side, the old gallery survives, encased in new skin of buttresses, hoodmoulded windows and crenellated parapet. Unfortunately, a misunderstanding between Atkinson and the clerk of works led to loss of 17th-century interiors in

south range. In their place, soberly elegant state rooms include dining room, linked by rib-vaulted ante room to well-proportioned drawing room, with early 19th-century silk wall coverings and wonderful gothic coffered ceiling, and spectacular **Long Gallery** with oak and bog oak floor. Landscape laid out between 1790 and 1812, partially realised from John Claudius Loudon's ambitious plans in his Treatise on Scone (1803) to make Scone 'the first place in the British Empire'. Loudon proposed to relocate the ancient Burgh of Scone, but medieval mercat **Cross of Old Scone**, late 16th-century **gateway** and graveyard remain.

Scone Palace Chapel, Moot Hill, remodelled 1807, William Atkinson

Pretty gothic mausoleum with huge spiky corner towers, remodelled from tiny chapel said to have been constructed 1604 for David Murray. Within, his splendid Italian alabaster **monument** (as 1st Viscount Stormont), 1618–19, started some 13 years before his death by premier London sculptor, Maximilian Colt. Murray is depicted kneeling between the Marquis of Tullibardine and the Earl Marischal. Outside, replica of **Stone of Scone**, or Stone of Destiny (original at Edinburgh Castle), brought here by Kenneth mac Alpin, which was, by legend, Jacob's pillow, becoming the seat on which the Scottish Kings were crowned.

Balboughty House and Steading, 1851–61, John Macdonald

Picturesque gothic house, and quirky Italianate tower with open cupola to large model steading.

St David's Chapel, Stormontfield, 1897, A Marshall Mackenzie

Built as chapel of ease to seat 100 bleachfield workers, simple gothic church after manner of Scots medieval parish kirks – long, low, aisleless rectangle with little external adornment and beautifully crafted interior.

Cambusmichael Kirk, late 15th century

The bellcote, two gables and parts of the side walls remain of this unicameral church, on a bluff above the Tay opposite Stanley Mills. A 12th-century chapel of Scone, Cambusmichael attained parochial status in the 15th century, when the current building was probably constructed incorporating ashlar blocks from an earlier structure. It was subsequently remodelled, but became ruinous by 1711 after the late 17th-century amalgamation with St Martin's Parish.

From top *Cross of Old Scone; Gateway; Chapel; Cambusmichael Kirk.*

Above *Newmiln Country Estate*.
Right *Stobhall Chapel*.

Newmiln Country Estate, 1855,
Andrew Heiton Sr & Son
Italianate mansion. Balustraded entrance tower anchors extended composition of gables and overhanging eaves.

Craigmakerran, *c.*1830
Small and picturesque Tudor-gothic mansion in whinstone, probably by Andrew Heiton Sr & Son for the Guildry Incorporation of Perth, who met in the west wing during visitations to their estates.

Stobhall has been associated with the Drummond family since the mid-14th century when Sir Malcolm Drummond acquired the lands from his aunt, Queen Margaret. In 1367 his sister Annabella married John Stewart, Earl of Carrick, later Robert III. In 1490 the 1st Lord Drummond constructed Drummond Castle (see p.92) 25 miles away, and Stobhall became a hunting lodge. Patrick, 3rd Lord Drummond built the new tower house and converted the chapel in 1578. His son earned the earldom of Perth for his part in securing James VI's peace treaty with Spain. The family's staunch support for the Stuart kings cost them their lands under Cromwell, and again after the Jacobite risings of 1715 and 1745. It was not until 1785 that the annexed lands were restored to Capt. James Drummond of Lundin. Stobhall descended through the female line until it was given to the 17th Earl of Perth, 1953.

Below *Chapel ceiling*. Bottom *Folly*.

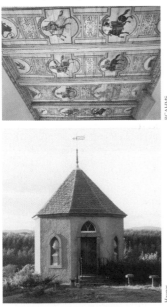

212 **Stobhall**, from 14th century
There is something magical about Stobhall: the fairy-tale setting, perched high on a promontory between the Tay and a romantic wooded gully; the perfect miniature scale of the house and manicured gardens; spectacular views west from the walled and terraced site to the mountains; and pervading sense of antiquity. Oldest of all, small rectangular **chapel**, possibly dating in part from the 14th century. It survived the Reformation by conversion in 1578 to form ground-floor hall of new house. Even more remarkable is the survival of the altar slab, stoup and aumbry door. Although much re-worked, an overtly Royalist painted ceiling exists from 1642, depicting the crowned heads of Europe and, more exotically, the rulers of Mauritania and Ethiopia. Restored as a chapel, 1858. To the west, single-storey **laundry**, **brewhouse** and **bakehouse**, late 16th century, with low walls, steep roof and catslide dormers, converted and linked to the tower in 1954. Entrance to the complex is past topiary gardens and sundials, through **gatehouse** archway, early 17th century, marked with the arms of 2nd Earl and Countess of Perth. Adjoining **Dower House**, dated 1671, typical of period with steep crowstepped gables, catslide dormers and moulded doorpiece; arched windows and tower are later modifications. South of the chapel, **library**, 1965, a tactful rebuilding of a pair of 18th-century

houses, which may in turn have incorporated parts of original castle. Small octagonal **folly**, 1987–9, Stewart Tod & Partners, enjoys sensational location above the Tay. It has an 18th-century flavour, custom-built to house genuine earlier 18th-century *trompe-l'oeil* panelling from the former Polton House gazebo (see *Midlothian* in this series).

Part of the great Strathmore glen, bounded by the Tay and its dramatic cliffs to the west, Cargill Parish rises to about 500ft before forming a plateau to the Sidlaw Hills in the east. Prehistoric burial mound, known as Macbeth's Law, exists at Lawton.

CARGILL
From 12th century, the monks of Coupar Angus established what was effectively a grange, or supply base for the abbey, high above the Linn of Campsie falls on the Tay. The footings of five buildings arranged around a courtyard, including the abbot's house, remain. Below the junction of the rivers Tay and Isla, only the ringwork survives of **Cargill Castle**, late 12th century, probably built by Richard de Montfiquet.

Easter Shian (former Cargill Parish Church), 1831, William Mackenzie
Something of a barn with four enormous arched windows facing towards the Tay, now maximised in its re-use as a house. Ruins of an old cruck-framed cottage, utilised as a rockery, stand in front. Opposite, beautifully tranquil **churchyard** containing remnants of medieval parish church and fine monument to the Thomsons and Macgregors of Wolfhill and Newbigging, 1765. Here too, a good vantage point for lattice-girdered **Cargill Viaduct**, mid-19th century, on the old Perth/Forfar railway.

Top *Easter Shian*. Above *Cargill Viaduct*.

Druidsmere House, Muirton of Ardblair, 1885, Andrew Heiton Jr
Large, idiosyncratic red sandstone Rhenish baronial mansion with cast-iron balconies overlooking White Loch.

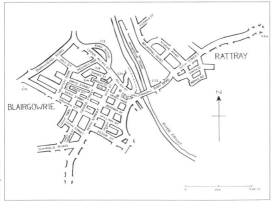

BLAIRGOWRIE & RATTRAY
Set on Highland Boundary Fault between lowland and highland, and divided by River Ericht into Blairgowrie and Old and New Rattrays, burgh has an unusually disparate urban character. Old village of Blairgowrie gathered round ancient site of parish kirk on Hill of Blair, until it became a free burgh of barony, 1809, when orderly grid plan of Blairgowrie proper was laid out. Old Rattray, on east bank of the Ericht, similarly had, and retains, nucleated plan round parish kirk. New Rattray a less sustained attempt at a grid pattern. Although officially united as Blairgowrie & Rattray Burgh in 1929, the old centres are still distinct, each with its own architectural character.

Top *Pagoda roof, Hill Church.*
Above *Brown Street.*

213 **Hill Church**, Hill of Blair, 1824, possibly William Stirling
Built on the commanding hilltop site of its predecessor above the Cuttle Burn Den, sadly derelict Hill Church remarkable for its tall slender tower capped with exaggerated pagoda roof.

Tulach, Kirk Wynd, *c.*1800
Small plain classical mansion with Roman Ionic columns to porch and pedimented side elevations.

The grid pattern of Blairgowrie is approached from the south by **Perth Road**, where an extraordinary number of original cast-iron railings and gates survived removal and melting down for the war effort. Now difficult to believe that virtually every street in the country was once enlivened by these highly decorative ironwork fences.

The density of building in the new grid pattern of Blairgowrie is at its greatest in **High Street**. **Queen's Hotel**, 21 High Street, late 18th century, has three-storey classical frontage to High Street, pedimented at the centre with urns on the skewputts. **Brown Street** leads up the hill from High Street in regimented steps on axis to **Old**
214 **Bank House**, 1837, handsome classical former
215 Commercial Bank. Red sandstone **Town Hall**, Brown Street, is early 19th century in origin, but reconstructed with two regal classical windows opening on to a balcony in a spirit of civic jubilation at the end of the war in 1939; hall to rear by John Carver of Kinloch, 1860. Solid early 19th-century domesticity in **George Street**, running parallel to High Street, and terminating at **13-15 James Street**, 1832. **St Catherine's Episcopal**
216 **Church**, George Street, 1841–2, John Henderson, has aisleless nave and chancel with five lancets to the front; four-centred ribbed timber ceiling.
217 Higher up the grid, **St Stephen's RC School**, 1841, single-storey symmetrical former parochial school with triple-arched and pedimented centre portico, terminates John
218 Street axis. **St Andrew's Church**, James Street, early 20th century, has West Coast look, probably heightened by use of red sandstone. Tall slender tower not quite resolved by dumpy pinnacles and short stone spire. Fine traceried east window.

Hawthornbank, Newton Terrace, 1839
Pretty little neoclassical villa with two-storey centre and wooden colonnade of Greek Doric columns between single-storey bay windows.

St Stephen's RC School.

Newton of Blairgowrie.

Reputedly sacked by both Cromwell and Montrose, **Newton of Blairgowrie** endured a troubled existence in the mid-17th century. **George Drummond**, 1687–1766, six times Lord Provost of Edinburgh, was born at Newton. Drummond was a great civic reformer in the capital, raising funds for the first infirmary, establishing five medical professorships at the University, and initiating construction of the North Bridge and the New Town. Thomas Graham, **Lord Lynedoch** (see p.81), was also born in the house.

219 **Newton of Blairgowrie**, Newton Street, late 16th century
High above the town and overlooking the broad sweep of Strathmore, Newton is a delightful harled Z-plan *château*. Main unvaulted three-storey-and-attic block has square stairtower adjoined at south-east corner, and circular tower, perhaps a fashionable bedroom stack, corbelled to square-plan at attic storey of north-west corner. 1883 wing to rear. Fine panelled principal rooms, *c*.1700.

Below *Royal Hotel*. Bottom *Wellmeadow*.

220 **Royal Hotel**, 53 Allan Street, 1852, makes an elegant classical full-stop on High Street as the main road takes a sharp right bend into Allan Street; three storeys of five windows, capped with scrolled blocking course. **Allan Street** itself broadens into **Wellmeadow**, effectively the town square. Western side a unified run of high quality
221 mid-19th-century shops and tenements, **Nos 29** and **30** with ground-floor arcade, probably Andrew Heiton Sr & Son, 1851, for Perth Banking Company. On east side, mixed bag including old 1930s' cinema and eccentric onion-domed corner shop with half-timbering, early 20th century. At the centre, **War Memorial**, 1920, Reginald Fairlie, comprises poignant bronze figure of a mourning soldier, sculpted by A Carrick, in front of octagonal column supporting carved stone pelican with upraised wings (colour p.223).

222 **Dome Café**, 14-20 Leslie Street, 1920s
Not promising of architectural delights from outside, but some of the gloriously florid interior survives, halfway between the refinement of a Glasgow tea-room and robust opulence of an Edwardian pub. Inside complete with flattened ribbed dome, horseshoe counter and embossed friezes. Unfortunately, painted glass seat-backs, bevelled mirrors, painted panelled walls do not survive.

Riverside Methodist Church.

NEW RATTRAY
Elegant arches of mid-19th-century **Bridge of Blair** survive beneath rather brutal later 20th-century concrete deck. **Ericht Bank**, off Boat Brae, *c.*1800, genteel cottage with delicate umbrella fanlight and wallhead nepus gable.

223 **Riverside Methodist Church**, Boat Brae, 1887, David Smart, with mid-Decorated style windows and broached stone spire, a picture-book image of an English country church, translated to red sandstone and bosky setting beside the Ericht. Surprisingly old-fashioned for date and architect is **Tordarroch**, Balmoral Road, 1862, John Honeyman, £1,577, for David Clarke, all cottagey gables and Tudor hoodmoulds.

OLD RATTRAY
224 **Rattray East Church**, High Street, 1820, William Stirling
A standard heritors' design with four large round-headed windows, modified by the addition of an unusually slender Italianate west tower.

Below Westfield, Brook Inn and Keathbank Mills. Bottom Old Mains of Rattray.

Blairgowrie was long a centre of extensive handloom and hand-spinning industry before construction of Meikle Mill on the River Ericht, 1798. From then abundant free power of the river and Lornty Burn spawned a rash of new linen and jute mills and associated owners' houses. A selection survives following the river northwards
225 from the town centre: **Keathbank Mill**, Westfield of Rattray, 1864–5, John Kerr & Co, probably best preserved and most unusual, combining water and steam power, now museum/visitor centre. Earlier water-powered mill, 1820–30, renewed and extended 1865 for Matthew Low, spinner, to accommodate brick chimneystack and single cylinder horizontal steam engine, still in situ. **Ashgrove Works**, mid-19th century, raised and interior reconstructed *c.*1950, the largest, driven by massive waterwheel, 24ft diameter and 19ft width. **Lornty Mill**, dated 1755, but thought to be built, 1814, for David Grimond, interesting early group, complete with gatehouse, offices, cottages and owner's house. Further north, beyond Bridge of Cally on the wild, scenic Black Water is **Netherton**, picturesque mid-19th-century vernacular grouping of rubble-built mill (rather severely converted to house) and whitewashed mill house, smithy, cottages and little gothic Free Church Mission, 1872.

Old Mains of Rattray, 1694
Sadly ruinous remains of two-storey, symmetrical

three-bay laird's house for David Crichton. Grotesque heads to skewputts. Wing dated 1720, incorporating tower house fragments.

Craighall-Rattray.

The Heitons
Another of the great architectural dynasties of Perth. Andrew Heiton Senior was born c.1793 and is first recorded as an architect undertaking repairs to Forteviot Church in association with William Stirling of Dunblane, 1830. His son, Andrew Heiton Junior, born in 1823, served his father and the Burn/Bryce office as an apprentice. From 1848, he joined his father in partnership as Andrew Heiton Sr & Son, continuing the family firm after his father's death in 1858, eventually establishing a branch office of this prolific practice in Dundee in 1865. From the late 1880s Heiton Jr was assisted by his nephew, Andrew Heiton Grainger, who in turn inherited the practice in 1894, reversing his name to become Andrew Grainger Heiton. Assistants and pupils in the office included John Murray Robertson (from 1859–73), William Leiper (briefly c.1862) and James Miller (from 1875–80).

Craighall-Rattray, *c.*1830, Andrew Heiton Sr
Dramatically sited on cliff above River Ericht, mansion incorporates earlier work, some *c.*1825, in centre tower. Pleasing combination of whinstone with red sandstone dressings, in Abbotsford-baronial style, perhaps in tribute to Walter Scott, who visited the old house in 1793 and made it part basis of his fictional Tullyveolain Castle in *Waverley*. Large three-storey tower added by Andrew Heiton Jr, *c.*1890. Fine mural monument and half-length effigy to Bartholomew Somerville, *c.*1640, from John Mylne's professor's house and six chambers (demolished 1790) at Edinburgh University, incorporated into east wall.

Gatehouse to Glenericht Lodge, A93, early 19th century
Wonderfully eccentric Gothick gatehouse with crazy glazing and little empty statue niches on either side of pedimented porch.

226 **Haughs of Drimmie Suspension Bridge**, *c.*1830, John Justice Jr (Dundee)
Beautifully delicate wrought-iron suspension bridge over River Ericht, built for Colonel Chalmers of Glenericht Lodge. Pairs of pylons at each end anchored to riverbank and attached rod-stays suspend the bridge deck across 32m span. Bridge wide enough to carry a carriageway and footpath. Enlarged and modified version of Kirkton of Glenisla Footbridge, Angus, by the same firm. Pretty Gothick lodge nearby.

227 **Cray Church**, Glenshee, 1844
Attractive plain gothic former Free Church, given small tower with fish-scale pyramidal roof, 1864. Horseshoe arrangement of pews.

Below *Haughs of Drimmie suspension bridge.* Bottom *Cray Church, Glenshee.*

Trevor Wain

Dalnaglar Castle.

Dalnaglar Castle, Glenshee, earlier 19th century
Given the Disneyland baronial treatment of
harled towers, crenellations and pepperpot
turrets in 1864. There appears to be an older,
more sedate house at the core of the baronial riot.

228 Glenshee Church of Scotland,
Spittal of Glenshee, 1831
Chapel of ease of traditional restrained design:
simple rectangle with three round-arched
windows and bellcote. Tiny gallery at one end,
pulpit at the other.

Glenshee Bridge, mid-18th century
Humpbacked rubble bridge on Blairgowrie to
Braemar military road, constructed 1749–63.

RCAHMS/J B White

Patrick Allan-Fraser, born Patrick
Allan, married the daughter and heiress
of the Revd James Fraser of
Hospitalfield. With his new wife, name,
and fortune, Allan-Fraser transformed
his properties at Hospitalfield and
Blackcraig in extravagantly romantic
medieval styles, amassed a large art
collection, and was generous in his
patronage of arts students, eventually
leaving Hospitalfield and its contents
for the purpose of art education.
Gladstone rented Blackcraig for at least
one summer.

Right *Blackcraig Castle*. Below *Blackcraig
Bridge*.

Irene Hemmings

229 Blackcraig Castle, Strathardle, from 16th century
Seriously baronial fantasy developed from 1856
by owner/architect Patrick Allan-Fraser, based
round substantial remains of tower house,
probably 16th century, clearly seen to the rear,
where original random rubble tower has been
completed with cap-house and parapet of cut
blocks. New mansion a very early and creditable
revival of the more vernacular/domestic end of
the baronial tradition: rubbly, asymmetrical, well-
studied proportions and grouping, not too flashy
in its detailing or skyline. Definitely more
fantastical is **Blackcraig Bridge**, 1870, also Patrick
Allan-Fraser, enclosed, mock-fortified medieval
bridge over the Ericht, worthy of Camelot itself.
Wonderful gothic gatepiers, 1856, with crouching
dogs; even the walled garden is fortified with
corner towers.

KIRKMICHAEL

Third largest of Perthshire's Highland parishes, encompassing most of the wild mountainous glens of Strathardle and Glen Shee, and stretching from Bridge of Cally in the south to the border with Aberdeenshire at the Cairnwell in the north. Remoter parts of the parish were largely untouched by destructive late 18th/early 19th-century Improvement farming methods and are therefore comparatively rich in archaeological remains, particularly prehistoric hut-circles and ring-ditches. Lower down, extensive remains of Improvement era lime kilns, notably those at Balnakilly, Dalnagairn and Milton.

Kirkmichael was once the centre of a thriving cattle trade. Bannerfield, now the recreation ground, is the site of the start of the 1715 Jacobite Rising, where the Earl of Mar first raised the banner of the Old Pretender.

230 **Kirkmichael & Straloch Parish Kirk**, 1791
Simple harled T-plan kirk with Venetian windows in gable walls and birdcage bellcote. Galleried interior renovated 1893, when porch probably added by John Sim (Montrose). No visible remains of medieval parish kirk of St Michael, recorded in 1189, which probably stood on the site. The 18th-century session house, former school, stands adjacent to the kirk.

Kirkmichael & Straloch Parish Kirk.

Kirkmichael Bridge, 1840
Fine two-arched bridge over River Ardle, built by public subscription.

Ashintully Castle, Strathardle, 1583
Remote, but fashionable, stepped L-plan mansion by Andro Spadyne (Spalding), perhaps in emulation of another Spalding property at Whitefield, almost identical in size and layout. Bold roll-moulded doorway with fine balusters framing armorial panel above, bearing motto 'THE LORD DEFEND THIS HOVS'. Corbelled viewing platform, built in the manner of a wallwalk, seems to have been an early feature. Ruinous by 1783, house revived and extended by four bays, probably 1831 – date of renewed crowsteps and wallwalk. Further late 19th-century additions and 20th-century modifications.

Below *Ashintully Castle.*
Bottom *Whitefield Castle.*

231 **Whitefield Castle**, Strathardle, 1577
Dramatic ruinous neighbour and antecedent of Ashintully. Over doorway in re-entrant angle, dated round-arched niche for armorial. Impressive groin-vaulted scale-and-platt stair to hall at principal floor. From here corbelled turnpike stair accessed upper floors. Plentiful gunloops. House altered, 18th century, and abandoned at beginning of 19th, when roof and some stones removed to build shepherd's house.

Balvarran House.

Balvarran House, Enochdhu, mid-18th century
Plain and solid harled five-bay house, probably
incorporating earlier structure, as suggested by
pronounced batter of walls and 1641
inscription. Curved porch and entrance hall,
1895, Robert Lorimer (colour p.156).

Appleton Studio, Enochdhu, 1980s, Ian Appleton
Earliest of Perthshire's new eco-houses. Timber
structure with turf roof planned around central
lookout tower.

232 **Kindrogan Field Centre**, Enochdhu,
earlier 19th century
Broad, low and symmetrical white harled
mansion, broad crowstepped gables with single
chimneys in outer bays; converted for Scottish
Field Studies Association, 1963.

Former Straloch Church, 1846
Built as chapel of ease to assist church attendance
for more remote parishioners. Surprising Greek-
Cross plan and exhibiting more than usual basic
level of decoration in its neo-perpendicular
traceried windows. Now converted to house.

Old Stronchavie Bridge, Dalnacarn,
earlier 19th century
Bypassed single-arch rubble bridge, part of
Thomas Telford's ambitious highland
road-building programme.

Edradour Distillery, Balnauld, 1837
Smallest distillery in Scotland, last of the
traditional 'farm' type containing some
outstanding early equipment, including malt-
mill, refrigerator and little spirit-still.
Public tours

In 1851 a missionary was appointed
from the Royal Bounty, an annual
Crown grant first established in 1725 by
George I for *fostering loyalty* and *putting
down popery* in the Highlands.

*Edradour Distillery, section through Still
House.*

Key to parts:
A   Mash Tun
B   Stirrers
C   Draff Door
D   Wash-pump
E   Wash-charger
F   Wash-still pipe
G   Wash-still
H   Old Furnace
I   Later steam pipes
J   Lyne arm
K   Wash-worm
L   Pot-ale pipe
M   Drain

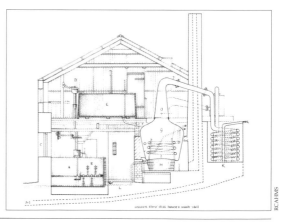

MOULIN

The village is dominated by the **Moulin Hotel**, large white harled L-plan with gabled dormers, partly dating from the early 18th century.

233 **Moulin Parish Church**, 1830–1
Constructed on a pre-Reformation site, present kirk, with angle buttresses, trefoil windows and dumpy tower, rebuilt by James Campbell Walker after fire, 1873. Tower altered by the addition of little spire, and gallery moved to south wall.

Caisteal Dubh Mhasthlinne, 13th century
Standing in a field south of the church, fragments of only remaining corner tower of quadrangular Black Castle of Moulin, reputedly destroyed by fire for fear of plague, *c.*1500. Surrounding shallow loch drained, early 18th century, now cultivated. Remains of stone path (possibly causeway) from Balnadrum visible in the 1920s.

Balnakeilly House, 1821, probably Charles Sim
Possibly some James Gillespie (Graham) involvement here. Five-bay classical mansion built of rubble with channelled long and short dressings. Centre pedimented with date stone, outer bays advanced. Fine Roman Doric doorpiece. Similar to Auchleeks House (see p.160).

The route of the guide now returns to Perth and starts out along the A94 to Coupar Angus.

NEW SCONE

Now a dormitory suburb of Perth, New Scone owes its existence to the 3rd Earl of Mansfield's decision to relocate the village of Scone from its ancient site beside Scone Palace to the Perth/Coupar Angus road in 1804. **Cross of New Scone**, 1841, is a replica of the original mercat cross, which remains at Scone Palace.

234 **Parish Church**, 1804
The first building to be moved from the old village, the parish church was only 20 years old when it was rebuilt on this site at the expense of the Earl of Mansfield. The severe rectangular box was augmented by a further aisle in 1870. Inside, exceptional Stormont Pew, 1616, huge and columned with two coats of arms and elaborate finials, presented to 1st Lord Stormont by Anne of Denmark, wife of James VI. **Monument** to David Douglas in the kirkyard.

Naturally divided in two by the mountains. The western Atholl portion of Moulin Parish is dominated by the distinctive features of Ben Vrackie, the man-made reservoir of Loch Faskally and turbulent rapids of the River Garry through the Pass of Killiecrankie. The less-populated eastern portion forms the upper reaches of Strathardle. Ancient sites include the stone circle at Faskally Cottages and the smaller one on the south-west flank of Faire na Paitig. Gaelic names predominate; the language was used at weekly kirk services until 1895.

Top *Moulin Hotel.* Above *Moulin Parish Church.*

The great botanist and seedsman, **David Douglas**, 1799–1834, after whom the Douglas Fir is named, was born at Scone and apprenticed to the head gardener at Scone Palace in 1809. As under-gardener at Glasgow Botanical Garden, Douglas was recommended by Professor William Hooker to take part in the Horticultural Society's plant-hunting expedition to China. Athough this did not take place, Douglas joined the replacement trip to North America in 1823. Subsequent visits to the west, particularly to what are now the states of Washington and Oregon, and the province of British Coumbia, introduced at least 215 new plants to Britain, including the Grand Fir, the Californian poppy and the flowering currant. On return from one of his trips via Hawaii in 1834, Douglas fell into a wild bull trap and was killed by the occupant.

Top *Scone New Church*. Above *Robert Douglas Memorial School*.

St Martin's
Said to derive its name from St Martin of Tours, the parish combined with Cambusmichael in the late 17th century, broadly to encompass the lands now falling between the Perth/Forfar and Perth/Blairgowrie roads. Balbeggie and Guildtown are the principal settlements, the latter established in 1818 by the Guildry Incorporation of Perth.

Below *St Martin's Parish Church*.
Bottom *St Martin's Abbey*.

Scone New Church, Perth Road, 1887, Sydney Mitchell & Wilson
Built as Free Church, distinguished Scots gothic in crisp red Corsehill sandstone from Dumfriesshire (colour p.222). Landmark tower with crowstepped cap-house and splendid wrought-iron finial. Plain, but impressive, interior to seat 400, lined with Alloa red brick; arcaded aisles and barrel-vaulted roof. Italianate former manse, **20 Murrayshall Road**, mid-19th century, possibly Andrew Heiton Sr & Son.

Robert Douglas Memorial School, Stormont Road, 1935
Striking red brick inter-war classical school, capped with splendid columned cupola. Established in memory of Robert Douglas (1859–1929), who made his fortune in the USA, and left money to his native town for charitable and educational purposes (colour p.224). Former Board School, Abbey Road, 1876, picturesque gothic with polygonal flèche, now **Robert Douglas Memorial Institute**.

Bonhard House, 1847–9
Red sandstone Jacobean mansion in Burn/Bryce mould, entered by three-storey tower with buckle quoins and ogee roof. Tall chimneys, square corner turrets and strapwork dormerheads. Half-timbered gardener's cottage an apprentice-piece by Robert Lorimer.

Two notable monuments adorn Murrayshall Hill. **McDuff's Monument**, 18th century, small and incomplete round tower erected by the McDuffs of Bonhard, partly as an eye-catcher. At the top of the hill, **Lynedoch Obelisk**, 1850, commemorating Thomas Graham, Lord Lynedoch (see p.35).

235 **St Martin's Parish Church**, 1842, Andrew Heiton Sr
Solid Tudor-gothic edifice, beautifully located on an ancient knoll, partly encircled by St Martin's Burn. Cruciform, with shallow transepts and distinctive octagonal bellcote. Fine original interior has particularly good pulpit with double stair and crocketed sounding board. Small pyramidal-roofed **session house** in churchyard; many interesting 18th-century gravestones.

St Martin's Abbey, 1791–3
Edinburgh lawyer and Writer to the Signet, William Farquharson McDonald, resolved: *to build a good house, tho' at considerable expense, and marked out the ground after 15 years' experience on the most*

commodious spot (Diary, 1791). Designed in typical post-Adam classical style with Venetian window and pediment to south entrance bay, and central bow to rear, the house and estate allowed McDonald to put into practice his agricultural theories, devised as a founder of the Royal Highland and Agricultural Society of Scotland. Little round-arched windowed **chapel** of 1842–3 adjoins to east. Policies re-landscaped by Craigie-Halket, 1858. Two years later David Bryce built a large addition, re-oriented to enter from north, and remodelled the interior. Apart from re-positioned porch, little of Bryce's work survives, as house was reduced and internally remodelled in retro 18th-century style by A G Heiton, 1921. **Stable block** unusual: single-storey north-east range appears to be early 18th century with doocot tower, probably

The colossal unexecuted 1869 Peddie & Kinnear scheme to rebuild St Martin's Abbey in the style of a French château.

heightened and capped with pyramidal roof by Peddie & Kinnear, *c.*1869; taller adjoining ranges enclose courtyard, entered through pedimented archway in elegant bowed south-west range, early 19th century. **Obelisk**, Dove Craig, 1834, memorial to Maj. Gen. Farquharson, Governor of St Lucia.

Rosefield, 1792, W Scott and D Davidson
Built for William McDonald of St Martin's as a post-house and inn. Two-storey, three-bay design with polygonal porch and single-storey wing.

KINROSSIE
Pretty broad linear fermtoun of single-storey cottages, largely dating from late 18th century, but retaining its **mercat cross**, dated 1686 (colour p.223). Many cottages were still reed-thatched well into the 20th century, but only **No 31** continues the tradition. Boxy Free Church, 1843, converted to **village hall**, 1962. Jerkin-roofed **Bonarwood**, 1848, on the Perth Road, was the manse.

Thatched cottages behind Kinrossie Market Cross, late 19th century.

236

COLLACE

Be lion-mettled, proud; and take no care Who chafes, who frets, or where conspirers are:
Macbeth shall never vanquish'd be, until Great Birnam wood to high Dunsinane hill Shall come against him.
William Shakespeare, *Macbeth*, Act IV, Scene I

From top *Dunsinane Hillfort; chancel arch, Collace Parish Church; Dunsinnan House; Drawing room, Keithick House.*

COLLACE

Largely flat apart from Dunsinane Hill, supposed site of Macbeth's castle. More certain is the spectacular prehistoric multivallate fort on the summit. Early history too has left its mark in the rare form of a broch, high up on Little Dunsinane Hill, probably dating from the early centuries AD.

Collace Parish Church, 1813, possibly James Gillespie (Graham)
Effectively a hall church with tower, but decked out in scholarly neo-perpendicular garb of some quality, possibly gleaned from John Britton's *Architectural Antiquities* of the same year. Landmark in the history of Gothic Revival church design in Scotland, marking the transition from generalised gothic forms to antiquarian gothic proper. Among the fine 18th-century gravestones of the churchyard, **Nairne Mausoleum**, constructed in 1812 from bits of the old kirk, including exceptional chancel arch, possibly dating from the church's dedication in 1242. Vaulted **mort-house**, also early 19th century.

Dunsinnan House, mid-18th century
Three-storey house, much extended earlier 19th century for James Mellis Nairne, and given an almost institutional long, low, classical front by John Wotherston, 1899. Symmetrical U-plan **stables** have slightly later Edwardian feel, with stylised thermal windows and tall entrance gatepiers. **Home Farm**, early 19th century, comprises modest pedimented house with single-storey pavilion wings, U-plan steading behind.

Old Bandirran House, 1811–12, David Whyte (demolished 1957)
Seven-bay classical house, three central bays bowed in late Adam manner. Unusually, the gentleman farmer-architect from Newtyle employed a U-plan, perhaps encasing, or re-using the footprint of an earlier structure. Surviving double lectern **doocot**, very similar to now collapsed Bonhard Doocot of 1709 (see p.178).

Keithick House, 1818–23, David Whyte
Built for W E Collinswood in earthy red sandstone. Elegant neoclassical design with projecting ends and central semicircular porch under overhanging shallow piended roof. Some remodelling already undertaken before David Bryce made minor alterations to porch and offices, 1839. Exceptional Adam Revival painted decorative scheme by Morant in drawing room. Symmetrical

180

stables/steading, c.1810, entered by tower with elliptical archway below arcaded doocot. Complementary **lodges** with proto-Doric columns.

Above *Keithick House*. Left *Coupar Angus, 1843.*

COUPAR ANGUS

Small settlement may have existed before Cistercians arrived from Melrose in 1161, but it was not until construction of the great abbey south of the large meandering loop in the River Isla that a lay community of any size took shape. Surviving street plan almost certainly has foundations in the medieval period, although there is no documentary and little archaeological evidence for its early form. Unusually for a Scottish burgh, the plan radiates from a central market place, The Cross, rather than the normal axial street with herringbone pattern of wynds or vennels leading off. As a result, High Street is reputedly the shortest in the country. Constituted a burgh of barony, 1607, and transferred from Angus to Perthshire in 1891. In the 18th century the town served as a resting place for Hanoverian troops on the route to the Highlands. Apart from its strategic location and agricultural market status, Coupar Angus thrived on the linen industry. The main thoroughfares of Calton Street and Causewayend were augmented by George Street and Union Street in early 19th century. Finally the A94 Relief Road, following the route of the 1837 railway, bisected the town in the late 1990s.

237 **Coupar Angus Abbey**, Queen Street, late 12th/earlier 13th century
All that remains of once rich and extensive Cistercian abbey is archway at meeting point of Queen Street and Dundee Road. Precise extent of abbey complex and its appearance are not known, as it was much damaged during the Reformation, and largely demolished, 1686, for new parish church. Parts of conventual buildings may have been incorporated into houses on

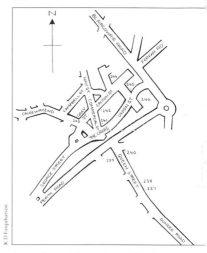

Coupar Angus Abbey: below *by Timothy Pont;* bottom *archway.*

opposite side of Queen Street. Even the function of surviving arch is obscure: purported as entrance gate through precinct wall, but close proximity to site of abbey church (thought to be where present Abbey Church stands) may suggest an entrance to another part of the complex, such as the cloister.

238 **Abbey Church**, Queen Street, 1859–60, John Carver
Replacement parish church for that of 1686. Restrained but effective design in Early Pointed gothic, presumably in recognition of abbey's original foundation in late 12th century. Buttressed aisles, large traceried west window and slated spirelet. Impressive interior with splendid hammerbeam roof and relics of previous churches including recumbent effigy of Sir Thomas Hay, 3rd Constable of Scotland, font created from part of an abbey column and 'The Weepers', early 16th-century low relief panel of figures in mourning. Polygonal **Watch House**, 1829, and **Murray of Simprin Mausoleum**, c.1850, plain Tudor, in kirkyard.

239 **The Steeple**, Queen Street, 1762
The town's landmark, six-storey tower with tall swept and fish-scale slated spire, clocks to each face, built by public subscription as the tolbooth. Ground floor housed gaol for Court of Regality, which sat in rooms above.

240 North of the Steeple is **Strathmore Hotel**, late 18th century, coaching inn with later log porch, originally known as White House or White Horse Inn. Across the Relief Road, High Street broadens into the triangular shape of **The Cross**, heart of the medieval street layout. **Royal Hotel**, High Street, c.1840 and later 19th-century mansard roof/corner tower, dominates west side of The Cross – two-storey adjunct in George Street was the town's Assembly Rooms. North-
241 east is **Corner Shop**, late 18th-century block with exotic ogee dome added at the corner. Unsympathetic glazing spoils adjacent **3 Commercial Street**, attractive early 19th-century town house with fine columned doorpiece and tympanum gable.

At the end of Commercial Street is
242 **Cumberland Barracks**, 2 Calton Street, dated 1766 on skews, but possibly in part of 17th-century origin. L-plan with re-entrant stairtower and broad harled frontage of five windows and central wallhead gable, but looks odd without any chimneys. Opposite, **2 Hay Street**, late 18th

century, has good moulded doorpiece. **Gray Street** has some handsome early 19th-century
243 town houses, in particular **No 7**, which sports blind Venetian window and pediment at first floor, topped with brick chimney. Old school, now **Masonic Buildings**, Gray Street, notable for round-arched windows at first floor, of similar date. From The Cross, **Causewayend** still has tight-knit urban density, with two-storey houses standing hard up against the pavement.

    Calton Street, old north-eastern route through town, with **Hill Street** leading off, retains vestiges of late 18th-century housing, **Aviemore** the smartest, with urns on the skewputts and typical Coupar Angus polygonal porch. At east
244 end, **Watson & Lyall Bowie**, elegant late 18th-century house with first-floor Venetian window, extended by early 19th-century bow-fronted wing. Some good villas on **Blairgowrie Road**.

Above *7 Gray Street*. Left *Town Hall and Library*.

245 **Town Hall and Library**, Union Street and Calton Street, 1887
Decorous French renaissance *château* erected with civic pride and £4,000 to celebrate Queen Victoria's jubilee.

246 **St Catherine's Lane Maltings**, later 19th century
Two distinctive kiln blocks with pyramid roofs front the Relief Road, clearly built at different times from the colour of stonework. Three large ranges of malt-barns adjoin behind.

247 **Bridge of Couttie**, River Isla, 1766, Major Caulfield
Graceful three-arch span over River Isla and two land arches, all widened by construction of secondary arches with lower centres on cutwaters.

Below *St Catherine's Lane Maltings*. Bottom *Bridge of Couttie*.

Above *John Cumming effigy, Bendochy Parish Kirk.* Right *Coupar Grange House.*

Bendochy Parish Kirk, 17th century
Gothicised long, low, rectangle, possibly incorporating pre-Reformation material, from when the parish included Coupar Angus. Blocked openings from 17th-century rebuilding still visible, although thoroughly remodelled with gothic windows, porch and transepts, 1885, Alexander Johnston (Dundee). Interesting remnants of past glories including early 16th-century aumbry donated by William Turnbull, Abbot of Coupar Angus, 16th-century pulpit minus sounding board, Burgerhuys bells and strangely medieval-looking **effigy** of John Cumming of Couttie (died 1606), decked out in armour with his feet resting on a dog. In 1885, 17th-century ogee-capped bellcote set up in garden of plain but picturesque **manse**, 1815. **War Memorial lych gate**, 1922, Reginald Fairlie, simple and beautifully crafted.

Coupar Grange House, *c.*1900, James Miller
Hermann Muthesius referred to Miller as one of *a small group of Scottish architects stirred by the wind of modernity* (*Das Englische Haus*, 1904). Well demonstrated at Coupar Grange, where external decorative treatment restrained, relying on more formal qualities of massing, and very definitely subordinate to the modern plan, function and materials. Result quite English-looking, after the manner of Voysey, with long, low gabled profile, tall corniced chimneys, broad strips of casement glazing and columned veranda. Interior was more conventionally opulent Jacobean in late 19th-century fashion. Pretty U-plan grouping of **Coupar Grange Cottages**, also by Miller, in English alms house tradition, also with small-pane casement windows, tall cornices, chimneys and columned porches.

Polcalk Farm, from 17th century
Interesting small farm complex which evolved gradually and escaped wholescale Improvement approach of building all functions into monolithic

steading. Harled **farmhouse** of three widely spaced bays with round-headed window in central wallhead gable, dated 1789. Lectern **doocot** may be 17th century in origin, crenellated 18th century and joined to earlier 19th-century water-powered **threshing mill**. Later 19th-century covered **cattle court**. Survival of little pitched roofed **bee house** particularly unusual.

248 **Kettins Parish Kirk**, from 1768
Approached by well-crafted English medieval style **lych gate**, 1902, J H Fowler Jones of York. Kirk itself standard heritors' design, originally entered and lit by south side, but now entered from north where small spired bell tower added, 1891, Alexander Hutcheson. Stained glass gifted by Lord Hallyburton, 1878. Interesting ancient kirkyard with remains of market cross, now topped with pre-Reformation font, old bellcote, complete with 1519 Flemish bell and 1768 dated finial, and much-weathered massive cross-slab. Lovely old **manse**, 1792, adjacent.

Pitcur Castle, early 16th century
Ruinous L-plan tower house of Hallyburtons, at centre of working farm. Severe blockish appearance, caused by squared-off wallheads. Circular stairtower in re-entrant angle, but entered by round-arched doorway in northern jamb. Remains of high courtyard wall.

Hallyburton House, from c.1680
Built to replace Pitcur. Much remodelled in 18th century, and again, c.1886, in Elizabethan manor-house style by Andrew Heiton Jr. New dining-room wing, 1903, Robert Lorimer.

Larghan House, mid to later 18th century
Manse-like two-storey house, extended by fashionable two-storey wing with tripartite windows, c.1790. Later log-columned veranda.

Isla Park, 1838
Quietly sophisticated classical house. Finely detailed ashlar three-window front with advanced centre, outer pilasters and Ionic-columned doorpiece.

From top *Polcalk Farmhouse; Kettins Parish Kirk; Lych gate; Pitcur Castle.*

249 **Arthurstone House**, c.1789
Impressive ivy-clad red sandstone classical mansion with angled centre rising full three storeys. Office wing 1797, and ogee-roofed water tower, 1838, George Steele. Doubly doomed fate attended William Burn's 1836 Jacobean north

wing for Patrick Murray of Simprim, demolished 1855, largely rebuilt at Cardean east of Meigle and demolished again, 1955. Spectacular castellated tower folly set behind greenhouses in **walled garden**, which also contains quirky Gothick summerhouse and 'Antiquarian Corner' of built-in fragments from Coupar Angus Abbey, including outstanding early 14th-century funereal slab depicting Christ in majesty. Lectern **doocot**, 1610, brought from beside UP Church in Coupar Angus by master mason, D Reid, 1883. Estate named after supposed relic of King Arthur, built into Arthurbank Farm, 1791.

250 **Ardler Village**, 1835, George Mathewson
Idyllic sleepy village, on grid plan, similar to nearby Newtyle, but with addition of two circular streets. Plan never fully completed and only three main streets, **Bentham Street**, **Church** (originally Kinloch) **Street** and **Wallace Street**, were feued and built, largely comprising single-storey cottages. Following demolition of the inn, **Washington House** is the only surviving two-storey building from first phase of construction, 1835–41, probably built by George Kinloch as a tenement. Plain Tudor-gothic **Ardler School**, 1839, extended in like fashion 1889. Former **Ardler Church**, 1881–5, Alexander Johnston, discreetly converted to house, 1988, has the scale of a cathedral in such a low-slung setting, but in spite of its incongruity forms very handsome Gothic Revival focus to the village. Renaissance burial enclosure to Carmichaels of Arthurstone, founders of the church.

Top *Arthurstone House*. Middle *Arthurstone greenhouses*. Above *Ardler Church*.

Ardler village was partially built to a plan drawn up for George Kinloch Jr, son of the Radical laird and first MP for Dundee, George Kinloch of Kinloch. The village was initially known as Washington, after the US president, and the streets were named in honour of Kinloch Senior's other political and philosophical heroes, Jeremy Bentham, William Wallace, Benjamin Franklin, John Hampden, and Major John Cartwright. Ambitious in its planned provision of an inn, station, school, church and nearly 200 dwelling plots, Washington was a partly philanthropic, partly commercial venture, as a transport depot for the surrounding farms, based on the arrival of the horse-drawn Dundee, Newtyle & Coupar Angus Railway.

Kings of Kinloch, A94, *c.*1800
Originally Kinloch House, square-plan copybook classical house, later uncomfortably sandwiched between entrance tower and rear wing, *c.*1860. On opposite side of A94, **Kinloch of Kinloch Mausoleum**, 1861, John Carver, Romanesque family burial aisle with little tower, reputedly on site of St Mary's Chapel, pre-Reformation chapel on Coupar Angus grange of Balbrogie.

MEIGLE
Picturesque qualities of warm red sandstone buildings gathered round hilltop kirk are slightly dissipated by A94 weaving through heart of the village. West of the square and right beyond the garage is **Old Bank House**, 1771, probably miller's house of some pretension with Venetian window in wallhead gable. At Wortley Place, old **Angel Inn**, coaching inn of 18th-century origins,

remodelled *c.*1840 behind more regular front with central gable. Neighbouring building has good example of wallhead or nepus gable.

Meigle Parish Kirk, 1869, John Carver
Unusually large galleried kirk, somewhere between heritors' box and Gothic Revival. Although not very refined close up, pinnacled tower is a successful landmark for village. Inside, elaborately carved stone font salvaged from old kirk. Sir Henry Campbell-Bannerman, Prime Minister 1905–8, buried in kirkyard.

Meigle House, off Alyth Road, later 18th century
Much-altered harled classical house with bowed stairtower, extended by large early 19th-century polygonal-ended wing and re-oriented by addition of modest Tudor wing and entrance, 1834, William Burn.

Above *Meigle Parish Kirk.* Left *Meigle House Steading.*

Meigle appears to have been an important centre, perhaps monastic, by the mid-9th century, as evidenced by the exceptional number and quality of sculptured stones found within the old kirk of 1431 when it was destroyed by fire in 1869. Further fragments were discovered in the fabric of a malt-kiln at nearby Templehall on demolition in 1858.

Meigle House Steading, Alyth Road, *c.*1815
Extraordinary Gothick steading with pointed barrel vaults to interlinking ranges, in a state of considerable collapse. Of two pinnacled outer pavilions of main north front, only that to left (east) survives. From the back (south) ruinous vaults and mossy overgrown roofs have an atmosphere of Piranesian grandeur and picturesque decay.

251 **Meigle Museum**, *c.*1845
Tudor-gothic old schoolroom houses remarkable collection of local Pictish sculptured stones from 8th and 9th centuries, largely cross-slabs or recumbent monuments, also probable architectural fragments. Most notable is massive cross-slab No 2, carved with fabulous animals and powerful depiction of Daniel in the lion's den.
Historic Scotland; open to the public; guidebook

Detail of cross-slab No 2, Meigle Museum.

Old Balmacron, 1762
Single-storey L-plan house with symmetrical front and pyramidal roof to large square ancillary building.

Top *Belmont Castle.* Above *Lodges at entrance to Belmont Centre.*

Henry Campbell-Bannerman, 1836–1908, was Prime Minister from 1905 on the resignation of Balfour, until ill-health forced his own resignation in 1908, two weeks before he died. Second son of Glasgow Lord provost, Sir James Campbell, the name Bannerman was added to Henry Campbell's name in accordance with the will of his maternal uncle, who left him a fortune. From 1868 until his death Campbell-Bannerman represented Stirling Burghs as Liberal MP. Following a succession of posts, including Secretary to the Admiralty, Chief Secretary for Ireland, and Secretary for War, he was knighted in 1895, and succeeded Sir William Harcourt as leader of the Liberal Party in 1899.

Drumkilbo House.

Belmont Castle, from *c.*1500
Wonderful agglomeration of real tower house, toy castle and baronial mansion, now an Eventide home. The 16th-century Kirkhill Tower, largely subsumed by later works, can be partly seen, clad in ivy in the middle of east side – ground and first-floor vaulting survives inside, along with part of turnpike stair. Tower regularised and quadrangular classical house added, 1752, given Tudor treatment in earlier 19th century, when crenellations, offset chimneys, hoodmoulds and three-storey entrance tower flanked by round towers added. Disastrous fire, 1884, provided opportunity for more fashionable baronialisation by James Thomson of Baird & Thomson, Glasgow, for new owner Henry Campbell-Bannerman. Turrets and cap-house on old entrance tower, new east porch, service wings and splendid **stable court** (i.e. everything that is bull-faced masonry rather than harled) formed part of this scheme, as did opulent French rococo transformation of interior (colour p.221). Most impressive of four **lodges**, a pretty pair of crenellated boxes to either side of archway, earlier 19th century, stands next to cup-marked stone known as **Macbeth's Stone**, at entrance to **Belmont Centre** on Ardler road.

Drumkilbo House, 1920, Robert Lorimer Rambling mansion set in delightful gardens created from 1950. Tower house, reputedly 14th century, forms core, extended 1811 and 1851, extensively remodelled and north and west wings added in 17th-century vernacular style by Lorimer. Panelled drawing room with magnificent compartmental plaster ceiling filled with modelled garlands and low-relief foliate motifs. East dining-room wing added in similar style, 1963, Robert Hurd & Partners.

Bridge of Dean, Cardean, mid-19th century
Large semicircular arch with small side arch of
rusticated ashlar, erected by Admiral Popham.
Old Bridge, or so-called Roman Bridge, probably
originally 17th-century packbridge, partially
blown up by the Admiral, reconstructed, 1878,
incorporating odd sculptural fragments; repaired
and sculptural collection augmented, 2000,
Stewart Tod & Partners.

Hallyards House, 1731
Small T-plan mansion, harled with wallhead
chimney at centre of five-window entrance front.
Early 19th-century tripartite porch. Built for
Hendersons of Hallyards.

Balhary House, 1817–21, John Carver
Remarkably intact, charming classical red
sandstone mansion for lawyer John Smyth.
Central portico and tripartite window above to
short three-window entrance front. Long garden
elevation has central bay window rising to full
height. Particularly unusual quadrant form of
office court, 1821. Quadrangular **stable court**
with pediment and timber *porte-cochère*, 1839.
Extraordinarily delicate braced iron **footbridge**,
1830, leads to walled garden.

Top *Old Bridge of Dean*. Above *Balhary House*.

Bardmony Bank House, 1830
Small, elegant neo-Greek mansion incorporating
earlier fabric to rear. Two-storey, three-window
ashlar front, centre advanced and pedimented,
with fluted Greek Doric porch and segmental-
arched fanlight, giant pilasters at corners.

Jordanstone House, from late 18th century
Now appears as substantial symmetrical mansion
with pedimented wings, but reached this state by a
series of additions. Centre block, incorporating
earlier remains, a little late 18th-century harled
classical house with advanced centre and
pediment, long and short quoins. John Murray
Robertson added right-hand gabled wing, 1890,
and Lorimer & Matthew added matching left-hand
wing, 1929, to re-instate the symmetry. Beautifully
crafted interior designed by Lorimer & Matthew,
executed by Scott Morton & Co, fire damaged
1964, but carefully repaired. **Admiral Knight
Burial Enclosure**, 1788, built to house remains of
the agnostic Admiral (1710–88), who scandalised
the parish by insisting on burial in his own garden.

Below *Bardmony Bank House*.
Bottom *Jordanstone House*.

Balendoch House, *c*.1800
Lovely small classical country house, from

Balendoch House.

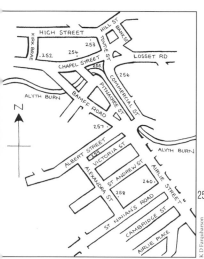

symmetrical manse/farmhouse tradition, but distinguished by Venetian doorpiece. Piend-roofed **doocot**, early 19th century.

Bridge of Ruim, Alyth Burn, 1713
Precarious nature of early 18th-century travel demonstrated by this unaltered narrow packhorse bridge, without parapets.

ALYTH

Irregular plan of old burgh of Alyth survives at The Cross, where Toutie, Hill and High Streets all meet, but demolitions have reduced density and picturesque jumble of buildings at the core. Further down the hill, the first new town of Alyth was laid out in a more sedate grid pattern from 1786. Tiny grid of New Alyth, outside the town proper, was established, 1833. Winding between old and new parts of town, Alyth Burn took on new importance in the townscape providing power to adjacent mills and a waterfront to the intermediate Commercial Street. The town flourished on linen manufacture and jute spinning in later 19th century, and was created a police burgh, 1875.

252 **Alyth Parish Kirk**, 1837–9, Thomas Hamilton
Perhaps not the most elegant design, but effective on commanding site at the top of the town. Hamilton's largest ecclesiastical building: idiosyncratic neo-Norman detailing married with Greek Cross plan and spire, all executed in warm red sandstone, quite unlike anything else in his oeuvre. Hamilton was called in by Court of Session to arbitrate on two competing designs and ended up producing his own more expensive replacement for the medieval kirk (colour p.222). Spacious galleried interior relatively plain, particularly after fire destroyed original organ case. Pictish cross-slab in porch.

253 **Old Parish Kirk of St Moluag**, late 15th century
Triple arcade of added south aisle, and piscina and aumbry in fragment of chancel wall, all that remain of the old kirk, abandoned 1839.

Old Parish Kirk of St Moluag.

Old Market Cross, 1670
In 1961, after several peregrinations, truncated shaft of the market cross returned to approximately its original position opposite the kirkyard gate, as first erected by the Earl of Airlie, 1670.

Some 18th-century remnants of the core of Alyth survive at **The Cross**, **5 High Street** (the old schoolhouse) and **7 Bamff Wynd**. Jostling

assortment of low and tall houses set tightly against the road on narrow winding **Toutie Street** best captures feel of the old village. Venetian window and bowed centre of some pretension to
254 **Leadenhall**, Chapel Street, c.1800, aptly built by cobbler-made-good who boasted of going to Leadenhall Market to buy his leather. On Bamff Road, former **Cornmill**, rebuilt 1834, has single-storey gabled entrance to street, disguising three-storey building behind and below.

Toutie Street.

Left Commercial Street. Below Bridge House. Middle Town Hall. Bottom St Ninian's Episcopal Church.

Old Packbridge, Alyth Burn, 1674, and **Bridge**
255 **House**, Old Bridge Lane, 1728, make picturesque grouping viewed from beside former **Carpet Factory**, Pitnacree Street. **Losset Inn**, Losset Road, 1730, harled with black-painted margins, former coaching inn. **Commercial Street** has curiously continental atmosphere, fronting canalised Alyth Burn and trees of Pitnacree Street. At north end is
256 former **Barony Church**, 1843, first generation Free Church with Gothick glazing and birdcage bellcote.

257 **Boer War Memorial**, corner of Albert Street, a slender granite obelisk. The later stages of the new town grid, west of Airlie Street, are broader and more leafy, housing largely late 19th- to early 20th-century villas, and the 1939 Saltire Award-
258 winning **Alexandra Street** local authority cottages by David Baxter of Johnston & Baxter.
259 Here too is the **Town Hall**, Albert Street, 1886, Andrew Heiton Jr, Old English in style with its half-timbered tower.

260 **St Ninian's Episcopal Church**, St Ninian's Road, 1856, David Bryce
Like Hamilton at the Parish Kirk, Bryce selected neo-Norman as most appropriate for this very handsome Episcopal chapel. The progress of the Gothic Revival ensured a much more archaeological approach from Bryce. Proportions are long and low with squat tower and stair-turret over porch, rounded apse and beautifully detailed round-arched columned windows. Good interior with open timber roof.

War Memorial.

Bamff House.

War Memorial, 1921, Kellock Brown
Striking seated female bronze on ashlar plinth.
Bronze panels.

Inverquiech Castle, late 12th century
Very ruinous remains of what was probably the
royal castle of Alyth, constructed at the same time
as the forest established by William I at Alyth,
late 1190s. Simple curtain wall appears to have
followed irregular topography of the site, on
steep bank above River Isla.

Pictish Stone, south of Bruceton Farmhouse,
8th century
Standing stone incised with horseshoe symbol
above what appears to be an elephant.

Bridge of Dillavaird, River Isla, 1850
Picturesque single arch of coursed rubble with
rock-faced voussoirs.

Bamff House, from late 16th century
Described as: *a respectable mansion of considerable
antiquity, and sufficiently improved in later times to
render it the elegant and commodious residence of a
country gentleman.* (*New Statistical Account*, 1843).
To reach this condition, the L-plan tower house,
built 1580–95, was extended 1828, and completely
remodelled for Sir James Ramsay, 1843–4, by
William Burn. Burn's work, more baronial than the
original, included new entrance tower and
corbelled turret, addition of dormers and heraldic
panels to 1828 wing and internal scheme of
Jacobean ceilings.

Returning to Perth, leaving the city on the Dundee
Road, the route past Kinnoull Hill to the Carse of
Gowrie is spectacular, verging on the sublime,
where bare rocky crags emanate from precipitous
wooded slopes at the end of the sleek **Friarton
Bridge**, 1975–8.

Matthew Gloag Headquarters, Walnut Grove,
1996, Building Design Partnership
Lightweight treatment of low profile and gently
curved canopy roof provides successful office
design for exceptional greenfield site. Visitors
are enticed through from north to south, past
relative darkness and solidity of the red
sandstone north wall, through asymmetrical
entrance drum, to wonderful views from
curtain-glazed southern side, where the
restaurant bows out gently towards the river
(colour p.154).

Kinfauns
The point where the lands north of the
Tay open into the Carse of Gowrie. The
route past **Kinnoull Hill** is spectacular,
verging on the sublime, where bare
rocky crags emanate from precipitous
wooded slopes. The similarities with the
junction of the Rhine and Moselle were
not lost on the early 19th-century
landowners, Lords Gray and Kinnoull,
who constructed mock-ruinous Rhenish
watchtowers on the skyline of Kinnoull
Hill and Binn Hill (colour p.221).

KINFAUNS

A single street leading to the church, built up only on the north side to maintain the views along the Tay. Here, as in a number of local villages, the parochial buildings were built or extended by Perth City Architect, William Mackenzie, in the earlier 19th century. T-plan **schoolhouse**, 1832; east addition to the 1799 manse, now **Kinfauns House**, 1840.

Kinfauns Parish Church, 1868–9, A Heiton Jr
Rather under-powered design, compensated by the sensational site. Roofless remains of the single chambered pre-Reformation parish church stand to east. Much-repaired **Charteris burial aisle**, dated 1598, retains its roof, ribbed groin vault and interesting memorial panels.

Top *Detail, Charteris burial aisle.* Above *Kinfauns Parish Church.* Left *Kinfauns Castle from* Views in Scotland.

261 **Kinfauns Castle Hotel**, 1820–6, Sir Robert Smirke
Nothing under-powered about Smirke's super-romantic gothic confection for Francis, 14th Lord Gray, dramatically sited on a bluff overlooking the Carse. Siting and design of the house were picturesque in the most literal sense – derived from 1809 watercolour proposals by Alexander Nasmyth. Building was raised on a massive artificial terrace to improve the tree-framed views to and from the house, and to heighten the skyline effect of towers, turrets and crenellations. Strip foundations demonstrate one of the earliest uses of mass-concrete in Scotland (colour p.222). Unusually for Smirke, composition is asymmetrical, although his classicist tendencies are barely suppressed in the garden front. Interior sumptuously fitted out in Tudor-gothic style, including 82ft coffered corridor or gallery to display family treasures and magnificent library, all originally furnished by the London firm of Dowbiggin. In spite of antiquarian veneer, the feel is Regency light, space and elegance. More serious baronial tone to refitted stair and first-floor corridor, c.1912, F W Deas.

Kinfauns Castle
The noble owner [Lord Gray] is a great lover of Mechanics … The Billiard Room is my Lord's workshop … here is everything to excite surprise and elicit admiration. How hard you can hit – how heavily you weigh – how swiftly you walk – electrifying machines in all shapes … clocks, watches, guns, swords, musical instruments …
T F Dibdin, 1838

W S Gilpin prepared formal plans for the shrubberies immediately surrounding the house in 1818.

Kinfauns Castle.

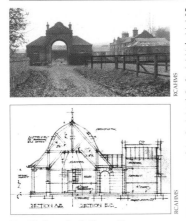

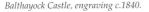

Top *Kinfauns Castle Farm.* Above *Kinfauns Home Farm Dairy by Robert Lorimer.*

Smirke was also responsible for **Kinfauns Castle Farm**, 1826, an impressive model courtyard in Jacobean style, now houses. Smirke's other estate farmhouse, **Tofthill**, was replaced in 1904 by F W Deas' finely crafted Scots 17th-century house, adjacent to the modern-day A90. Deas also designed **gateway** to the walled garden, with beautiful wrought-ironwork of 1910. **Home Farmhouse**, an attractive plain classical house, c.1800, ogee-roofed **dairy** (colour p.222) and adjoining **scullery**, 1928, a late and charming work by Sir Robert Lorimer, at his best on a small scale.

Balthayock House, 1870, James MacLaren Derelict mansion house, built from the fruits of railway contracting. Relatively restrained gabled exterior with odd flourishes of railway detailing, such as decorative steel arches of the *porte-cochère* and sliding front door. Interior was exuberant French Second Empire affair of statues, stained glass, scagliola columns and Corinthian capitals. Railway technology also inspired the spectacular 92ft span of cast-iron **bridge** on drive over Hail Pool.

Balthayock Castle, late 14th century
Severe and diminutive tower, remarkably early survival for the area, occupying precipitous position next to ravine and commanding wonderful views along Glen Carse. Rectangular plan, three storeys with massive 3m thick walls. Straight mural stair links ground floor to vaulted hall above, turnpike rises to upper floor and wallwalk. Hall also entered directly from outside by round-arched doorway. Side arch carries initials of Alexander Blair and his wife, dated 1578, probably when more comfortable accommodation began to be added in L-plan on the north-east side of the tower. Complex was long derelict in 1870 when James MacLaren demolished later buildings and restored the tower, recasting the interior and adding battlements and forestair.

Balthayock Castle, engraving c.1840.

KILSPINDIE
The variety of landscape is remarkable, ranging from the rich agricultural lands of the Carse to the moorlands and barren tops of the Sidlaw Hills. From Evelick Hill, the spectacular view takes in Schiehallion and Ben Vorlich to the north, Strathmore, the Carse of Gowrie and beyond to Fife and the Lomond Hills. Three small settlements, Pitroddie, Kilspindie and Rait, developed where their respective glens open into the Carse. Little remains of Pitroddie.

262 Parish Church, plain but attractive gothic box *c.*1815, built on an ancient site. Behind, slightly eccentric **Stuart of Rait Mausoleum**, erected in filial affection, 1822. In relation to the size of the church, the old **manse** is very commodious indeed, the 18th-century core extended in L-plan by William Mackenzie, 1850. Magnificent seat of the Douglases of Kilspindie, recorded on Pont's late 16th-century map, probably stood on the site of the farmhouse, or possibly the manse, but all that remains is an estate wall running from the church and large dilapidated lectern **doocot**. Fine old **school**, 1821, David Neave, three-bay house with schoolroom wing.

Evelick, late 16th century
Substantial ruinous remains of seat of the Lindsays of Evelick. Broad circular stairtower rising the full height of the re-entrant angle in offset L-plan, a harled precursor of more famous 1606 stairtower at Glamis. Smaller scale and less elaborate detail, but here too genealogy was important, as is evident from the moulded frame for a heraldic panel which survives on the tower and stones embedded in **steading**. Timothy Pont's late 16th-century map depicts a symmetrical arrangement of structures in front of the house, perhaps a forecourt. Vanished two-storey wing added to east gable in the 17th century.

RAIT
Extremely picturesque village straddling the burn, now famous for its antique traders, based in the
263 steading of **Rait Farm**. Adjacent, beautifully proportioned early 19th-century farmhouse, now known as **Rait House**. Nearby too, remains of the

Top *Parish Church.* Above *Stuart of Rait Mausoleum.* Left *Evelick.*

Evelick was the scene of a tragic fight between step-brothers William Douglas and Thomas Lindsay in 1682, which ended in the murder of the latter. Following a trial, Douglas was executed. Further scandal engulfed the house in 1752 when Allan Ramsay, later court painter to George III, eloped to Edinburgh with Margaret Lindsay, elder daughter of Sir Alexander and Lady Amelia Lindsay. The Lindsays strongly disapproved of Ramsay's lowly social position, in spite of his wigmaker father's reputation as a poet, and considerable rancour ensued for many years. Ramsay's tender portrait (*c.*1758) of his second wife clasping a pink rose, now in the National Gallery of Scotland, is justifiably his best-known work.

Rait, 1903.

3-6 Westend.

Once in the same ownership, the estates of Fingask and Kinnaird were linked by a footpath, and reputedly a series of underground passages, along the ridge. A triple-arched Gothick folly, **The Monument**, marks the halfway resting point above Flawcraig Farm, with magnificent views across the Tay.

pre-Reformation church, abandoned on uniting with Kilspindie, and churchyard. West end of the village is an exceptional survival of a pre-Improvement fermtoun – a number of cottages here date from the 18th century and some sustain the 19th-century native tradition of reed thatching, originally supplied from the margins of the Tay. **Westend Cottage** and the curved row at **3-6 Westend** are notable examples.

Right *Fingask Castle, 1903.* Below *Fingask Castle.* Bottom *Tam O'Shanter garden sculpture.*

Fingask Castle, from 1594
L-plan tower house, expanded to T-plan, 1670s, considerably altered and extended throughout 18th and 19th centuries. Radical re-ordering and pruning by Mills and Shepherd of Dundee in 1925 removed the Georgian Gothick bow-fronted and crenellated drawing-room wing and tower, and mid-19th-century ogee-roofed octagonal entrance tower. The result, both internally and externally, a very stripped back version of Lorimer – Arts without Crafts. Glory of Fingask is its setting, high on the Braes of the Carse, beautiful topiary and **sculpture gardens**. Many by David and William Anderson of Perth and local mason, Charles Spence, are figures drawn from literature, history and legend: Last Minstrel, Tam O'Shanter and Kate's Watty and Meg; Willie brewed a peck o' Maut; Prince Charles Edward; Flora MacDonald; and Ossian. Among the numerous architectural fragments are the shaft and surmounting lion rampant of **Perth Mercat Cross**, 1669, by Robert Mylne, extraordinary 17th-century faceted **sundial** reputedly from the Palace of Holyroodhouse, and **sundial** from Linlithgow Palace. Derelict **sawmill**, *c.*1910, expensively built in dark whinstone with red sandstone dressings and pantiled roof. Arcaded ground floor, balconied loft door and steep crowstepped gables all beautifully detailed.

KINNAIRD
An informal cluster of houses around the church. Perth City Architect, William Mackenzie, was responsible for the fashionable **Delford House**, the former manse of 1831, and the old **school**, 1834 (raised and dormers added, 1858).

Kinnaird Parish Church, 1815
Church specialist Hippolyte Blanc sought to give the plain rectangular box some decent French gothic trimmings in 1879. His alternative schemes for a steeply pitched roof, flèche and apse are unexecuted.

Kinnaird Castle, late 15th century
At four storeys tall and perched high on the Braes of the Carse, Kinnaird is a tower house designed to impress. Several peculiarities: part stone-vaulted and part corbelled timber ceiling to ground floor; full-height buttress with external doorway and drawbridge to the wallwalk of former single-storey wing or courtyard to west (shown on Pont's map but long demolished); and detached kitchen wing, dated 1610 on the dormer. Behind the sturdy yett, straight mural stair to first-floor hall belies the defensive appearance of the exterior. Roofless by 1855, garret is an addition of the later 19th-century restoration. Below the house, 17th-century lectern **doocot**, probably recast 18th century, incorporating medieval graveslab as lintel.

Top *Kinnaird Parish Church.*
Above *Kinnaird Castle.*

BALLINDEAN
Easter and **Wester Ballindean**, both earlier 19th-century, two-storey, three-bay farmhouses, one piended, the other gabled, mark the boundaries of this picturesque estate hamlet. In between, charming red sandstone **Wester Ballindean Cottages** and **The Cottage** of *c.*1835 retain their lattice windows.

Below *Wester Ballindean Cottages.*
Bottom *Ballindean House, 1832 design.*

264 **Ballindean House**, 1832, probably Thomas Hamilton with Sir William Trotter Long, low, triple-pile classical design with pediments and glazed porch, made distinctly exotic by enormous circular cupola rising above central stairhall. Planning eccentric too, incorporating lower two-storey service wing across the length of the rear elevation and large ballroom spilling out into glazed bay window on east elevation. Trotter's highly successful Edinburgh cabinet-making business supplied the wherewithal for the house and the know-how for the sumptuous kitting out, now largely

Sir William Trotter, d.1834
The fortunes of Trotter's Princes Street
furnishing business were based largely
on his association with leading
Edinburgh architects, such as James
Gillespie Graham, Thomas Hamilton,
and W H Playfair, and his near
monopoly on supplying their clients,
particularly in the New Town. The
furniture is characterised by the use of
top quality timber and deep-cut carving,
much of it in neoclassical or Grecian
style, although commercial dexterity
allowed the adoption of every style from
gothic to Louis XV on demand. Also an
astute politician, Trotter became Lord
Provost of Edinburgh in 1825.

*From top Abernyte; Parish school;
Abernyte Parish Church; Gavintown House.*

dispersed. Old house of 1711, adapted to an office
wing, was demolished early 1960s. Behind the
house to west, 18th- and 19th-century
compartments of the **walled garden** and nearly
symmetrical arrangement of **farmhouse** and
pyramid-roofed **pavilions**. Stylistically eclectic
South, **West** and **Nursery Lodges**.

ABERNYTE
Noted for its views, 40ft waterfall and spring
carpet of primroses at Milton Den. Village
comprises a single street on the site of the hamlet
of Balfour, winding gently down Abernyte Glen.
Mostly late 18th-century single-storey cottages of
whinstone rubble, but some, like the **Smithy,**
raised to two storeys. **Parish school**, 1906,
distinctive red brick with swept eaves, opposite
the junction to the church road. **Abernyte House**,
for Professor Bannerman of Edinburgh, later 19th
century, sited aloofly outside the village at foot of
Kirktoun Craig: semi-baronial, with pedimented
dormers and crowstepped gables, now rather
gap-toothed without its window mullions.

265 **Abernyte Parish Church**, remodelled 1870,
T S Robertson
Although dated 1672, and incorporating earlier
pre-Reformation fabric, small cruciform church
owes its current appearance to Robertson's
almost Episcopalian remodelling nearly 200 years
later. Gothicised by new steeply pitched roof with
intricate timber bracing, triple-arched belfry,
pitched pine furnishings and stained glass
windows. Interesting 18th-century headstones,
particularly that of James Lowson 'Flesher in
Glenlyon in Longforgan' in **churchyard** (colour
p.224) **Gavintown House**, the old manse, dated
1666, also incorporates pre-Reformation fabric at
east end. Largely rebuilt by John Beveridge of
Baledgarno in 1727, first slated rather than
thatched in 1736, the bowed drawing/dining-
room wing added, 1821, Revd James Wilson, and
all saved from demolition by repairs report of
Kinnear & Peddie, 1883.

266 **Rossie Priory**, 1807–15, William Atkinson
Set high above the Carse among the woodlands
of Rossie Hill, and commanding magnificent
views across the Tay, Rossie Priory was a vast
castellated gothic fantasy for the 8th Lord
Kinnaird, more monastic than domestic in scale,
as befitted its new name (previous house was
called Drimmie House). Bulk of the main house
demolished *c.*1949, a garden terrace created on

the foundations. Rump adapted by Basil Spence, including a new bay window to banish finally the gothic gloom. Remaining west wing includes second storey of 1839 and chapel of 1866. Below the garden terraces stand two rustic timber and rosemary-tiled **sports pavilions**, *c.*1900, the larger still in use for cricket. Now divided from the estate by the A90, old principal drive and roguish gothic **Inchture Lodge**, *c.*1870, probably T S Robertson, complete with geometric-patterned windows, bands of fish-scale slates, decorative ridging and octagonal chimneys. *One of the most magnificent edifices of its kind* (*New Statistical Account*, 1845).

Left *Rossie Priory from* Views in Scotland, *early 19th century.* Top *Inchture Lodge.* Above *Old Rossie Kirk.*

Old Rossie Kirk, rebuilt 1875, T S Robertson Medieval kirk abandoned in 1670 on amalgamation of the parish with Inchture. Ruins almost entirely rebuilt, 1875, as Episcopal chapel for Rossie Priory estate, incorporating heavily restored north doorway and north and east walls. Interesting interior including beautiful 8th-century interlaced Pictish cross-slab. Now private mausoleum.

Old Rossie Mercat Cross, 1746
In the glen below the kirk, the extremely fine mercat cross is all that remains of Rossie village, transplanted to Baledgarno in the late 18th century. Square fluted Corinthian column crowned with rampant lions and unicorns supporting ball-finial. Monogrammed 'KG RH' and dated at shaft collar.

Moncur Castle, late 16th century
Ruinous three-storey, Z-plan house comprising principal hall range with square entrance tower to north-east corner, and circular bedroom tower and turnpike stair attached to south-west. Main stair accessed only the hall on *piano nobile*. Mock defensive gunloops pepper vaulted ground floor.

Moncur Castle
Timothy Pont's late 16th-century map shows a substantial tower house. If the map is accurate, the tower must have been replaced shortly afterwards by the more fashionable and smaller Z-plan house which has remained ruinous since a fire in the early 18th century.

Crop marks have revealed a ditched enclosure around **Moncur Castle**, which may be the remnant of a genuine bailey, or continuation of the mock defences into the landscape. Beyond this, both the crop marks and General Roy's mid-18th-century map show the house as the focus of formal approaches and planting.

Old Rossie Mercat Cross.

Baledgarno.

Baledgarno, rebuilt from 1790
Pretty estate village, distinguished by rich red local
sandstone dressings. Single-storey groups flanking
the west entrance to Rossie Priory are the oldest,
but largely remodelled *c*.1880, some with gabled
porches, the bowed one as library. Remaining two-
storey groups, *c*.1840, with varying degrees of later
work. **Burnside**, more picturesque Tudor gothic
with deep eaves, the old schoolhouse of the same
date. Original **Baledgarno Farmhouse**, guarding
the entrance to the village, has gothic windows to
match 1839 alterations to Rossie Priory and large
western addition dated 1879. Gothic trimmings too
on the dairy of **Castlehill Farm**, the harled complex
above and behind the village, probably on the site
and containing fragments of 16th- or 17th-century
Edgar House.

LONGFORGAN
(see *Dundee* in this series)

INCHTURE
Derived from the Gaelic *'Innis-tuir'* meaning
island of the tower. Both tower and island were
long vanished by the earlier 19th century, when
the village was largely rebuilt along the new
Perth/Dundee turnpike road. Many single-storey
houses and **Inchture Hotel** were designed in
Tudor-gothic, probably by David Mackenzie, as a
gentle limbering-up for passing visitors to the
super-gothic Rossie Priory. Duncan D Stewart,
estate factor and architect, was probably
responsible for the houses of the 1880s and '90s,
some with rustic log-columned porches.
Schoolhouse, mid-19th century, two storey, brick,
with latticed windows, former schoolrooms
behind. Detached at the west end, **Crossgates**,
1849, again Tudor, built for Dundee and Perth
Railway as terminus of tramway link to Inchture
Station, a mile south. On closure of the single
horse-drawn tram service in 1916, track was
removed to France for the war effort.

267 **Inchture Parish Church**, 1834, David Mackenzie
Sparer, scaled-down version of spiky gothic
already employed by Atkinson at Rossie Priory,
here symmetrically arranged in T-plan. Fiery red

Below *Inchture Hotel*. Bottom *Inchture Parish Church.*

local sandstone now badly weather worn, but carved grotesques on the drip stones survive. Interior destroyed by fire, 1890, and rebuilt the following year by Duncan D Stewart.

Inchmartine House, from late 17th century
Tall, broad classical mansion remodelled *c.*1800 from remains of an earlier house. Generous sash windows in an unusual arrangement of six bays with doorway squeezed in the middle, entered from smart Roman Doric porch. Distinguished **stables**, also *c.*1800, have octagonal lantern tower doocot over entrance. Small derelict later 19th-century **chapel** to east.

Westown Kirk, 16th century
Beautifully sited on the ridge at Westown and draped in ivy are the ruins of old Inchmartin Parish Kirk. Chancel largely removed leaving only the nave with its precarious belfry.

Errol Station, 1847,
possibly Andrew Heiton Sr
Fine example of Tudor-gothic house style of the Dundee and Perth Railway, characterised by broad overhanging eaves, hoodmoulded windows and tall chimneys (now rebuilt in brick). The mile-and-a-half distance from Errol weighed against its survival as a station. Station Master's house and brick signal box complete the ensemble.

Top *Inchmartine House.* Middle *Westown Kirk.* Above *Errol Station.* Left *Megginch.*

268 **Megginch**, from 15th century
Large, and much-altered tower house lies at the heart of the complex of later wings and additions. Details such as the roll-moulded windows and the round tower corbelled to square cap-house are consistent with a major late 16th-century remodelling, as recorded over one of the windows: *Petrus Hay, aedificium extruxit an: 1575.* Castellated and bow-ended south-west wing,

North Lodge, Megginch, late 19th century.

thought to have been initiated by Robert and James Adam, 1780s, contains very fine drawing room. W M Mackenzie completed this wing in 1820, and added north-east wing and porch, again all castellated. Wonderfully picturesque Gothick court of offices, used as a location in the 1994 film *Rob Roy*, were begun in brick in 1707, and altered/extended in 1809, with the addition of the ornamental doocot. Contemporary atmospheric **North Lodge**, adjacent to the A90, perfectly evoking the entrance to a place of great antiquity with its spiky gatepiers, ogee windows and crenellated screen walls. Small crowstepped **chapel** dates from 1679, largely rebuilt in 1781.

Gourdiehill House, early 19th century (demolished)
Poor Gourdiehill stood fire-damaged for over 20 years before its final demise in 1991. A rectilinear classical villa in red ashlar sandstone, regimented by paired Ionic pilasters at the corners and entrance bay – a miniature version of Inchyra House – tacked on at right angles to the old house.

Gourdiehill House.

Pattrick Matthew, 1790–1874, known as 'Old Gourdie' was responsible for building the new front to Gourdiehill. An eccentric character, living as a recluse, *he neither believed in God or deevil*. However, he did believe in the transmigration of souls, and that one very near and dear to him had become a blackbird. Even though the fruit in his orchard became ravaged, he refused to allow the blackbirds to be shot! Matthew is also reputed to have gone to live in a travelling van to escape the threat of cholera.

Waterybutts Doocot.

Waterybutts Doocot, 1733
Showpiece pigeon house, now lacking its roof, but retaining three small crowstepped gables with ball-finials and double doors to protect the valuable contents of the hundreds of stone nesting boxes, so vital to the laird's winter dinner table. Inner door a gate, keeping pigeons in but allowing light for the keeper to carry out his work. Nearby **Newbigging Doocot**, *c.*1730, a similar double-chambered lectern design, but taller, with stepped *rat course*, thought to prevent vermin from climbing the walls and entering through the flight holes.

Seasyde House, early 19th century, possibly John Paterson
Neat and compact classical country house. Columned doorpiece and broad umbrella fanlight adorn the entrance front, while central bays of the rear are bowed to maximise the southerly views across the Tay to Fife. Galleried circular central hall.

ERROL

Largest of the Carse parishes, traditional fiefdom of the earls of Errol and the Hays and Drummonds of Megginch, bounding the Tay and containing some of the best agricultural lands in the country. Unique winding main street of the village, almost French in character, notable for its clay-wall construction. High Street climbs gently from the east, opening into a small square around polished red granite **fountain** and **market cross**, 1900, Johnston & Baxter. Here, a number of early 19th-century three-storey tenements with tall roofs and broad chimneys survive, for example **Keir's Land**, 1-8 High Street, small windows under the eaves probably indicating weavers' workshops. A little later, but definitely not artisan, is **Dalgleish House**, like a manse with infilled arch at the ground floor of its additional bay. Next door, late 19th-century **Albert House** and **Victoria Hall** of local polychromatic brick. Similar polychromy and Venetian round-headed windows to match at **Library Buildings** (now flats). Like many buildings throughout Errol, particularly in High Street and Church Lane, **Commercial Hotel**, dated 1793 over the doorway, is likely to conceal a clay-wall construction behind harling.

To the rear of the *c*.1800 **schoolhouse**, School Wynd, is the **old kirkyard**, site of the former parish kirk, containing a few 17th-century tomb chests and good 18th-century gravestones. Former **Free Church**, Church Lane, one of the early Disruption churches of 1843, has an unusual shallow-roofed tower seemingly derived from steading design.

In Church Avenue, off the north side of High Street, a surprisingly metropolitan tenement block of 1904, built in red sandstone and sporting crowstepped gables with modishly offset chimneys. **Errol Parish Church**, 1831–3, James Gillespie Graham, a 1,450-seat neo-Norman giant with unaccountably spiky skyline in typical Gillespie Graham manner. No doubt to save the occupants from Puginian industrial hell, former

Top *Seasyde House.* Middle *Market cross.* Above *Keir's Land.*

Below *Roof, former Free Church.* Bottom *Errol Parish Church, 'The Cathedral of the Carse'.*

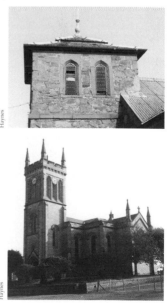

269

Female Industrial School.

Errol village developed as a kirkton under the patronage of the Hays of Errol and achieved burghal status in 1648, allowing limited trading privileges. By the end of the 19th century the village was still largely populated by farmworkers and weavers, but possessed its own post office, bank branch, two inns, a gasworks, two schools, and a library.

Above *Inchcoonans Brickworks.*
Right *Flatfield Farmhouse.*

*... **the houses in the village** are as paltry as the situation is pleasant. As there is no stone in the neighbourhood, they are mostly built of clay, and huddled together without much order or regularity. Excepting gentlemens seats, all the old buildings in the parish are of that substance, which when properly cemented, is reckoned the warmest and most durable of any ... It is thought that the people have now in some measure lost the art of preparing the materials, and compacting them together, so as to give the clay-houses the solidity they had in past times. They are, however, adopting a plan of building much more agreeable to the eye, and certainly no less useful for accommodation, moulding the mortar into bricks, and with these forming their dwellings.*
First Statistical Account, 1792

Female Industrial School and **Schoolhouse**, 1855–6, by J, J M, & W H Hay of Liverpool, are very firmly gothic with tall pointed gables, shouldered windows and splendid latticed oriel window to house.

Errol Park House, 1875–7, Alexander Johnston Pont depicts a large house at Errol. The later 18th-century house, similar to Glendoick, destroyed by fire, 1874. Replacement a low, broad renaissance design, surprisingly vigorous in its symmetry for its date. Opulent **stables**, 1811, designed by John Paterson, former lieutenant to Robert Adam. They take the form of a round square with extraordinary octagonal tower over the entrance; top stage added 1899 by Johnston & Baxter for village cistern.

Inchcoonans Brickworks, 1950
Site of a brickworks for at least 200 years, the oldest parts of the current complex are the two Temco beehive kilns, one of which was in operation from 1950 to 1986. Distinctive red bricks can be found throughout the area, and traditional brick-making skills are being rekindled by the modern Errol Brick Company. *'Follow the Errol brick road!'*

Flatfield Farm, 1785
Independent of the local estates from its formation by Alexander Clark, Flatfield is an exceptional example of an autonomous Improvement farm. Farmhouse itself is of handmade clay bricks and was almost certainly thatched. Unusually large for the acreage. Detached farm buildings were built of *pisé*, or shuttered rammed clay, and arranged to form a courtyard north of the house. Unique constructional feature of the barn is the continuation of joists through the walls, where the

ends are fixed with timber plates and pegs. Orchard and walled garden are contemporary with the house.

Robert Craigie, 1685–1760, son of Laurence Craigie of nearby Kilgraston, bought the Glendoick estate in 1726. His rise through the legal profession was slow but steady, achieving the position of Lord Advocate in 1742, and Lord President in 1754 following the death of Robert Dundas of Arniston. It has been suggested that Craigie supplemented his official earnings as Lord Advocate during the '45 uprising by trading information on Jacobite activities, and that the house was built on the profits.

Glendoick House.

270 Glendoick House, *c.*1747

Picture-book image of a medium-sized mid-18th-century classical country house: white harled symmetrical box with contrasting stone dressings, central pediment, high piended roof and ridge chimneys. Unknown architect tucked the service court modestly behind, rather than bringing forward pavilion wings. Above ground or basement storey, *piano nobile* distinguished by broad set of steps up to Venetian doorway and pediments over windows. Inside, house is panelled in pine from top to bottom and, dining room apart, the principal rooms contain sensuous rococo plasterwork, probably by Thomas Clayton, William Adam's plasterer at The Drum and Palace of Holyroodhouse (see *Edinburgh* in this series). In compensation, the dining room has a magnificent Ionic pilastered niche, originally shelved for china display. House restored and east service wing raised a storey, 1910, A G Heiton, who also designed **South-East Lodge** to main road, with distinctive roof forming eyebrows over the windows. In walled garden, curious **sundial chair**, 1776, constructed of stone slabs and engraved dial. **Doocot** of rarer square-plan with pyramid roof, probably pre-dates house by 20 years or so.

Sundial chair.

Glendoick School and Schoolhouse,
earlier 19th century

Schoolroom at ground floor, with forestair to schoolhouse above. Fusion of traditional clay-wall construction with fashionable plain classical arrangement and stylish lying-pane windows.

PITFOUR

Cottown Schoolhouse.

271 **Cottown School and Schoolhouse**, 1745
Most complete and fascinating survival of much-
altered remnants of this 18th-century cottertoun,
strung out along a single street, is the school.
Cotters worked the lands of tenant farmers, or
plied a craft such as shoemaking. Although
thought to date from 1745, the school was
remodelled several times, most notably in 1766,
the 1770s, 1818, the 1940s and '50s. Beautifully
long, low, lime-rendered and reed-thatched, the
school was meticulously repaired in 1996 by the
National Trust for Scotland and Historic Scotland.
Like many buildings of its date throughout
Scotland, it was constructed of clay-wall and kept
dry by an overhanging thatched roof. An entirely
renewable building of natural materials, 250
years ahead of the Green movement.

Pitfour Castle, late 19th century.

Pitfour Stables, drawn by David Walker.

272 **Pitfour Castle**, 1784, attributed to Robert Adam
Conceived on an ancient site for John Richardson
as a fairy-tale castle of round and square towers,
pepperpot turrets, mock gunloops and
battlements, all symmetrical and elegantly
proportioned in the late 18th-century classical
manner and surrounded by landscaped park
with ha-ha. Entrance court formed by similarly
styled stables, offices, gateways and enclosing
walls. Although plasterwork inside is fairly plain,
the wonderful domed oval staircase contained
painted panels by Zucchi. Architect not known,
but it is certainly in the 'castle style' of the Adam
brothers at Oxenfoord, 1780 (see *Midlothian* in this
series), and Dalquharran, 1786 (see *Ayrshire &
Arran*). By 1825, when William Burn was called
in, the fashion for medievalising was reaching its
zenith, led by royal patronage of Jeffry Wyatville

at Windsor Castle. Deliberately breaking up the symmetry and increasing the picturesque qualities of the skyline, Burn added gothic library, Windsor-style round tower as a music room, and clocktower, and heightened one of the stable block towers. It seems likely that the house was stripped of its unifying harl to reveal the dark whinstone rubble at this time, again for picturesque effect. Now converted to flats.

Pitfour Doocot, Upper Mains, *c*.1730
Like Newbigging and Waterybutts along the Carse, splendid two-chamber lean-to, with three crowstepped gables along the back wall to shelter sun-loving birds. Such architectural display suggests that the previous house at Pitfour was of some significance.

ST MADOES
Small fertile flatland parish in the crook of the Tay opposite the confluence of the River Earn. Substantial engineering schemes reclaimed much of the lowest lying land in the late 18th and early 19th centuries. Name is said to be derived from a 4th-century French missionary, Madoch, whose converts dedicated a church to him on the site of the present parish church.

St Madoes Parish Church, 1799
Dark whinstone T-plan with elegant Venetian windows and delicate birdcage belfry. Laird's loft in the projection. Remarkable 8th-century Pictish **cross-slab**, now housed in Perth Museum, came from the burial ground.

Inchyra House, *c*.1810,
probably James Gillespie (Graham)
Built for successful Edinburgh lawyer, John Anderson, Inchyra reflected the fashionable 'Grecian' classicism sweeping the country's urban terraces and public buildings. Razor-sharp ashlar front, articulated by paired pilasters and Tuscan columns, an expanded version of Gillespie (Graham)'s 1813 Commercial Bank in New Assembly Close (see *Edinburgh* in this series).

GLENCARSE
Estate village, laid out in a straight line along the old Perth/Dundee road, single-storey cottages to south, one-and-a-half storeys to north, and two hotels to catch passing trade. **All Saints Episcopal Church**, 1878, Mr Blackadder of Perth, a rather incongruous, but attractive, half-timbered and rosemary-tiled interloper.

Below Pictish cross-slab, St Madoes Churchyard. *Middle* Inchyra House. *Bottom* All Saints Episcopal Church, Glencarse.

RCAHMS

Stephen Stuart

Haynes

273

207

Top *Glencarse House*. Above *Seggieden House*.

Ayton House.

Route of the guide now heads southwards from Perth to Glenfarg, taking in Abernethy.

Glencarse House, 1790, Robert & James Adam
Late work in classical style for Thomas Hunter, much altered in 1889 and 1923. Original scheme comprised five-bay house with attached single-storey temple-fronted wings projecting to north. South (garden) front was three bay with full-height central bow and incorporated channelled basement, which served as a plinth. While of undoubted practicality, the major alterations of 1889, including rendering, extensions to the east and west, and infilling the north court, contrast with the formality of the Adam work.

Seggieden House, remodelled *c*.1795, John Paterson (demolished *c*.1975)
Heavily influenced by Robert and James Adam (Paterson's previous employers until he was dismissed in 1791), Seggieden bore close resemblance with the centre block of nearby Glencarse House of 1790. Perhaps the most distinctive debt to the Adams could be found in the horseshoe staircase and series of oval rooms, culminating in the drawing room, bowed out at the centre of the south elevation. Large west wing added, 1866.

Seggieden Ice House, early 19th century
Small commercial ice house in the garden of Seggieden Cottage. Stone vaulted structure was packed with crushed ice in winter and sealed until the fishing season began. Ice was then used to pack freshly caught salmon from the Kinfauns fishings for onward transport.

Ayton House, 18th century
(Core of) Ayton at centre of entrance front probably formed from old farmhouse of Craigpottie estate. House already much extended

and altered by 1830, when William Burn added new south wing of public rooms with long balcony, and updated the planning of what was now a small mansion. Classical detailing of pediments and quoins, but arrangement is deliberately asymmetrical, firmly placing function before form. Robert Lorimer probably added the bay window to the left of Burn's porch c.1905. Tudor-gothic **South-West Lodge** and nearby **bridge**, c.1830, also likely to be by William Burn.

ABERNETHY

274 **Round Tower**, late 11th century
Extraordinary sentinel over village, with spectacular views of the Tay. Built of coursed hewn sandstone walls 3½ft thick, 72ft high and 15ft in diameter at the base, tapering by about a foot to the top. Bottom 12 courses appear to be earliest part. Different stonework of narrow round-arched doorway and tower above suggest later rebuilding. Inside, old arrangement of timber ladders and landings replaced by modern stair. Medieval iron **jougs**, or punishment collar, attached to tower next to churchyard gate and broken 7th-century Pictish symbol stone.
Open to the public

275 **Abernethy Parish Church**, 1802, James Balingall
Old Parish Church, probably incorporating parts of a pre-Reformation collegiate church, was demolished in 1802, when this new preaching box was erected a short distance away. Burial ground contains mainly 19th-century monuments, including unusual stone of 1831 depicting shuttle and carding tools of weaver John Young.

Most of the historic core of the village dates from 18th and 19th centuries, although the gently curving plan of **Main Street** or 'Highgait' follows the classic arrangement of a medieval burgh: long, narrow feus in herringbone pattern; wynds leading off at right angles; broadening at the middle to accommodate a market. Houses here are generally of traditional two-storey, two- or three-bay design, some set gable end to street, many 19th-century examples sporting 'long and short' window surrounds and quoins. At the 276 centre, **War Memorial**, 1920, Mills & Shepherd, in the form of a market cross, stands on the site of the Town House. On the south side of the small square further east, a noticeably polite earlier 19th-century **former bank** or shop, with channelled ground floor and quoins.

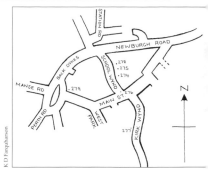

K D Farquharson

Abernethy Round Tower, with the tower at Brechin, are the only mainland survivals of a building type most commonly associated with the Irish Celtic Church. Nineteenth-century speculation about the purpose of the towers ranged wildly from Buddhist temples to Pictish royal burial chambers. More recent research suggests they were designed to carry the sound of hand-bells, rung from each belfry opening in turn. At Abernethy, the tower always stood as a separate campanile, detached from the church it served.

Below *Round Tower*. Middle *Abernethy Parish Church*. Bottom *Main Street*.

RCAHMS

Haynes

Perth Museum & Art Gallery

Top *South United Free Church.*
Above *Skewputt, Corner Shop.*

Abernethy is a large and varied parish, bordered by Fife to south and east, the Rivers Earn and Tay to north and Glen Farg to west. Taking advantage of the key strategic position at the confluence of the rivers, the Romans began, and soon abandoned, an ambitious legionary fort at Carpow in the early 3rd century. At the heart of Abernethy parish lies the ancient Pictish and early Christian centre of the same name. The topography divides: to the north, flat fertile carse lands of the Earn and to the south, dramatic glens and tops of the Ochil Hills.

Old House of Carpow, later 19th-century: the stairtower then had a thatched roof, doocot openings, and a corner sundial.

Kirk Wynd leads south, past picturesque early 19th-century **Pitkeathly Cottage** (once reed-thatched, like many houses), to former **South United Free Church** or **Williamson Kirk**, 1866, by C S Robertson. Reflecting the strong local tradition of dissenting worship, the kirk is enormous – a craggy gothic barn with rose windows, double transepts, and powerful gableted spire. Now converted to housing.

School Wynd leads north from the war memorial, passing early 19th-century **Mornington Cottage** with unusually carved skewputts and adjoining coach house, converted to local museum, 1998. **Back Dykes**, once the northern limit of the Main Street feus, now forms village bypass. At west end, where it once joined Main Street, **Corner Shop**, *c.*1840, with odd skewputts depicting pointing hands and capped by small sphinxes. The new line of the road here expunged a wonderfully dilapidated and characterful 18th-century thatched house opposite. Further east, several 18th-century single-storey vernacular cottages survive in various states of alteration. The arrival of the Edinburgh & Northern Railway in 1848 transformed the fortunes of the backlands to a small, but fashionable, villa suburb.

Glenfarg House, 1907, James B Dunn
Highly idiosyncratic Arts & Crafts mansion – harled with graded Scots slate roof. Low and rambling scale, incorporating ogee-roofed octagonal tower and two ingleneuk chimneys. **Stable block** and **lodge** are contemporary.

Old House of Carpow, early 17th century
Ruinous remains of once fine laird's house. Initially T-plan, with projecting stairtower, lower thatched wings were added, early 18th century, to make Z-plan.

Pottiehill Farmhouse, early 19th century
Attractive three-bay farmhouse rendered mildly exotic by ogee arches over door and windows.

Blairstruie House, 1853
Picturesque cottage style of gothic porch, low first floor, broad eaves, and lying-pane glazing, more generally in use in the 1820s and '30s.

Fordel, 1784
Once a neat and fashionable neoclassical arrangement of pedimented five-bay *corps-de-logis* linked at the ground floor to single-storey

Venetian-windowed pavilions. Regrettable
recasting of the house by Andrew Heiton Jr, 1875,
when pavilions and links were heightened to two
storeys, bay windows and fireclay balustrade
added, and the interior completely remodelled.
Ruins of the Brown family's **Old House of Fordel**
remain at Easter Fordel: late 16th-century
rectangular laird's house with circular stairtower
at north-west corner and 17th-century wing
(heated by an ingleneuk) forming L-plan.
Cromwell spent two nights here in August 1651.

Fordel.

The *Old Statistical Account* (1794)
describes the agriculture as unimproved
until 1782, when a number of farmers
from the Carse of Gowrie settled in the
parish. **Glentarkie** and **Gattaway**, with
their walled gardens typical of the Carse,
appear to date from this time, the latter
farmhouse boasting a very genteel
Venetian doorpiece. The early 19th
century saw much investment in the land
and the construction of steadings and
farmhouses. The finest is **Catochill**,
hidden away off Abernethy Glen, large
and classical with pretensions to
mansionhood. Plainer classical, but
notable farmhouses at **Elliothead**, *c.*1820,
Pittuncarty, 1826, and **Carey**, *c.*1835.

GLENFARG
The arrival of the railway in 1890 transformed the
old fermtoun of Damhead into a thriving village
and something of a resort, supporting four hotels.
281 The red sandstone tower of **The Glenfarg**, *c.*1890,
still a prominent landmark. At the centre of the
village, Lord Rowallan donated the former
Arngask Library (Corbett Institute), 1892, a gem
of Scots renaissance Freestyle by top Glasgow
architect, A N Paterson. Quality shines through
in the beautifully detailed red sandstone
dressings, rear ingleneuk and clocktower with
oversized ogee roof (colour p.223). **Arngask
Parish Church**, 1906–7, set into bank of the
Newhill road, is another outstanding import, this
time by A G Sydney Mitchell & Wilson of
Edinburgh, incorporating old Free Church of
1844. Whinstone tower is particularly notable for
the hint of Art Nouveau in stylised flowing
tracery and tapered buttresses of top stage.
Myrtlebank, *c.*1830, has canted porch indicating
its origins as tollhouse, erected to service the
newly constructed Perth/Milnathort turnpike
road. **Dunalisdair**, the old manse, 1828–9, by
Perth City Architect William Mackenzie, is
appropriately chaste classical with the tiniest
dash of ostentation in the splayed doorway.

*Left Arngask Library. Below The
Glenfarg. Bottom Arngask Parish Church.*

211

Top *Old Abbot's Deuglie House.*
Above *Arngask Old Parish Church.*

Heraldic panels, Balvaird Castle.

Old Abbot's Deuglie House, 1730
Initialled AB.KB (for Burt). Small but fascinating house at lower end of lairdly scale, fusing aristocratic and civic fashion for symmetry with strong native tradition of crowstepped gables. Roof was probably thatched and interior has been gutted as a byre, but openings appear unaltered.

Arngask is an upland parish of the Ochils, sharing a boundary with Fife and Kinross-shire. Bisected by Glen Farg, the natural communication route through the rolling hills, and now dominated by the motorway.

Duncrievie
Arngask's second village, a considerably altered fermtoun. Best is **Rose Cottage** at the junction with the Glenfarg road, a late 18th-century cottage with cable-moulded scroll skews.

Arngask House, earlier 19th century
Small and quietly distinguished classical mansion. Western block is of whinstone with sandstone channelled quoins, cornice, blocking course and diamond-plan chimneys. Roman Doric porch appears to be contemporary, but has been infilled, and the small-pane windows have been replaced.

Arngask Old Parish Church, 1806
Built before the turnpike road through Glenfarg, the old church suffered from its isolated position on Arngask Hill. A plain rectangular preaching box with galleries of 1821. Two significant architects were later associated with the building: James Campbell Walker renovated the interior and inserted two windows under the gallery in 1879; Sir George Washington Browne added the bellcote in 1907. Abandoned in 1950, now ruinous.

New Fargie, 1868, Andrew Heiton Jr
House much-altered, but an interesting L-plan stable block survives with pedimented dormers and strange stone-roofed circular tower.

Balvaird Castle, late 15th century
The most spectacular modern approach is by the long straight on the Arngask road, from which the dramatic view of 'the Place of Balward' brooding over open countryside demands a closer visit (colour p.224). Footpath winds up past the tower to less-forbidding **gatehouse**, 1567, along with now ruinous courtyard buildings. To the east lies

282

vast walled garden, probably an orchard, to the south a smaller pleasure garden and, at some distance to the north, crowstepped remains of associated buildings. Wall thicknesses of L-plan tower vary between 8ft and 4ft, suggesting significant later alterations. Luxurious in its final form, boasting stairtower and two-storey caphouse in re-entrant angle, heraldic panels over doorway, corbelled parapets and open corner rounds, sophisticated system of chimney flues, joining in one vent, and flushing latrines. Hall is especially atmospheric containing splendid carved lintel over the fireplace, elaborate imported aumbry, water basin and three large window seats, all perhaps part of general remodelling, 1567.
Historic Scotland; public access

The indistinct arms of Sir Andrew Murray and Balvaird heiress, Margaret Barclay, can be found over the entrance to the tower, probably placing its construction somewhere in the last years of the 15th century. The same heraldry appears at Tullibardine Chapel (see p.74), where Sir Andrew added transeptal chapels and a small tower to his father's building. The Balvaird estate was inherited by Sir David Murray, and it was his son, another Sir Andrew, who transformed the tower into a sumptuous courtyard *'place'* or palace in 1567. The estate passed by descent to the earls of Mansfield.

Left *Balvaird.* Below *Yew Walk, Cleish Castle.* Bottom *Garden Gates, Kinross House.*

KINROSS-SHIRE

Kinross-shire was once the second smallest county, after Clackmannanshire. In spite of its size, it has a richly varied landscape and even its own microclimates. The county is bounded by the Ochils on the north and north-west, the Lomond Hills on the east, and Benarty and the Cleish Hills on the south, effectively forming a flat-bottomed bowl around and to the west of Loch Leven. Apart from the burgh of Kinross, Milnathort is the only settlement of more than village or fermtoun size. Agriculture continues to predominate, in spite of the notoriously wet Cleish hill-lands which presented cultivation problems well into the 19th century. The pattern of land ownership perhaps reflected these difficulties, since the western estates are relatively numerous and small in terms of acreage. Architectural brinkmanship prevailed in

The name **Kinross** is derived from the Gaelic 'ceann-rois', indicating the former position of the town at the head of the promontory to Loch Leven, where the old kirkyard still survives. Kinross became a Burgh of Barony in 1540. As wool and linen weaving prospered, still evidenced by the dominant **Todd & Duncan Factory**, 1963 (colour p.221), the town spread west to the Sandport, and eventually gravitated to its current site in the early 18th century. A number of date stones and marriage lintels exist from this period. There is evidence, from an 18th-century plan after Alexander Edward, that the town was intended to integrate with the great axial avenue of Kinross House, Sir William Bruce's masterpiece, which dominates the lochside.

the county during the later 16th and early 17th centuries, led by Regent Morton at Loch Leven, as almost all the old tower houses sprouted new great halls, kitchens, ancillary buildings, courtyards and gardens. Both emerging from this tradition, and reacting against it, Sir William Bruce built his extraordinary new classical house and formal garden at Kinross (see p.218).

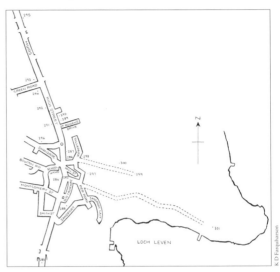

Below South Queich Bridge. Bottom Old Kirk Tower.

KINROSS

Kinross developed as county capital and staging post on the Great North Road, which forms the spine of the mile-long straggling plan along the western side of Loch Leven. Long, linear, twisting, broadening and narrowing, the town never submitted to the formal plan proposed to integrate it with the layout of Kinross House. Kinross was renowned for the manufacture of cutlery, damasks and plaids, and for excellent fishing on the loch. The southern end of High
283 Street begins at **South Queich Bridge**, an elegant shallow single-span, 1812, replacing the old triple-arched bridge, 1687, Sir William Bruce, and runs in a straight line of assorted terraced houses, largely from late 18th century.

At the heart of the town is the group of public
284 buildings clustered round the **Old Kirk Tower**, 108 High Street, 1751, and the little gothic octagonal **Cross Well Fountain**, 1893. Kirk itself (1741) demolished after 1832 leaving the old-fashioned square-plan tower with re-used lion rampant panel over doorway, corbelled balustrade and slated broached spire; clock faces from 1875. Plain two-storey market hall,

later **Town Hall**, built on the site of the kirk, 1841; tall single-storey extension, 1868–9. **Carnegie Library**, 112-114 High Street, 1905, sparing baronial.

285 **Old County Building**, 1771, Robert Adam
Adam's re-fronting of Old County Building or Tolbooth also sparing, but much more sophisticated townscape, using dog-leg of road to maximise axial impact from the southern approach. Instead of finishing with a gable, Adam extended into three-bay bow-end, articulated by giant order pilasters, and deep cornice and frieze. Two niches flank central window at first floor, and prominent second-floor plaque records *This County House was repaired by the Crown AD 1771 Robert Adam, Knight of the Shire, decorated this front at his own expense.* Well-detailed ground-floor shopfronts probably installed, 1826 (colour p.222).

98-102 High Street is a good piece of earlier 19th-century burgh architecture: original pilastered shopfront at No 102, later 19th-century shop at No 98, single storey of tenements above, and nepus gable, all slightly angled at centre to follow the bend in the road.

286 **Salutation Hotel**, 99 High Street, 1721
Harled with painted window margins, forming L-plan on corner of Avenue Road. The Salutation almost certainly remodelled and heightened, early 19th century, subsequently thoroughly restored and extended twice. Sadly, fine classical doorway to High Street now blocked up as window. Front elevation of fairly regular three bays, but side elevation shows a jumble of different-sized windows and lumps and bumps of the early inn.

287 **65-79 High Street** appears to be a run of early 19th-century tenements and houses, but **No 75** incorporates some re-used 17th-century painted beams in basement, possibly from demolition of New House (see Kinross House p.218), and weaver's date stone of 1701 to rear.
    Western backlands of High Street core still tightly knit, and bear testimony to their origins in names such as Curate Wynd, Smith Street and Piper Row. Good rows of much-restored early 18th-century vernacular houses in School Wynd and Brewery Lane, all two storey, cement-harled and pantiled. Of particular note are **10 Brewery Lane**, initialled WM.KW and dated 1720 over

Old County Building

Robert Adam was elected MP, or 'Knight of the Shire', for Kinross-shire in 1768. Whatever Robert's political motivation, the Adam brothers almost certainly viewed his election as an opportunity to promote the family firm of William Adam & Company in the best London club. Just months before the spectacular collapse of the brothers' Adelphi project in London, Robert paid for the refurbishment of Kinross-shire's civic buildings. Here too the motivation is ambiguous. On the one hand, the building is an expression in miniature of his urban planning principles for public spaces – order, harmony, scale, and unity (as a full-stop on the vista). On the other hand, as contemporary local critics recognised, it is a blatant piece of self-advertisement at fairly minimal expense.

Salutation Hotel.

Top *Mercat Cross*. Above *Clydesdale Bank*. Right *County Buildings*.

Kinross was a staging post on the old Great North Road between Queensferry and Perth. The importance of coaching to the 18th- and early 19th-century economy can be seen in the number of surviving inns. Robert Burns is said to have spent a colic-ridden night at the **Old Red Lion**, now a much-altered annexe to the Victoria Bar, 121-123 High Street. The **Loch Leven Inn**, 6 Swansacre, was briefly the Theological Hall of the Secession Church in 1765-6. At three storeys, the **Salutation** is the largest and most impressive of the central inns. Further north, **Kirkland's** and the **Green** took advantage of their less constricted sites in the early 19th century to vie for trade.

Kirkland's Hotel.

former doorway, and crowstepped **3-5 School Wynd**, with stair corbelled across chamfered corner of the building. **5 Swansacre**, fine symmetrical two-storey, three-bay early 18th-century town house. Rare shuttered window recently discovered in attic.

288 Old **mercat cross** and **jougs** removed from their original site outside the Tolbooth in 1824, and now in Sandport Park *c*.1955. Simple cross shaft of at least 17th-century origin. Jougs, or iron collar and chain, were used to secure miscreants on display to public contempt. **Auld Manse**, 8 Sandport, dated 1769 on skewputt to rear, typical two-storey, three-bay, harled with classical doorpiece, widened ground-floor windows and bow dormers.

North of junction with Station Road, High Street loosens into a villa suburb. **41 High Street**, early 19th century in origin, Edwardianised with full-height bay windows
289 linked by porch. **Clydesdale Bank**, 37-39 High Street, fine classical villa, *c*.1820, set back from road to accommodate carriage drive, and distinguished by giant pilaster quoins, columned doorpiece and round-arched panels to ground-floor windows.

290 **County Buildings**, 21-25 High Street, 1826–7, Thomas Brown
Handsome neoclassical courthouse and prison, built to replace Old County Building refronted 1771, Robert Adam. **War Memorial** in the form of market cross.

291 **Kirkland's Hotel**, 20 High Street, and its neighbour, **Burgh Chambers**, 18 High Street, both earlier 19th century, in smart three-bay villa
292 format. **Kinross High School** has nicely balanced arrangement of Dutch-gabled boys' and girls' entrances to High Street, both with pairs of umbrella fanlights. Later 19th-century villas with frilly bargeboards mark end of High Street and beginning of Muirs. **1 High Street** has mildly

293 baronial corner tower of 1896. **Green Hotel**, 1829, was extremely large coaching inn for its time, purpose-built with 16th-century styling of diagonally set chimneys and broad mullioned
294 windows (colour p.223). **Bank of Scotland**, 2-4 High Street, *c.*1835, elegant symmetrical villa with notable doorpiece of fluted Ionic columns set *in antis* and octagonal chimneys (colour p.224). **Moss Grove**, 18 Muirs, earlier 19th century, also refined with generous multi-pane windows and broad bowed bay.

295 **St Paul's Episcopal Church**, Muirs, 1875
Curious polygonal tower with open arcaded belfry fronts the road. Inside, the white walls and plentiful timber of the pews and roof are transformed to a glowing richness by the light from the stained glass.

296 **Kinross West Church**, Station Road, 1831–2, George Angus
Not one to waste a successful design, Angus built identical perpendicular churches at Kincardine and Kingskettle (see *The Kingdom of Fife* in this series), all of which are variations on Archibald Elliot's Cockpen Church of 1818 (see *Midlothian*). Main trunk of T-plan is M-gabled, with tall hoodmoulded windows. Tower is capped with latticed parapet and octagonal pinnacles. **West Manse**, 15 Station Road, follows the traditional design of its predecessor in Sandport, with the addition of a porch and bipartite ground-floor windows.

Top *St Paul's Episcopal Church.* Above *Kinross West Church.* Left *Rachel House.*

297 **Rachel House**, Avenue Road, 1995, Gray Marshall & Associates
Beautifully sited in old kitchen garden to Kinross House, Scotland's first children's hospice successfully performs its difficult task. Far from daunting, exotic fancy-dress appearance of main block as a 'mandarin's hat' is light-hearted and welcoming. Scale is low in embracing crescent-plan to the entrance, and emphasis is on light – the stone and timber-clad walls are amply glazed under broad eaves of the slate roof.

Haynes

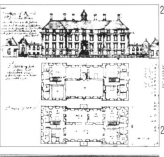

RCAHMS

298 Kinross House Lodges, 1905, Thomas Ross
Original ogee-roofed lodges and main gates built
c.1685 by the celebrated Alloa architect/mason
Tobias Bauchop from wooden models by William
Bruce. Buildings demolished, c.1810, and
reconstructed in present beautifully crafted form,
1905, by Thomas Ross, with splendid wrought-
iron gates (colour p.221).

299 Kinross House and Gardens, 1679–93,
Sir William Bruce
Exceptional in almost every respect, Kinross has
the rare and serene beauty of a true masterpiece.
Bruce's own house arose slowly and carefully
over 14 years of declining political and financial
fortune. Begun in 1686, it was entirely executed in
fine ashlar. Apart from native precedents at
Culross, Berwick and other houses, indirect
European patternbook influences can also be
found. Great charm and beauty of the house is
the uncontrived harmony of all parts, combined
with the very highest levels of craftsmanship –
Alexander Eizatt, wright; James Horn, smith;
Peter Paul Boyse and Cornelius van Nerven,
responsible for magnificent stone carving over
doorways, all appear in surviving accounts, but
key tradesmen such as plasterer and wood-carver
not known (colour p.221). Internally, Bruce's
panelled **entrance hall** survives, complete with
screens of Ionic columns. Many family rooms on
this floor remain largely intact, retaining
panelling and Dutch-style fireplaces, some set
fashionably across corner of room. Staircase too,
wreathed in intricately carved oak foliage,
original, but state rooms on first floor, including
enormous 'Sallon', not completed in Bruce's time.
Based around lengthwise corridor through centre

Haynes

*Kinross House: top garden front; middle
elevation and plan of house by Alexander
Edward; above carving over doorways by
Dutchmen, Peter Paul Boyse and Cornelius
van Nerven, who also worked at Drumlanrig
for 1st Duke of Queensberry, 1686.*

*… by much the finest seat I have yet seen
in Scotland.*
John Macky, *A Journey Through Scotland*,
1723

of house, near-symmetrical plan incorporates curious mezzanine floors reached by turnpike stairs at north and south ends. 'Houses of office' demolished, 1852, and roof replaced, 1869, John Lessels. Dr Thomas Ross and Fred MacGibbon (son of late partner David MacGibbon) carried out extensive, but discreet, restoration of the long-empty house for Sir Basil Montgomery in 1902, including adaptation of staircase ceiling to complete Bruce's Great Dining Room ceiling, and alteration of recessed entrance portico as porch (as close as possible to the original concept).

Bruce moved to the old house (confusingly called New House, demolished 1723) of the earls of Morton in 1679 to supervise the laying out of the gardens. Contemporary survey drawing by Alexander Edward shows that the formal landscape setting was significant from the start, aligned axially from the town, through the centre of the house and the **Fish Gate** (colour p.222), to the island ruins of Lochleven Castle. Both the Fish Gate and New House were originally closer to the water – level of loch lowered, 1830. Enchanting character of the garden today, with lawns, topiary, hedges and large herbaceous beds, essentially Edwardian, planned by Thomas Ross, and dating from Sir Basil's 1902–28 rescue of the estate (colour p.224). North garden **loggia** appears to be late 18th century, **loggia** adjacent to south pavilion, early 20th century.

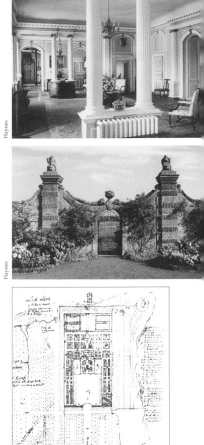

Top *Entrance hall.* Middle *Fish Gate celebrates the wealth of aquatic life in the loch, including the famous trout, which have distinctive red flesh.* Above *Plan of garden by Alexander Edward.* Left *Stables.*

The New House of the earls of Morton, which stood just outside the north-east corner of Kinross House gardens, was built *c.*1554, with an L-plan lodging within a courtyard. Likely to have been a structure of some prestige, as the Danish Ambassadors to the Court of James VI were entertained here in 1590, and it is known to have had a superb collection of wall hangings. Stones from the garden walls of New House are said to be incorporated into the present garden walls, and it is possible that fragments of the house itself were re-used about the town following demolition *c.*1723.

300 **Stables** attributed to Bruce, but there was already a stable court at the house and design looks rather later, perhaps incorporating earlier fabric: two symmetrical ogee-roofed pavilions linked by single-storey range with central archway, all with round-headed openings and raised long and short dressings in William Adam style. Two-storey, conical-roofed **doocot** stands at centre of courtyard.

301 Bruce Mortuary Chapel, East Burial Ground, 1860
Old parish kirk of 1675 abandoned 1742. This
small stone-roofed burial aisle for the Bruces of
Arnot reconstructed on the site, 1860. Small
crenellated **Watch Tower**, 1853, safeguarded
against resurrectionists.

*Top Bruce Mortuary Chapel. Above Loch
Leven and Castle. Right Lochleven Castle.*

Following the power struggle at
Carberry, Mary, Queen of Scots, was
held prisoner here from 17th June 1567
until her escape on 2nd May 1568. The
escape was effected by 'Daft Willie', who
stole the keys from his uncle, Sir William
Douglas, and locked him in the castle.

The first split from the established
Church of Scotland centred on the
issues of heritors' patronage,
diminishing orthodoxy, and perceived
weakness of the General Assembly.
Revd Ebenezer Erskine, former minister
of Portmoak Parish, led the breakaway
movement from its foundation at
Gairneybridge, creating an Associate
Presbytery. As a result he was deposed
from his living in 1740. Members of the
new **Secession Church** wanted the right
to appoint their own minister, rather
than landowners' nominees, and
countered wavering beliefs by renewing
the Covenant in 1743.

Parenwell Bridge.

302 Lochleven Castle, *c.*1400
Romantic and picturesque qualities of the castle
and its island setting appreciated at an early date
by Sir William Bruce, who made it the focus of
the vista from his projected new house at Kinross,
1679. Curtain wall probably predates four-storey
tower of squared rubble, entered by forestair and
grand round-arched doorway at level of hall,
above two vaulted storeys. Enclosing wall, later
15th century, with 16th-century modifications for
Regent Morton, including circular bedroom
tower at south-east corner and large window to
new hall in west wall. Little remains of numerous
associated structures which lined courtyard.
Historic Scotland; open to the public; guidebook

Secession Church Monument,
Gairneybridge Farm, 1883
Obelisk commemorating formation of first
Presbytery of the Secession Church, 1733, at an
inn on site now occupied by farm steading.
Gairney Bridge, late 18th century, broad, shallow
arch with channelled voussoirs, said to date from
completion of Queensferry/Perth turnpike road,
1753, but looks later.

PARENWELL
Ornamental **Bridge**, 1838, has inscribed panels
recording that it was built by Lord Chief
Commissioner Adam to mark the site of Lord
Rothes' attempt to seize Mary, Queen of Scots,
and Lord Darnley in 1565. **Binn Cottage and
Monument**, early 19th-century, single-storey
cottage with central porch.

Clockwise from top *Kinross-shire from Dowhill; Todd & Duncan, Kinross; Armorial panel, Kinross House Lodge; Belmont Castle, Meigle; Kinnoull Hill; Kinross House.*

221

Top *Fish Gates, Kinross House*. Top right *Alyth Parish Church*. Middle *Old County Building, Kinross*. Above right *Kinfauns Dairy*. Right *Kinfauns Castle Hotel*. Above *Scone New Church, New Scone*.

Top *Arngask Library, Glenfarg.* Above *War memorial, Blairgowrie.* Left *Green Hotel, Kinross.* Below *Kinrossie Market Cross.*

Top *Bank of Scotland, Kinross*. Top right *Balvaird*. Middle *Dowhill Castle*. Above right *Robert Douglas Memorial School, New Scone*. Right *View to Lochleven Castle from Kinross House*. Above *Abernyte Parish Churchyard*.

Blairforge Smiddy, early 19th century, possibly Daniel Robertson
Behind modern porch, pantiled house and workshop to smiddy have identical three-bay frontages with segmental-arched windows.

303 MARYBURGH

Once picturesque single-storey cottages stepped up the hill, now much altered. Small planned village, named after William Adam's wife, Mary Robertson, established, 1740, to house estate coal miners. Non-commissioned officers of the Dragoons lodged in the village during summer grazing for their horses at Blair Adam.

304 **Blair Adam**, from 1733, William Adam
Perversely, least 'Adam' house in the country, family home of the architectural dynasty a fantastic hotchpotch of buildings and styles, added over course of century and a half to form courtyard behind comfortably scaled, but rigorously unornamented house *'upon the plan of an ordinary manse'* (William Adam II) on ancient site by William Adam for his own and his factor's use. This house still lies at the centre of main east front. His son, John, added the porch, remodelled wings and linked the house to rear steading, 1775. William Adam, later Lord Chief Commissioner, built southern range of offices, 1805, linked by covered walkway to house, and then the two towers. Major replanning scheme, 1859, including construction of new dining room with enormous cast-iron Adam Revival fireplace, entrance hall and hub known as 'the Corridor', by David Bryce for William Patrick Adam. Three-sided **walled garden**, laid out, 1755–61, by John Adam, contains contemporary **Gardener's House**, with blind Venetian doorway, rusticated **gateways** in east and west walls and pedestal **monument** of 1833 to the estate improvements by William and John Adam.

William Adam, 1689–1748, 'Scotland's universal architect' and founding father of the famous architectural dynasty, bought the 'wild unsheltered moor' (*New Statistical Account*) of Blair Crambeth from the Colviles of Cleish in 1733. He built a house for his factor, added the estates of Dowhill, Woodend and Dichindad, and began an ambitious programme of planting and improvements. Adam's lairdly ambitions were financed by a huge range of entrepreneurial pursuits, including his own large architectural practice and interests in coal, salt, barley, timber, brick, stone, iron, glass and other businesses. John Adam, 1721–92, laid out the South Avenue to complement his father's North Avenue, and elsewhere continued planting on a prodigious scale in a less formal manner. Picturesque ruins were planned for The Hill (1760) and The Glen (1763), but never built. Robert Adam, 1728–92, prepared remodelling plans for his father in the 1740s, and a new house for his brother John in 1772. The disastrous speculative scheme at the Adelphi in London ended any prospect of a new Blair Adam. The house was mortgaged and stood empty between 1785 and 1796. John's son, William, 1751–1854, an eminent lawyer and Whig politician, reoccupied the house and revived the landscaping of the gardens. Various re-casting schemes for the house, including a Tudor-gothic one by Sir Jeffry Wyatville, came to nothing.

Left *Blair Adam.* Below *Robert Adam's unexecuted plans for a new house at Blair Adam.*

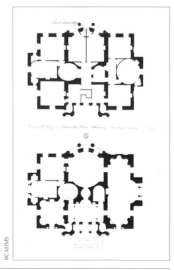

Coach House appears to be late 18th century, again probably John Adam, but altered to form curious mix of pediments and pantiles. **North Blair**, now standing sentinel over motorway, is fragment of very grand court of offices designed, 1760, John Adam, but never finished. Converted to house for Commissioner Adam's clerk, 1814. **Blairfordel Lodge**, early 19th century, probably by John Adam's protégé Daniel Robertson, pretty octagonal gatehouse.

Middleton House, mid-18th century
Idyllic traditional farmhouse. Surely originally harled to show off smart channelled quoins, eaves course and window margins. Wallhead above first-floor windows unusually high, reminiscent of Shetland 'haa hooses'.

Dullomuir House, c.1755, possibly John Adam
Restrained but extremely beguiling two-storey, three-bay house with oddly anachronistic crowstepped gables, neat margins, triple flued chimneystacks and 19th-century timber porch. Originally harled, built as replacement accommodation for estate factor, who had lived in Blair Adam House during William Adam's time. Former **stables** and linen **mill** adjoin.

Top Coach House. Middle Middleton House. Above Dullomuir House.

KELTYBRIDGE
Straddling the boundary with Fife, the **Kelty Bridge** itself is mid-18th century, distinguished by neatly rusticated voussoirs. Village laid out from mid-18th century as mixture of single- and two-storey houses for mineworkers.

Dowhill, from 1710
Developed from Barns House built by Mr Burt, later factor to William Adam. Charmingly remodelled and extended, earlier 19th century, in manner of William Burn with Tudor-gothic hoodmoulds, mullioned windows, and tall octagonal and square chimneys.

Dowhill Castle in 1770 from an engraving after John Clerk of Eldin, brother-in-law of the then owner, Robert Adam. On his father's death in 1748, Robert inherited the Dowhill estate and styled himself Robert Adam of Dowhill.

305 **Dowhill Castle**, from early 16th century
Even field boundary walls here, made of massive boulders, have an air of antiquity. Long ruinous, Dowhill was once a palace of considerable sophistication belonging to the Lindsays of Dowhill. Rectangular-plan tower house, perhaps incorporating earlier building, is clearly visible at eastern end of remaining palace block. Probably extended and refaced in prestigious ashlar, mid-16th century, changing vertical emphasis to horizontal L-plan hinged round circular tower on

south-west corner. Broad south-facing windows maximised light and views from the hilltop. Another circular tower to north-east, incorporating doocot, all that remains of courtyard wall. Little survives above principal first-floor level, but tempting to speculate on the possibility of gallery behind central oriel of west range, which looked out over rolling countryside (colour pp.221&224).

KIRKTON OF CLEISH

306 **St Mary's Parish Kirk**, 1832, Daniel McIntosh
Built as preaching box on ancient and tranquil site at the centre of the parish to replace John Adam church of 1775, destroyed by fire. Minimal decorative treatment enlivened by addition of chancel and crenellated tower, 1897, Hardy & Wright. Small crowstepped **session house** stands next to gates. Back part of adjacent **manse** dates from 1744, and front from 1837, James Macfarlane.

Cleish Public School, 1835, small T-plan parochial school, with clock set into front gable. Unusually, adjacent **Old Schoolhouse**, 18th century, had boxbeds in attic for boarders. **Cleish House**, 1765, broad three-bay, with widely spaced windows extended by *faux* early 19th-century wing, 1960s, W Schomberg Scott.

Top *St Mary's Parish Kirk*. Middle *Cleish Public School*. Above *Cleish House*. Left *Cleish Castle*.

Cleish Castle, from 15th century
Much altered and little-documented, old Place of Cleish is difficult to unravel. Likely that taller, narrower south wing was original tower house. Unusual feature here is buttress effect of series of offsets in massive south gable wall, suggesting a number of remodellings. Broad lower wing added to form L-plan house in courtyard, with generous circular stair to second floor inside re-entrant angle and smaller ashlar turret stair corbelled from

second floor in centre of east elevation. Relocated pediment on turret, bearing date of 1600, and initials of Robert Colville and his wife Beatrice Haldane, probably contemporary with these additions. By 1840, house was roofless and John Lessels called in to revamp it, probably removing remains of original harling. Interiors and Lessels' charming forestair and first-floor porch stripped away, early 1970s, as part of Saltire and Civic Trust Award-winning restoration scheme by Michael Spens. Resulting light and airy interior of exposed steel beams and tiled flooring in hall, incorporating ceiling (now at Dean Centre, Edinburgh) and hangings by Eduardo Paolozzi, has since been remodelled in more traditional style. Earliest surviving yew walk in Scotland (see p.213), dating from early 17th century, once formed part of formal gardens.

Hardiston Farmhouse, late 18th century
Fine two-storey, three-bay Improvement farmhouse, harled with rusticated quoins, scrolled skewputts, later flat-roofed porch and Edwardian curvy dormerheads to rear wing.

Top *Hardiston Farmhouse*. Above *Aldie Castle*.

307 **Aldie Castle**, 1464
Stronghold of powerful Mercer family, in commanding position and arranged in the standard manner with vaulted ground floor, hall at first floor and accommodation above. Angle turrets and top storey of tower rebuilt, 1585. Tall southern wing pre-dated existing two-storey south wing, which contains new kitchen, and perhaps replacement hall above. Further three-storey wing added to east, and central entrance and stair installed to rationalise the plan, probably in mid-17th century. Tower was unusually and expensively built of ashlar, additions were of rubble, but whole building harled during restoration by Ian G Lindsay, started late 1930s, interrupted by Second World War and continued into 1960s. Scheme was ground-breaking and pointed the way for many post-war tower house restorations.

Blairingone Church, 1836
Extension church, built to serve remoter western part of Fossoway Parish. T-plan with porch in right hand angle of the T.

Vicar's Bridge Cairn
Small cairn incorporating panel from old Vicar's Bridge commemorating Revd Thomas Forrest of Dollar, martyred in Edinburgh, 1538.

Briglands, 1759

Originally long, low seven-bay classical house of considerable charm, mauled and extended, 19th century. From 1899 Robert Lorimer remodelled the house in his best 17th-century style for the advocate J Avon Clyde, later Lord President. First came the **lodge**, a loose interpretation of Queen Mary's Bath House at the Palace of Holyroodhouse, and pretty bellcast **garden pavilion**. New entrance wing and courtyard followed, 1903, complete with scrolled dormerheads, crowstepped gables, carved panel over door and corner sundial. More remodelling of old house, 1907, this time running a gallery through the attic to new guest wing and billiard room at west end. Details are engaging, but whole scheme definitely at the expense of the early house.

Fossoway and Tulliebole Kirk, Crook of Devon, 1806

Plain symmetrical preaching box, with bellcote of baluster columns and pagoda roof, probably from earlier church, 1729, on the site. Interior recast, 1926, and two-storey session house added in remarkably sensitive vernacular Georgian style, 1966. **Kirkyard** contains 18th-century gravestones and table tombs.

Top *Perspective elevation of Briglands by V D Horsburgh.* Above *Fossoway and Tulliebole Kirk.*

308 **Tulliebole Castle**, from 16th century

Captivating tower house and hall. In spite of baronial trimmings, decidedly domestic rather than defensive in setting beside fish-ponds, doocot and wash house. Described by MacGibbon and Ross as all of one period. More plausible explanation for differing roof heights, proliferation of staircases and massive internal wall is that Tulliebole started life as the tower at the west end, maybe early 16th century. Next came lower east range, housing spacious new kitchen and hall. This latter room contains astonishing fireplace with moulded lintel of over 11ft in length and possible evidence of gallery at eastern end.

Tulliebole Castle.

First mention of buildings at Tulliebole is made in a grant by James IV confirming the lands to the Hering family. It was sold to John Haliday in 1598. His son, John, was responsible for the entrance tower. Henry Welwood purchased the house in 1749, since when it has passed by descent to the Moncreiff family.

Tulliebole Castle.

Although dormer on this range and bartizaned entrance tower both bear the date 1608 and initials IHHO for John Haliday and Helen Oliphant, junction between the two parts of the building is awkward, suggesting different construction dates. Entrance tower most likely to be 1608, but curiously baronial for this period, with lots of gunloops and roofline features including strange serpentine waterspout. Inside, broad ceremonial stair rises to hall at first floor, and corbelled turnpike stair services floors above. By the time of Lord Cockburn's *Circuit Journeys*, 1801, roof had been removed to Glendevon Castle. Tulliebole repaired shortly afterwards by Sir Henry Moncreiff and narrowly escaped proposal of 1875 for large and charmless baronial addition by Robert Matheson. Bathroom tower to rear, 1926, and kitchen conversion of woodstore by Ian G Lindsay, who restored the house in 1956. Roofless lectern **doocot** dated 1751 above door; no timber nesting boxes remain. Crenellated lean-to ornamental **wash house**, early 19th century, stands beside fish-ponds.

Below *Balado Bridge*. Middle *Turfhills Farmhouse*. Bottom *NATO Early Warning Centre*.

Wellwood-Moncreiff Monument, Old Tulliebole Kirkyard, 1855
Obelisk memorial to the celebrated Lord of Session, Sir James Wellwood-Moncreiff of Tulliebole, 9th Baronet, set among cypress trees.

Middle Coldrain Farmhouse, mid-18th century
Traditional two-storey, three-bay farmhouse, with small widely spaced windows, later central porch and lower single-storey wings. Difference in height and angle between existing slated roof and skews suggests it was probably originally thatched.

Balado Bridge, 1777
Fine segmental-arched, humpback bridge, now superseded on Crook of Devon/Kinross road.

Turfhills Farmhouse, early 19th century
Handsome and generously proportioned two-storey, three-bay house, unbalanced by later bay window and single-storey wing.

NATO Early Warning Centre, 1981
Distinctive swollen white 'golf balls' in landscape, early warning radar detectors of late Cold War era.

The Lecker Stane, 18th century
Large slab, set near B918 turn-off to Dalqueich, said to be resting place for coffin bearers on the way to church in Kinross.

Balado Home Farm, late 18th century
Near-symmetrical arrangement of two-storey
house and single-storey, piend-roofed wings. Main
house appears to have early 19th-century roof and
porch and 20th-century bipartite windows.
Polygonal **horse-mill** incorporates doocot in the
pantiled roof.

Below *Hilton House*. Left *Market Street,
with Town Hall steeple*. Middle *New
Road*. Bottom *Thornton House.*

Ballingall Farm, from early 18th century
Original laird's house now ruinous, as is attached
steading. New house of soft red Milnathort
sandstone with contrasting dressings, mid-19th
century, sits a little aloof on a knoll.

Hilton House, *c.*1830
Small classical laird's house of two storeys over
basement, with steps to Doric-columned
doorcase. House and pretty octagonal milk-
house, *c.*1860, enjoy commanding views, blighted
only by motorway.

MILNATHORT
Known locally as 'Milsie' or 'Millaforth', the town
developed as a market and weaving centre. Streets
radiate from The Cross, distinguished by 95ft
tower and steeple of **Town Hall**, 1855. To the south
is **High Street**, where a number of weavers'
workshops survive at ground and basement level
below houses. In **Wester Loan**, the old market
place, **Cross Keys Inn**, mid-18th century, like most
of the early houses here, was probably thatched.
Back Loan contains dated lintels from 1698 to 1750.
13 Manse Road, *c.*1815, is manse-like apart from
unusually high wallhead above first-floor
windows, but **Orwell House** further up the road
was the actual manse, built 1798, remodelled 1825.
New Road appears late 18th century in origin, to
judge from scrolled skewputts of **nos 21-23** and
others. Opposite, a restrained touch of Art Deco.
Symmetrical pair of forestairs lead to pilastered
doorpiece of **Thornton House**, 1 Perth Road, finest
earlier 19th-century house in Milnathort. **Meal mill**
has gone, but **Mill House**, 2 Stirling Road, dated
1792, remains.

309

231

Orwell Parish Kirk, Milnathort, 1729
Distinct building line runs just below the level of the roundels, indicating it has been raised in height, probably at the time of internal recasting, 1880s. Design of kirk very Presbyterian in symmetry of long south elevation and T-plan, but residue of Episcopalian form found in 17th-century bellcote with its baluster columns, re-used from previous church on the old site next to Loch Leven.

Former United Presbyterian Church, South Street, 1867–9, J & W Ingram (Kilmarnock)
Fairly muscular gothic externally, apart from broached spire, too slim and gawky to be convincing. Inside, horseshoe gallery revealed true character of the building: a God box to accommodate 700 people. Now converted to flats.

Hattonburn House, mid-19th century
Hattonburn grew from relatively modest house into rambling mansion, complete with Italianate tower, late 19th century. Recently it has shrunk back again to more manageable size, by shedding tower wing and numerous dormers.

Arlary House, mid-18th century
Very accomplished laird's house, symmetrical, long and low in proportion, and beautifully detailed with long and short quoins and window surrounds. North side pedimented, and south side has late 18th-century porch. Early 19th-century **steading** has impressive series of cart-arches and circular horse-mill.

Top Orwell Parish Kirk. *Middle* Hattonburn House, *from a visiting album kept by Violet Montgomery. Above* Arlary House.

Sir James Balfour of Pittendreich, 1525–83, masterful political opportunist and lawyer, probably involved in the murder of Lord Darnley. Lord President from 1567. Extended Burleigh Castle in 1582.

Right and below Burleigh Castle.

310 **Burleigh Castle**, from early 16th century
Four storeys of tower complete to corbels of parapet and angle turrets, but fragmentary above this level. Sir James Balfour of Pittendreich responsible for incorporation of old tower into courtyard layout of a palace, 1582. Two-storey entrance range appears to have had additional

storey, perhaps timber gallery. At south-west corner, rounded (possibly bedroom) tower corbelled to square and gabled at second floor. Further range enclosed southern side of courtyard, probably new kitchen and hall, on the basis of contemporary developments nearby.
Historic Scotland; open to the public; guidebook

From top *Lethangie House; gazebo; Michael Bruce's Cottage; Michael Bruce Memorial.*

Burleigh Farmhouse and Steading, *c.*1820
New farmhouse, *c.*1820, added to back of existing house. Parts of steading appear to pre-date this, but cartshed and granary range contemporary. Steading converted to housing, 1996.

Lethangie House, from early 19th century
Lethangie started life as modest T-plan farmhouse, but grew like Topsy with the addition of bow-fronted wing and ingleneuk, *c.*1870, rear wing and remodelling, *c.*1910, William Kerr of Alloa, and further wing to east by Kerr, *c.*1923. Extraordinary survival is early 19th-century **rustic summerhouse**, walled with rustic logs and heather, roofed with fish-scale slates and lined internally with twigs laid in geometric patterns. Interesting estate buildings include pretty Tudor-gothic **south lodge**, *c.*1820, crowstepped **stables**, *c.*1870, early 19th-century **gazebo**, and **kitchen garden** and square-plan **doocot**, which appear to be marked on Alexander Edward's Kinross House estate plan of late 17th century.

Easter and Wester Balgedie
Two fermtouns, picturesquely grouped around their respective farmhouses on slopes of Bishops Hill, retaining much of their layout.

KINNESSWOOD
Famed for its production of vellum in 18th century. Oldest and most attractive part of village, **The Cobbles**, straggles up steep slope of Bishops Hill.

311 **Michael Bruce's Cottage**, earlier 18th century, now museum to poet Bruce and the village, is the best preserved of the traditional 18th-century houses. More modern part of the old village, **Main Street**, has good early 19th-century houses, particularly **Douglas House**. Traffic, unsympathetic alterations to some houses and some ugly 1970s and '80s developments have taken their toll on the once-charming character of the village.

312 **Portmoak Parish Kirk**, 1832
Precipitously sited on the side of Bishops Hill, plain God box incorporating birdcage belfry of previous 1659 building. Among traditional 18th-

St Serf or Servanus was a 6th century scholar saint, who established a number of chapels of ease around the margins of the loch. His pet robin was brought back to life by his follower, St Mungo, or Kentigern, as symbolised in the City of Glasgow's coat of arms. Brude, last king of the Picts, is reputed to have given the largest island of Loch Leven to the hermit Culdees in 838. David I subsequently granted it to the Augustinian Canons of St Andrews in 1153, who probably constructed the priory here in the late 12th century. From 1395 the prior was Andrew of Wyntoun, author of The Orygynale Cronykil of Scotland.

Above *Well and wash house.* Right *Arnot Mill.*

Called Fons Scotiae by the Romans, and site of a Red Friars hospital (1250–1587), Scotlandwell is famed for its curative waters. The medieval field system, a form of lowland crofting known as the 'crooked rigs', operated into the 1920s, and is still visible above the village.

St Serf's Priory.

and 19th-century headstones of kirkyard stands remarkably urbane **Michael Bruce Memorial** – monumental Greek Revival sarcophagus in the manner of W H Playfair erected to the poet and Secession hero, 1842, 76 years after his death, and months before the Disruption split the Kirk again.

SCOTLANDWELL

Much of the village dates from 18th century. From 1857–60 Thomas Bruce of Arnot carried out improvements in the village, including handsome 313 **well** and **wash house**, to designs by David Bryce.

Arnot Tower, late 15th century

Prestigious seat of the Arnots of that Ilk. Long ruinous four-storey rectangular tower, expensively built in coursed ashlar. Ground-floor vaults also of ashlar. Remains of later additions against east and south walls. In 15th century the lands were held from the king, as Earl of Fife, but in 1507 Walter Arnot's '*manor or place, tower and fortalice*' were incorporated in a free barony. Sir William Bruce acquired the estate in 1705 in payment of a debt. Adjacent half-piend roofed **house**, 1882, Kinnear & Peddie, much altered.

Arnot Mill and House, mid-19th century

Unusual three-storey estate mill, incorporating lintel, *1593. VA.MB*, presumably from tower house. Fine traditional harled mill house with piended roof. **Greenside Arnot**, 18th century, pretty 1½-storey symmetrical cottage, with lean-to wings, incorporating scrolled skewputts.

New Gullet Bridge, *c.*1835

Elegant elliptical arch over new cut of River Leven.

314 **St Serf's Priory**, St Serf's Island, Loch Leven, late 12th century

Small roofless rectangular-plan fragment of priory church secularised at the Reformation. Remains of arches to chancel and perhaps to tower at east and west ends respectively. Foundations of substantial (83ft by 22ft) structure lie to the west.

ACKNOWLEDGEMENTS

A large number of people have contributed their time, expertise and enthusiasm to the completion of this volume. David Walker's meticulous scholarship informed the original statutory lists for Perthshire, which still remain the best source of information on many of the buildings. Without his invaluable advice and encyclopaedic knowledge I could never have begun such a task, and to him I am enormously indebted. Charles McKean's energy and devotion to the architecture of Scotland founded this series, and his commitment to this volume has proved similarly uplifting.

The eventual completion of the book owes everything to the saintly patience, constant encouragement and hard work of Helen Leng and Susan Skinner of the Rutland Press, who have both contributed far more than should be reasonably expected of any publishers. Thanks too are due to the copy editor, Kate Blackadder, to Adrian Hallam of Almond Consultancy, who brought order and harmony to the sprawling muddle of text and pictures, to Kevin Farquharson, who produced the maps, to Eilidh Donaldson for a wide range of help and to Oula Jones for the index.

My family and friends have provided endless support and assistance during the long gestation of this book. I am particularly grateful to Christine Haynes, John and Juliet Haynes, Sara, Tony and Ben Wills, David Taylor, Simon Montgomery, Sarah Montgomery, Debbie Mays, Victoria Ball, Bruce Ritchie, Tony Cairns, Geoff Pearson, Anthony and Alison Montgomery, Althea, Kirsty and Henny Dundas-Bekker, Pippa Robeson, Andrew Fleming, Cathy Orton, Ian Elder-Cheyne, Alex von der Becke, Mark Pedroz, Joanna White and Hanisa Santimano.

John Freeman of Perth & Kinross Heritage Trust nobly waded through the draft text at very short notice, saved me from numerous howlers, provided many valuable suggestions for improvements and helped enormously with the photography. Particular thanks also to Rachel Tilling and Bill Beaton of Perth & Kinross Heritage Trust, Bertram Zank of Perth & Kinross Council, Revd Fergus Harris of Perth Civic Trust, Mr and Mrs R Moncreiff, Dr David Munro and Mrs Elizabeth Adam of Kinross Civic Trust, who assisted greatly in the research and willingly put their detailed knowledge of the area at my disposal. Stephen Connelly of the A K Bell Library Archives was exceptionally helpful in tracking down material from the Dean of Guild records and other local sources. Paul Adair, Perth Museum & Art Gallery, first introduced me to the delights of the Magnus Jackson and John Wood Collections.

Past and present friends and colleagues at Historic Scotland have been unstinting in their support and practical assistance, most notably Gordon Barclay, Kirsty Burrell, Paul Byrne, Krysia Campbell, Richard Emerson, Sally Foster, Bernadette Goslin, Claire Hunt, Caroline Kernan, Holly Kinnear, Chris MacGregor, Aonghus MacKechnie, Daniel Maudlin, Graeme Munro, Sara Newman, Alan Rutherford, Norma Smith, Jim Souness and Mark Watson. Pam Craig, Cathie Dodds, Ann Spears, Fiona Scott, Sarah Gosman and Iain Fuller of the Listing Section deserve special thanks. I am also indebted to Historic Scotland's Library staff, Paulette Hill and Billy McColm, and to Iain Shaw and David Ritchie of the Photographic Library for their untiring efforts on my behalf.

As always, the staff of RCAHMS and the National Monuments Record of Scotland have been unfailingly helpful, especially Ruth Wimberley, Jane Thomas, Veronica Steele, Philip Graham, Simon Green, Miriam McDonald and Miles Oglethorpe. Graham Douglas, formerly of RCAHMS, undertook valuable photography. Chris Fleet of the National Library of Scotland Map Library provided much help and information on the Pont manuscripts. My thanks also to Christopher Dingwall and Scott Cooper of the Garden History Society.

Last, and certainly not least, I am deeply indebted to the many owners and architects who shared their knowledge and love of the buildings of Perth & Kinross with me.

SELECT BIBLIOGRAPHY
Historic Scotland Inventory of Gardens & Designed Landscapes in Scotland, **Schedule of Ancient Monuments and Statutory List of Listed Buildings** (various dates); **Encyclopaedia Perthensis** (1772); **New Statistical Account of Scotland Vol X** (1815); **Statistical Account of Scotland** (1791–9); H Colvin, **A Biographical Dictionary of British Architects, 1600–1840** (1995 edition); P Dennison & R Coleman, **Historic Coupar Angus** (1997); R Fawcett, **Scottish Architecture from the Accession of the Stewarts to the Reformation** (1994); W R Findlay, **Heritage of Perth** (1985); M Glendinning, R MacInnes & A MacKechnie, **A History of Scottish Architecture** (1996); D Graham-Campbell, **Perth – The Fair City** (1994); F Groome, **Ordnance Gazetteer of Scotland** (1884); D Howard, **Scottish Architecture from the Reformation to the Restoration, 1560–1660** (1995); J & J Keay, **Collins Encyclopaedia of Scotland** (1994); D MacGibbon & T Ross, **The Castellated and Domestic Architecture of Scotland Vols I-V** (1887); L J Macgregor & R D Oram, **Atholl & Gowrie** (2000); L Melville, **The Fair Lands of Gowrie** (1939); R & A Moncreiff (eds), **The Annals of Kinross-shire** (1990); D Omand (ed), **The Perthshire Book** (1999); RCAHMS, **Inventory of Monuments & Constructions of Fife, Kinross & Clackmannan** (1933); RCAHMS, **North-East Perth – An Archaeological Landscape** (1990); RCAHMS, **South-East Perth – An Archaeological Landscape** (1994); W Scott, **The Fair Maid of Perth** (1828); J W & R E Seath, **Dunbarney – A Parish with a Past** (1991); M L Stavert, **Perth – A Short History** (1991); D B Taylor (ed), **3rd Statistical Account of Scotland – Perth & Kinross** (1979); N Tranter, **The Fortified House in Scotland Vol II** (1962); A R Urquhart, **Auld Perth** (1906); B Walker, **The Agricultural Buildings of Greater Strathmore, 1770–1920** (unpublished PhD thesis, University of Dundee, 1983); B Walker & W S Gauldie, **Architects & Architecture on Tayside** (1984); B Walker & G Ritchie, **Exploring Scotland's Heritage – Fife & Tayside** (1987); N H Walker, **Kinross House** (1990); J Zeune, **The Last Scottish Castles** (1992).

In addition, many further parish histories, newspaper cuttings, biographies and much other information can be found in the excellent local history section of the A K Bell Library.

Selected web sites:
Dunning Parish Historical Society: http://www.dunning.mcmail.com/
British Architectural Library: http://store.yahoo.com/riba-library/
Historic Scotland: http://www.historic-scotland.gov.uk/
Kinross-shire bibliography: http://www.tulbol.demon.co.uk/bibliography.htm
National Library of Scotland: http://www.nls.ac.uk/
Perth & Kinross Council: http://www.pkc.gov.uk/
Royal Commission on Ancient & Historical Monuments of Scotland: http://www.rcahms.gov.uk/
Scottish Cultural Resources Access Network: http://www.scran.ac.uk/

INDEX

GLOSSARY

1. Architrave (projecting ornamental frame)
2. Astragal (glazing bar)
3. Barge (gable board)
4. Basement, raised
5. Bullseye, keyblocked (circular window with projecting blocks punctuating frame)
6. Buttress (supporting projection)
7. Caphouse (top chamber)
8. Cartouche (decorative tablet)
9. Cherrycocking (masonry joints filled with small stones)
10. Channelled ashlar (recessed horizontal joints in smooth masonry)
11. Chimneycope, corniced
12. Chimneycope, moulded
13. Close (alley)
14. Cobbles
15. Console (scroll bracket)
16. Corbel (projection support)
17. Crowsteps
18. Cutwater (wedge-shaped end of bridge pier)
19. Doocot, lectern
20. Dormer, canted & piended
21. Dormer, pedimented (qv) wallhead
22. Dormer, piended (see under 'roof')
23. Dormer, swept wallhead
24. Fanlight (glazed panel above door)
25. Finial (crowning ornament)
26. Fly-over stair
27. Forestair, pillared
28. Gable, wallhead
29. Gable, wallhead chimney
30. Gable, Dutch (curved)
31. Gibbs doorway (framed with projecting stonework)
32. Harling
33. Hoist, fishing net
34. Hoodmoulding (projection over opening to divert rainwater)
35. Jettied (overhanging)
36. Lucarne (small dormer on spire)
37. Margin, stone
38. Mercat Cross
39. Marriage Lintel
40. Mullion (vertical division of window)
41. Nave (main body of church)
42. Pavilion (building attached by wing to main building)
43. Pediment (triangular ornamental feature above windows etc)
44. Portico
45. Quoins, rusticated (corner stones with recessed joints)
46. Refuge (recess in bridge parapet)
47. Ridge, crested
48. Roof, flared pyramidal
49. Roof, leanto
50. Roof, ogival (with S-curve pitch generally rising from square plan and meeting at point)
51. Roof, pantiled
52. Roof, piended (formed by intersecting roof slopes)
53. Roof, slated
54. Skew (gable coping)
55. Skewputt, moulded (lowest stone of skew, qv)
56. Skewputt, scroll
57. Stair jamb (projection containing stairway)
58. Stringcourse (horizontal projecting wall moulding)
59. Transept (transverse wing of cruciform church)
60. Transom (horizontal division of window)
61. Voussoir (wedge-shaped stone forming archway)
62. Tympanum (area within pediment qv)
63. Window, bay (projecting full-height from ground level)
64. Window, oriel (corbelled bay qv)
65. Window, sash & case (sliding sashes within case)